SOME ACCOUNT

OF

𝕯𝖔𝖒𝖊𝖘𝖙𝖎𝖈 𝕬𝖗𝖈𝖍𝖎𝖙𝖊𝖈𝖙𝖚𝖗𝖊

IN

ENGLAND,

FROM RICHARD II. TO HENRY VIII.

WITH NUMEROUS ILLUSTRATIONS OF EXISTING REMAINS
FROM ORIGINAL DRAWINGS.

BY

THE EDITOR OF "THE GLOSSARY OF ARCHITECTURE."

PART I.

OXFORD,
AND 377, STRAND, LONDON:
JOHN HENRY AND JAMES PARKER.
M DCCC LIX.

Kessinger Publishing's
Rare Mystical Reprints

THOUSANDS OF SCARCE BOOKS
ON THESE AND OTHER SUBJECTS:

Freemasonry * Akashic * Alchemy * Alternative Health * Ancient Civilizations * Anthroposophy * Astrology * Astronomy * Aura * Bible Study * Cabalah * Cartomancy * Chakras * Clairvoyance * Comparative Religions * Divination * Druids * Eastern Thought * Egyptology * Esoterism * Essenes * Etheric * ESP * Gnosticism * Great White Brotherhood * Hermetics * Kabalah * Karma * Knights Templar * Kundalini * Magic * Meditation * Mediumship * Mesmerism * Metaphysics * Mithraism * Mystery Schools * Mysticism * Mythology * Numerology * Occultism * Palmistry * Pantheism * Parapsychology * Philosophy * Prosperity * Psychokinesis * Psychology * Pyramids * Qabalah * Reincarnation * Rosicrucian * Sacred Geometry * Secret Rituals * Secret Societies * Spiritism * Symbolism * Tarot * Telepathy * Theosophy * Transcendentalism * Upanishads * Vedanta * Wisdom * Yoga * *Plus Much More!*

DOWNLOAD A FREE CATALOG
AND
SEARCH OUR TITLES AT:

www.kessinger.net

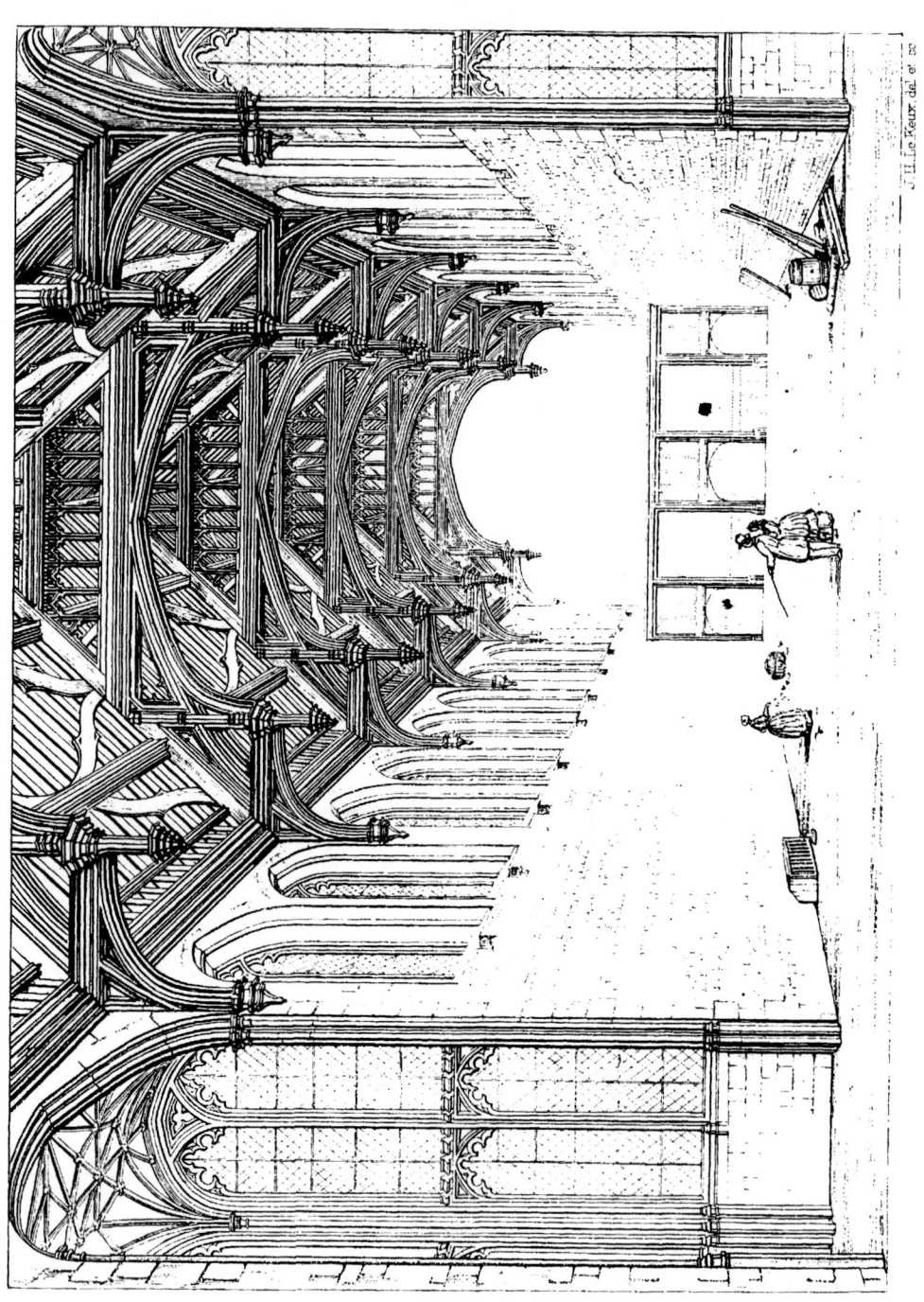

PREFACE.

More than twenty years have elapsed since the Editor of the present work first put forth the "Glossary of Architecture." One object of that work was to awaken the attention of the clergy and the educated classes generally to the merits and beauties of Medieval ecclesiastical architecture by numerous pictorial representations of the characteristic details of the buildings of each succeeding century, and to afford such information as would facilitate the study of the true principles of the Gothic style.

The object of the present work is also in part to do for the houses of our ancestors what the "Glossary" has done for their churches,—to awaken the attention of their owners and of all who are concerned in them, to the value and importance of those remains which are daily disappearing from our eyes,—to bring public opinion to bear upon the subject,—and to cry shame upon the noblemen and gentlemen who wantonly destroy, or allow their agents to destroy, valuable relics of ancient art, or historical memorials of the highest interest and value.

But if these works have had any practical effect it has been in a great degree incidental; their primary object was historical, to accustom people to remember the dates of the different styles, and to connect them with the history of their respective periods. The "Glossary" was the first work in which an attempt was made to apply Rickman's system and assign dates to several hundred examples by the style only, where historical dates were not forthcoming. Many of these dates have been confirmed by subsequent investigation, and very few have been found to be erroneous.

At the present time, also, there seems a desire among the more educated classes of the country to enquire for themselves into the claims which different styles of architecture have upon us; and there is no doubt the more the architectural history of the country is studied, the more it will become apparent not only that English Gothic was a style by itself, and most suitable for the requirements of this climate and this country in the Middle Ages; but also that with fair and proper development and adaptation it is still the most suited to meet the various requirements of the present time.

The Editor has endeavoured to obtain as much information from personal observation as possible, because experience and the habit of comparing one building with another have enabled him to see and understand the meaning and use of fragments which others might perhaps overlook. But he has not scrupled to avail himself of every other means in his power of obtaining such information as he required, either by the help of friends or of books; and he has made free use of the various county histories in endeavouring to ascertain what remains there are of the various houses or castles for which the "licences to crenellate" are recorded. This part of his work has been the most difficult and the least satisfactory, for the authors of those works were seldom possessed of the simple key to the dates of buildings which is now possessed by every one who has enjoyed a liberal education, and as they often made no distinction between the remains of a building of the twelfth century and one of the fifteenth, their information cannot always be relied upon. In this manner the Editor was led into a few mistakes in the notices of existing remains in the second volume, and he can hardly expect to have escaped altogether in the present one, although his experience has led him to use greater caution in dealing with the works of authors of the last generation.

The first volume of this work bore the name of the late Mr. Hudson Turner, who had been employed to search the Records which were indispensable for the proper understanding of that early period. His thorough acquaintance with these documents rendered his services invaluable, and it was felt to be a fitting compliment to place his name in the title-page, although he was, in fact, only one of several persons employed upon the work, and the present Editor is responsible for the architectural portion of that volume also.

In the second volume, which was printed after the death of Mr. Turner, the Editor was responsible not only for the architectural portion, but for much of the documentary information, which was collected in order to throw light upon the manners and customs of the Middle Ages, as explanatory of the uses to which the different parts of the buildings were applied. The materials which Mr. Turner left behind were far from sufficient for this purpose, and he had therefore to take a far more prominent part in the production of the work than he had originally intended. He was, however, ably assisted by numerous friends on whose knowledge of these subjects he could rely.

For the present volume he is obliged to accept a still greater share of the responsibility: nearly the whole of the documentary portion has been collected by himself, assisted by his son and by friends. He has to record his obligations to E. A. Freeman, Esq., for many architectural notes; to George Ormerod, Esq., the venerable and respected historian of Cheshire, for useful historical information; to the Messrs. Buckler for the free use of their valuable collection of drawings, and for many notices of existing remains which had escaped other observers; and most of the friends whose names have been mentioned in the previous volumes have again assisted him. Visits to Scotland in the summer of 1857, and to Ireland in 1858, have enabled him to add chapters on the chief peculiarities of the Domestic Architecture of those countries, which were omitted in the previous volumes.

The number of houses of the fifteenth century which remain in all parts of Europe, and the different character of them in each country and each province, renders it impossible to include those of Foreign countries in the present volume, which has already exceeded the limits prescribed for it, and the Editor has been reluctantly compelled to omit the numerous Foreign examples which he had collected.

France alone affords ample materials for a separate work on the subject, but this want has been in some degree supplied both by the excellent work of M. Verdier, and the concise popular volume of M. de Caumont, both of which have appeared since the present undertaking was commenced. Germany, Italy, and Belgium would each afford materials for a similar work.

He is indebted to M. Viollet-le-Duc of Paris for the following interesting letter on the subject of the Domestic Architecture of France in the fifteenth century, which affords so much information in a short space, and gives the result of so much experience and observation in an unpretending form, that he cannot refrain from giving it publicity here, although it may be considered somewhat out of place:—

"*Paris*, 31 *Mars*, 1859.

"CHER MONSIEUR,

"Vous savez que les deux prémiers tiers du xve. siècle ont été, chez nous, employés à nous battre tantôt contre les Bourguignons tantôt contre les Anglais, tantôt contre Bourguignons et Anglais réunis. Les bourgeois des villes, dans ces temps des misères publiques, n'ont eu ni le loisir, ni l'argent nécessaire pour rebâtir des maisons neuves. Ils avaient leur affaire de conserver celles qui leur restaient; aussi n'est-ce guère qu' à dater du règne de Louis XI. que nous voyons des maisons neuves s'élever dans les villes du nord et du centre de la France. C'est à dire a partir de la 2e. moitié du xve. siècle.

"Il existe encore à Chartres quelques morceaux des maisons de cette époque. Il en existaient autres à Tours et à Angers.

"Vous connaissez l'hotel de ville d'Orléans bâti sous le règne de Charles VII. et qui présente cette particularité curieuse d'une construction du milieu du xve. siècle dans laquelle on trouve déja tous les éléments de l'architecture de notre Renaissance développée sous Louis XII.: c'est aujourd'hui le musée d'Orléans.

"A Rouen beaucoup de maisons de la fin du xve. siècle existent encore, mais ces maisons sont fort mutilés. Cependant elles donnent une haute idée de l'art appliquée aux habitations de cette époque.

"A Gallardon, sur l'ancienne roûte de Chartres, il existait encore il y a quelques années, dans la grande rue, une belle maison du xve. siècle en bois; je ne sais si elle est conservée aujourd'hui.

"A Reims, sur l'ancienne grande place, on voit encore deux jolies maisons en bois du xve. siècle (1470 environ).

"A Paris nous possédons encore l'hotel de Sens, qui date du règne de Louis XI. mais fort mutilé.

"A Beauvais, une grande partie de l'ancien évêché (palais de justice aujourd'hui) date de cette époque.

"A Nevers, vous voyez l'ancien palais des Ducs, qui vient d'être restauré et qui date des dernières années du xve. siècle.

"Je n'ai pas besoin de vous citer la maison de Jacques Cœur à Bourges qui donne un magnifique spécimen de l'architecture privée du milieu du xve. siècle.

"Dans le midi, à Cordes il existe encore dans la grande rue, des maisons du xve. siècle ; on en trouve des restes à Saint Antonin, à Caylus, à Caussade, à Toulouse, à Alby. Mais tout cela est fort gâté. Quelques restes assez curieux à Montferrand près Clermont, au Puy en Vélay, à Issoire. * * * *

"Tout à vous comme toujours si vous avez besoin de moi

"Et mille amitiés.

"E. Viollet-le-Duc."

In conclusion, the Editor can only hope that the present work will in some measure assist towards the attainment of his object, and that in future the remains of the houses of our ancestors will be as well looked after and as carefully studied as our ancient churches have recently been. Several of the fine structures engraved in this work have actually been destroyed during its progress through the press: so marked and so disastrous in its results has been the general apathy on the subject. He trusts that the rest may be spared, and that as monuments of our national history, if on no other grounds, we may hand them down in at least as perfect a state as we received them. He will hope, also, that the same improvement will take place in the erection of new houses and public buildings during the next twenty-five years that may be observed in the churches built during the last quarter of a century.

The Turl, Oxford,
July 20, 1859.

TABLE OF CONTENTS.

CHAPTER I. General Remarks.

The houses of the fifteenth century well adapted to their purpose.—The arrangement not the work of one mind, but the growth of centuries.—The architecture kept pace with the change in manners and customs.—The development of the castle: first the Norman keep, then outworks gradually extended.—The different chambers and buildings brought together in one block.—Kenilworth Castle a good example.—Development shewn.—In the beginning of the fifteenth century the type of the fortified castle dies out, and the domestic house comes into existence.—Warwick Castle an example of transition.—Berkeley Castle a similar example.—In this century the large body of retainers no longer needed.—The old modes of defence rendered useless by the introduction of gunpowder.—Alnwick Castle an example of the developed type of the fourteenth century.—Survey *temp.* Queen Elizabeth.—Linlithgow Palace part domestic, part military.—Peles, or fortified tower-built houses.—In Scotland and in the border counties.—In Ireland tower-built houses very numerous.—The manor-houses in the interior of England.—Houses similar to tower-houses.—Parsonage houses.—Town houses.—London houses.—Progress of English luxury.—The decline of the Common Dining Hall, and the causes.—The rise of the Middle Classes.—Vassalage.—Increase of number of separate chambers.—The drawing-room.—College halls.—Houses of the peasantry.—Cottages in Kent.—Materials for building houses.—Use of brick.—Flint used in chalk districts.—Stone used in Ireland.—Timber and half-timber houses.—Overhanging stories.   pp. 1—24

CHAPTER II. Towns and Town Houses.

Extension of cities by suburbs.—City fortifications.—Buildings outside the walls separately fortified.—Arrangement of streets meet-

CONTENTS.

ing in a centre.—Market crosses, wells, and cisterns.—Noblemen's houses fortified.—Houses of merchant princes.—Guild-halls.—City walls rebuilt.—Houses, lower part of brick, and upper part of wood.—The corner post.—Doorways of timber-houses.—Windows.—ornamental plaster.—Panelled fronts.—London mansions.—The shops.—Signs.—Bedrooms, kitchen, cellar, garret, &c., in small town houses.—Documentary evidence.—Illuminations.—Extracts from Romances.—Paving of the streets.—Bridges.—Repair of bridges mentioned in wills.—Abingdon bridge.—Bridges with towers.—Celebrated bridges.—Almshouses.—Hospitals.—Inns and taverns.

pp. 25—48

CHAPTER III. THE HALL.

The arrangements of the hall same as in previous centuries.—The entrance porch.—Squints, or openings.—Internal porch.—The screens.—Buttery-hatches.—Lavatory.—Music-gallery.—The dais.—Furniture of the hall.—The bay-window.—The cupboard and buffet.—Inventory of a hall.—The brazier.—The fireplace.—Timber roofs.—Gable window.—Ceilings.—External covering by tiles.—Decorations of the hall.—Arras and hangings.—Tapestry.—Linen panel.—Flooring of the hall.—Inventories of furniture and utensils.—Chairs.—Tables and table linen.—Almeries and lockers.—Lavers.—Lavatory.—Water-drain.—Decline of the custom of dining in the hall.—Eating in chambers.—Great chamber.—Dining parlour.—Reception room.—Banqueting room in Wanswell Court and at Hampton Court.—Rooms over the hall introduced.—CUSTOMS AT FEASTS.—Ewerer.—Borde cloths.—Panterer.—Carver.—Butler.—Almoner.—Etiquette.—Furniture of the hall.

pp. 49—87

CHAPTER IV. THE CHAMBERS AND OFFICES.

General arrangement.—Usual plan.—Bridge.—Gate-house.—Outer bailey, or farm-yard.—Inner bailey, or principal court.—Servants' court.—Vaulted substructures, or cellars.—Arrangement of chief apartments.—Warwick.—Chepstow.—Chalfield.—Fawsley.—Coventry.—Aula.—Camera.—INVENTORIES OF FURNITURE.—Bed-chambers.—Wardrobe.—Dormitory.—Furniture.—Beds.—Hangings.—Bed of Henry v.—Beds in the Priory of Durham in 1446.—Tapestry of Bed-chamber.—Bed of Henry VIII.—Cradles.—Apparel of State

CONTENTS.

Chamber of silk and arras.—Panels.—Scrolls.—Ornaments.—Wainscot.—Linen pattern.—Cornice.—Carpets.—The couch.—The bench. The settle.—Chests.—Standards.—Inventory of Reginald de la Pole. —Chairs.—Tables.—Buffet-stool.—Chimney-piece.—Chimney-shafts. —Glass windows.—Casements moveable.—Painted Glass.—Ceilings.—Articles of glass.—Water-drains.—Wash-hand stands.—Cupboards.—Almery.—Dresser.—Paintings.—Books.—Letterns.—Staircases.—The porch.—Doorways and doors.—Passages and corridors. —Projections.—Bartizans.—Garderobes, as at Compton Castle and Conway.—Covered ways.—Wells.—Cisterns.—Water-pipes.—Gurgoyles.—Kitchens at Stanton Harcourt, Oxford, Hampton Court, and Warwick.—Inventories of kitchen furniture.—Andyrons.—Pantry. —Buttery.—Cellar.—Furniture of offices.—Larder.—Provisions.— Ewery.—Salsarium.—Bakehouse.—Brewhouse.—Dairy.—Granary. —Mill.—Stables.—Barns.—Granges. pp. 88—172

CHAPTER V. THE DOMESTIC CHAPEL.

Usually placed near the upper end of the hall, with a passage from the dais, but in various situations, as at Kidwelly, St. David's, Raglan, Ightham, Haddon, Linlithgow, Hawarden, Warwick, Stanton Harcourt, Cothele, Berkeley, Trelawney.—Over the gateway, as at Prudhoe.—Detached.—Sacrarium the whole height.—Western part in two stories.—East Hendred.—Berkeley.—Trecarrel.—Godstow.— Sherborne.—Alnwick.—Oratory.—Chepstow.—Brougham.—Linlithgow.—Beverstone.—Squints.—Illustrations from Romances.—Inventories of chapel furniture.—Oriel window. pp. 173—185

CHAPTER VI. MEDIEVAL GATEHOUSES.

Infinite variety.—But two great divisions.—Detached, and attached to, or forming part of, other buildings, as castles, colleges.—Gatehouse with flanking towers.—The military type.—Rhuddlan.— Tunbridge.—Chepstow.—Pennard.—Penrice.—Denbigh.—Rye.—Carisbrooke.—Llawhaden.—Allington.—Llandaff.—Raglan.—Wells.— Change from military to domestic.—Herstmonceux.—Cowdray.— Oxburgh.—Layer Marney.—Cambridge.—St. Pierre.—Norwich.— Without corner turrets.—Colleges at Oxford.—Wykeham's towers. —Winchester.—Windsor.—St. Cross.—Crickhowell.—Itton.—Tre-

CONTENTS.

tower.—Bosbury.—Anomalous, as at Mackworth.—Detached.—At Saltwood.—Athelhampton.—Of monasteries and cathedral closes, as Bury St. Edmund's, West Walton, Malvern, Castle Acre, Leicester, Chichester, Malling, Thornton, Maidstone, St. Ethelbert's, Norwich, Kingswood, Bayham, Battle. Montacute, Canterbury, Congleton, South Wraxhall. pp. 186—200

LIST OF ENGRAVINGS.

CHAPTER I. General Remarks.

	PAGE
HALL of Eltham Palace, Kent	*Frontispiece.*
General plan of Warwick Castle	5
(See also p. 92.)	
Hurstmonceux, or Herstmonceux Castle, Sussex	7
Pele tower, Kirk-Andrews-on-Eske, Cumberland	9
Tattershall Castle, Lincolnshire	10
Rectory farm, Chesterton, Cambridgeshire	12
(See also p. 298.)	
Parapet of moulded brick, Layer Marney, Essex	23
(See also pp. 67, 118, 300.)	
Agecroft Hall, Lancashire, (a timber-house)	24
(See also p. 213.)	

CHAPTER II. Towns and Town Houses.

Corner-post, Great Chesterford, Essex	29
Bracket, pavement, York	ib.
Corner-post, Salisbury	30
Part of a house in Eastgate-street, Bury St. Edmund's, Suffolk	ib.
Timber-house in St. Mildred's, Canterbury	33
Panelled house in Small-street, Bristol	35
Timber-house, from a MS. in Douce's Collection	36
Shops in the Butcher-row, Shrewsbury	36
Inn, Norton St. Philip's, Somersetshire	47

CHAPTER III. The Hall.

Hall of Westminster School, with the brazier (or reredos) and louvre	49
Niche and iron hook in the hall, Little Wenham	51
Exterior of the hall, &c., Great Chalfield, Wiltshire	52

LIST OF ENGRAVINGS.

	PAGE
Bay-window, Thornbury Castle, Gloucestershire	54
Enamelled burette, from a MS. in the Bibl. Paris	56
Fireplace, Southwell Palace, Notts.	58
Interior of hall, Great Chalfield, Wiltshire	60
Openings or masks in ditto	ib.
Wainscot with the linen panel, Layer Marney	67
Interior of the hall, Yanwath, Westmoreland	68
(See also p. 122.)	
Locker in a house in the Close, Lincoln	73
Water-drain, Moat-house, Appleby, Leicestershire	ib.
Interior of a hall, shewing the dais, the plate cupboard, the minstrels' gallery, &c. from a MS. of the fifteenth century of Quintus Curtius in the Bodleian Library	77
Interior of the hall, Wanswell Court, Gloucestershire	78
(See also p. 267.)	

CHAPTER IV. THE CHAMBERS AND OFFICES.

	PAGE
Porch of the hall and window of the chapel? and gateway of the inner court, with turrets, manor-house, South Wingfield, Derbyshire	89
Plans of ground-floor and first story of the domestic buildings in Warwick Castle	92
Plan of Haddon Hall, Derbyshire	97
Dormitory, Layer Marney, Essex	98
Beds from MSS. of the fifteenth century in the Bodleian	103
Cradles from MSS. in Douce's Collection	106
Wooden panels from Syon House, Middlesex, and Colchester, Essex	107
Panelled chamber, Thame Park, Oxon.	109
Cornices and barge-boards from Rochester, Winchester, and the Mote, Ightham, Kent	110
Wooden bench, from a MS. in Douce's Collection	112
Wooden settle at Combe St. Nicholas, Somerset	ib.
Long settle and money-chest, from a MS. in the Bodleian	114
Standard chest, Rockingham Castle, Northants.	ib.
Chairs from MSS. in Douce's Collection	115
Chimney-pieces, Sherborne, Salisbury, and Cerne Abbas	116
Chimney-shafts, Mellingham, Suffolk; St. Osyth, Essex; Droitwich, Worcestershire; Layer Marney, Essex	118

LIST OF ENGRAVINGS.

	PAGE
Chimney-shafts, Maxstoke Castle, Warwickshire; Aslackby, Lincolnshire; Thornbury Castle, Gloucestershire; Tonbridge School, Kent	120
Windows and iron grating, Yanwath, Westmoreland	122
Windows carved in oak, Coventry, and Smithell's Hall, Lancashire	125
Ditto, at Lewes, Sussex	126
Ditto, at Wingham, Kent	127
Plaster ceiling and inner porch, with panelling, Thame Park, Oxon	128
Water-drain, Abbot's House, Wenlock	129
Ditto, Warwick Castle	130
Wash-hand stand, with basins, soap-dish and towel; seat, distaff, spindle and reel; from MSS. in Douce's Collection	ib.
Pottery and glass, and cupboard, from ditto	132
Furniture, reading-desks, blacksmith's forge, sculptor's bench and tools, from ditto	141
External staircase, Archbishop's Palace, Maidstone, Kent	142
Porch, doorways, and doors, Weobley, Herefordshire; Sherborne, Dorsetshire; and Norwich	143
Double cloister, front of Abbot's House, Wenlock, Shropshire	145
Plan of a room and window, with doorway in the jamb, Wetherall Priory, Cumberland	146
Compton Castle, Devonshire, with bartizans	148
Corbel-table and water-spouts, Kirk-Andrews-on-Eske, Cumberland	150
Interior of kitchen, Stanton Harcourt, Oxfordshire	151
Kitchen fireplace and furniture, from MSS. in Bodleian	155
Mill, with sluice and overshot-wheel, from ditto	166
Bakehouse, fireplaces, tables, and seats, from ditto	171

CHAPTER V. The Domestic Chapel.

The Mote, Ightham, Kent	173
Stanton Harcourt, Oxon.	175
Plan of Berkeley Castle, Gloucestershire	ib.
Section and plan, East Hendred, Berks.	177
Oriel in chapel, Berkeley Castle	178
Almshouse with chapel, Sherborne, Dorset	179
Plans of chapel and oratory, Beverstone Castle, Gloucestershire	181
Section of ditto	182
Oriel window, Sherborne, Dorset	185

LIST OF ENGRAVINGS.

CHAPTER VI. MEDIEVAL GATEHOUSES.

	PAGE
Layer Marney, Essex	187
Oxburgh Hall, Norfolk	189
Jesus College, Cambridge	191
Mackworth Castle, Derbyshire	193
Athelhampton, Dorsetshire	194
Thornton Abbey, Lincolnshire	197
South Wraxhall, Wiltshire	199

DOMESTIC ARCHITECTURE OF THE FIFTEENTH CENTURY.

CHAPTER I.

GENERAL REMARKS.

THE houses of the middle ages were always well adapted for the purposes for which they were intended, and so long as it was necessary to support a large body of retainers to defend the building, or to maintain the dignity of the family, it would be difficult to contrive a more convenient arrangement than that which we find adopted by our ancestors at the commencement of the fifteenth century.

This arrangement was not, however, the result of the working of any one powerful mind; it was not the design of some one great architect who gave the key-note which other builders followed; it was not even the work of one generation; but it was the growth of centuries. Side by side with the gradual development of the civilization, wealth, and power of England, grew the domestic habitations of the country; in each age reflecting not only the manners and customs of the people, but the position and prosperity of the English as a nation: each progressive step in the gradual development of the style and plan, down to the time of which we are now treating, is but an illustration to a page of history.

This is most apparent in the CASTLE, properly so called. The small unfortified manor-houses of the earlier centuries retained, to a great extent, their original plan and arrangements throughout; as also the border-towers, usually known by the name of Peles or Pele-towers, which, intended but for resisting encroachments, as long as they were necessary at all, so long were built in strict accordance with the object in view, and thus retained a military aspect to the last. Some of the houses in connection with monastic institutions, and houses in towns, would naturally fall beneath another category; but the history of the plan of our English castles, which, after all, were but the dwelling-places of the principal landowners in the kingdom, is much as follows:—

First, we find the plain square keep-tower of the Normans, protected both by moats and earth-work, and by the essential thickness of its own walls, defying every battering-ram and other engine of war. These moats and earth-works gradually gave place to walls of enceinte, or, at most, took the inferior position of only an outer line of defence. These walls, however, enclosed a much larger space than the old moat, leaving court-yards round the centre fortress; and were provided with towers and bastions, in which probably, in times of peace, at least, the internal arrangements were far more of a domestic character than the military aspect of the exterior would lead one to suppose. Added to this, on the inner side of this wall were erected sheds or other wooden buildings, accommodating the serfs and lower orders of domestics, while the bastion-towers were probably occupied by the officers or warders of the castle. This was the first step towards forming, or rather congregating, a household; and these wooden buildings for a long time held their ground, partly because of the ease with which they were erected, and partly because, in the case of an attack, their destruction was not of consequence, and they could easily be removed in those places where their presence might have afforded facilities to the enemy for entering the castle. But in process of time the wood made way for stone, and different apartments were built along the line of the fortification wall, which were often inhabited by the owner of the castle himself, when fear of an approaching enemy did not deter him from consulting his own will and convenience.

This arrangement brings us into the middle of the thirteenth century; and the next development may be said to consist in the gathering together of these different chambers into one whole, in some part of the ground within the fortification. In this block of buildings the hall was the chief feature; and round the hall the other chambers, offices, &c., were grouped. Gradually divest the building of the military character, take away the wall of enceinte, and we find, with but few modifications, the arrangement which existed down to the time of Elizabeth.

To make our remarks better understood, we may, perhaps, take an example,—such a one as Kenilworth, which is well known, and easy of access; though, perhaps, few may have ever taken the trouble to examine the different changes in plan and extent which it has at different periods undergone. It is also an important example, inasmuch as there is sufficient evidence to be derived from the documents which exist, scattered here and there, and treating of different periods, to fix the exact date to a great portion of the walls which remain standing to tell of its ancient splendour.

In the centre we find the first type, which has been mentioned above, the large square tower. All traces of the early moat have, naturally, long been swept away, but it could not have been far distant from this tower. From 1180 to 1187 are entries for building and repairing walls and fortifications; but in the beginning of the thirteenth century, from 1212 to 1216, very large sums were expended; one of these sums is especially mentioned as being for the king's chamber and garderobe. This king's chamber remains, and is identified by the description; close to it are the two towers known as Lunn's Tower and the Water Tower, all on the line of the fortifications. Many buildings continued still, no doubt, of wood, on the inner side of the wall; and although, perhaps, the retainers at this time may scarcely have increased at all, accommodation for them must have increased tenfold.

Again we turn to Kenilworth for the third development, namely, the great hall, which, next to the old keep, still left standing throughout all the changes, is the great object of attraction there. Near to this can be traced the remains of many buildings of the same period,—the chapel, the kitchen, the cellars, and other rooms. The old thirteenth century buildings were left standing. They may have been used as servants' apartments, or as stables, but there is little doubt that the chief household took up its abode far away in the later group of which we have been speaking. From time to time also it seems clear that the walls of enceinte were extended, and a larger space thus enclosed. This development might easily be traced in other castles where the architecture of successive periods appears; and from the massive character of that Norman keep, the centre round which the later buildings turned, we believe that there is no castle originally built in the twelfth century which does not to this day retain this keep within its walls of enceinte, and in almost all cases as perfect as any of the other parts of the buildings. Moreover, it should be borne in mind that

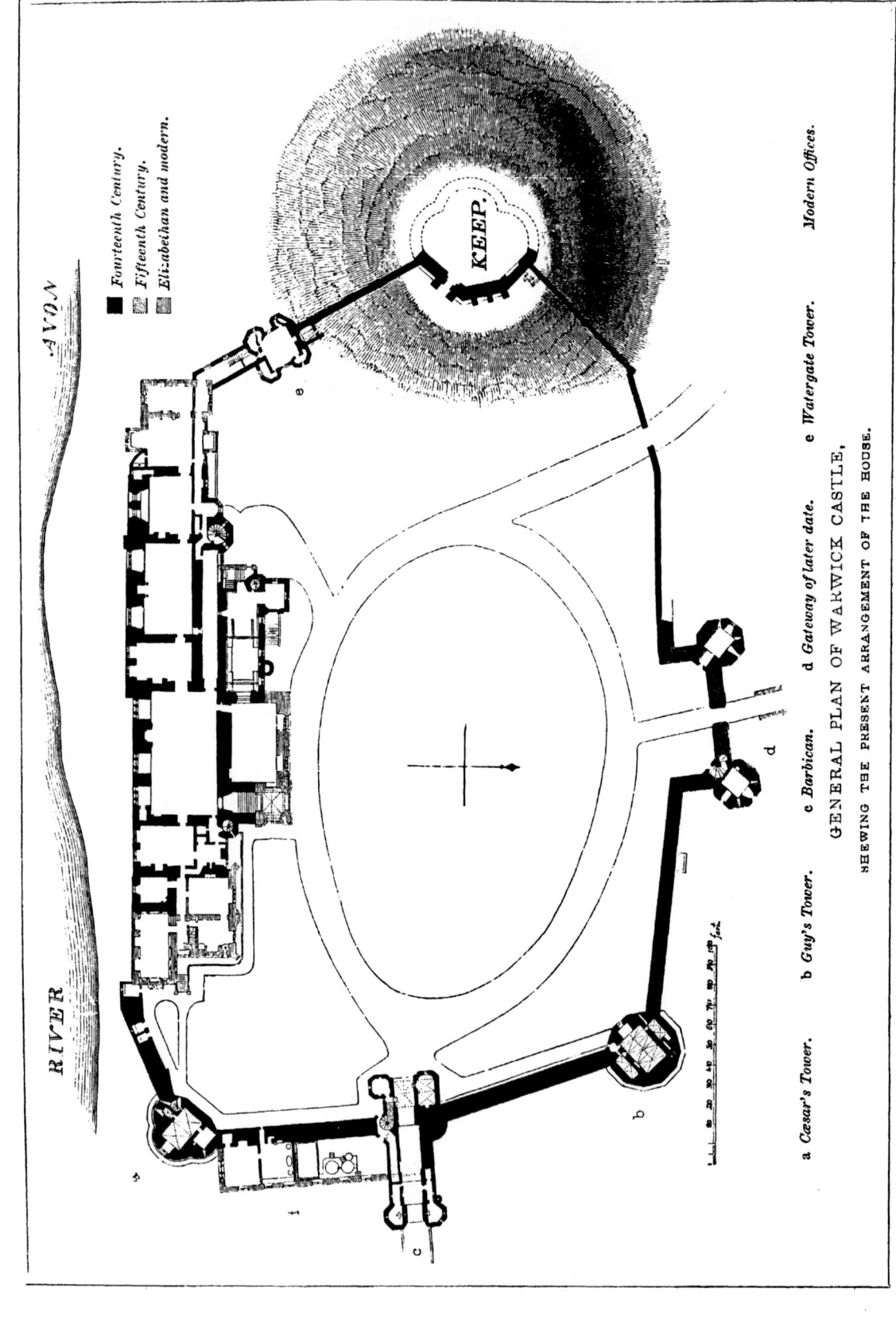

throughout these periods the type of the newly-built castle seems to be nearly the same with that found in the gradually developed example. The principal buildings were mainly scattered along the whole wall of enceinte in the thirteenth century, and seem to be, as a rule, gathered up much more compactly together as we progress in the fourteenth; gradually preparing, as it were, for the time when the wall of enceinte would be dismissed altogether.

At the time, then, of which the volume before us treats, we find the house and castle, so to speak, combined,—the type of the castle gently dying out, the type of the domestic house breaking forth into existence. The military character has not yet left, and the civil is perhaps, to a great extent, made subordinate to it. We open our volume upon a transitional state of plan, like as we find in the designs of Gothic architecture a transitional period was clearly marked, as one style made way for another.

Warwick Castle is an excellent example of this transition, and in remarkably perfect preservation; built partly at the end of the fourteenth century, but not finished until the fifteenth. Externally it is a strong fortress, and before the use of gunpowder must have been almost impregnable. The walls of enceinte, with the towers, the battlements, the alures behind them, the covered ways, the bastions carried upon corbels, with open intervals between them for throwing down stones or other missiles, and commonly known by the name of *machecoulis*, are still so perfect that they might be used at any time, and the portcullis is still actually used, being let down every night, more perhaps to keep up a stately tradition than for actual use. Within these walls, and gathered up, as we have shewn, on one side, where the river protects it externally, is the dwelling-house, the upper part of which, occupied by the family, is modernised according to the requirements of modern life, and affords a splendid suite of apartments, with a stately entrance-hall, still occasionally used as a dining-hall when the tenantry are assembled, or any large party. Beneath these are the servants' apartments, almost an equally fine suite in their way, and in a more original state, with their stone-vaulted ceilings, Gothic doorways and windows, the corridor or passage from one end to the other, with the kitchen, offices, and cellars opening out of it. (See the ground-plan.) Berkeley Castle is another fine example of the same period, almost equally perfect, but not exactly on the same plan, the buildings there forming two sides of a quadrangle, with the chapel at the angle. In both cases the hall, although an important feature, has ceased to have such a decided prominence; there is a separate dining-room, and a withdrawing-room of considerable importance, and the bed-chambers are numerous.

But during the fifteenth century the necessity of continuing to support a large body of retainers ceased in many instances, and the castles were modified accordingly; some built on one plan, and some on another, according to the wants of the owners. Again, the introduction of the use of gunpowder in warfare had rendered the old mode of fortification in a great degree useless, except to protect the house against any sudden attack of a party of marauders; and the builders became gradually aware of the fact, so that the gatehouse and the walls, and battlements and towers, began to be considered more in the light of ornaments, and indications of state and grandeur, than as actually necessary for defence against an enemy, and the more palace-like character of the building was gradually developed. The more peaceful

DOMESTIC ARCHITECTURE: FIFTEENTH CENTURY.

HURSTMONCEUX CASTLE, SUSSEX.

and civilized state of the country also had its effect; and notwithstanding the wars of the Roses, England appears to have made more rapid progress in the peaceful arts during this century than any other country. In Thornbury Castle and Cowdray House, the fortifications appear to be intended more for show than for use; in Hurstmonceux Castle, perhaps as much for one as the other.

Before quitting the larger castles, an example should be mentioned which, while reflecting faithfully the picture which has been drawn of the developed castle of the fourteenth century, underwent few material changes afterwards. The reason for this is evident. That peace which the rest of England enjoyed seems never to have exercised its civilizing influence over those parts where Alnwick Castle was situated; and thus we find, from a survey of the time of Queen Elizabeth, that the castle down to that date still retained the same military character which it possessed in earlier ages:—

"The keep or donjon, as Clarkson calls it, formed a polygon, with a court-yard in the centre, which was encircled by seven round towers and one square tower, under which was the gateway. The approach was by a drawbridge over the moat, and on either side in advance semi-octagonal towers, added by the second Lord Percy, about 1350, to the original square Norman tower. These semi-octagonal towers rise four stories high, and contain on the entrance-floor accommodation for a porter, and under the chamber, to the right, is a deep dungeon-prison, the only access to which is through the bottle-shaped ceiling by a trap in the floor, and there are loopholes in the walls. The outer face of the archway next the court consists of a noble series of Norman mouldings, carved with enrichments, and there were originally two columns with their capitals on each side. Within the court, to the right, is a draw-well in the thickness of the wall, with three pointed arches, surmounted by one large discharging arch, forming a very picturesque object; beyond which is a doorway, leading into a vaulted chamber, called by Clarkson 'a fayre vaulte, which is the buttereye, in length xvii yards, in breadth vi.' Above this 'fayre vaulte' was the hall, approached by an external flight of steps, and over the hall was the peculiar feature of two chambers. In the tower next that of the hall were contained the kitchen, sculleries, buttery, larder, &c. The lord's and lady's lodging was over the gatehouse.

"The other towers contained the accommodation for the household. They were all detached, except in one case, forming separate dwellings, united by curtain-walls for the purposes of defence. And again, to use Clarkson's own words, 'uppon the sayde lead ys a trimme walk and a fayre prospect.' 'There is raysed on the west side of the said donjeone one lyttle square tower, called ye watche tower, above the lead xiv yeard, wherein ys place for a watchman to be, and a beaken to be sett or hung.'

"Between the constable's tower and the postern tower was a brew-house, with all proper plant and fittings, and adjoining the postern tower a bakehouse; and near to them two houses, one for a slaughter-house, the other for stores; and there was a chancery-house, and a wood-garth attached to the middle ward; in fact, a complete series of domestic offices close in upon the keep. The keep itself was surrounded by a deep moat, which was dry; and the recent works have brought to light the retaining wall of the sloping ground next the keep-towers."

Now this retaining of the military character being especially remarkable in border counties, or near the sea-coast,—in a word, in all disturbed districts,—it is not to be wondered at that in these parts, when new houses or castles were erected, they should have followed also rather the old and fortified plan than the modern development which had taken its place in the other parts of England. In Linlithgow Palace, Scotland, for instance, although the buildings towards the court are quite of a domestic character, yet on the exterior and in the gatehouse the embrasures for cannon, as well as the loopholes and *machecoulis*, shew that it was well calculated to resist a siege for a considerable time. And it is according to the same principle that we find, especially in the north, the Border manor-house, or Pele-tower, built in the fifteenth, or even sixteenth century, exactly after the original models which had existed from the earliest times.

DOMESTIC ARCHITECTURE: FOURTEENTH CENTURY.

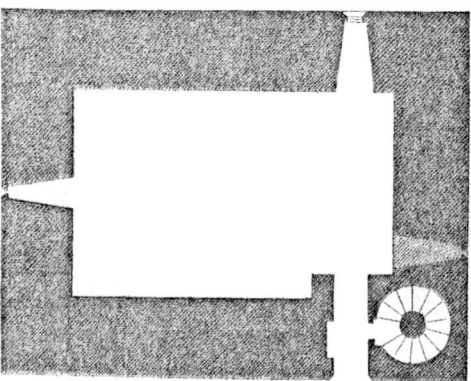

North.

TOWER KIRK ANDREWS ON ESKE CUMBERLAND

These peles, or tower-built houses fortified, may still be found in great numbers in Scotland and the border counties, and in Ireland. In Scotland they are frequently as late as the sixteenth century, built in close imitation of a Norman keep, and with a singular fondness for Norman ornaments, often very closely imitated, particularly the billet and the cable. The most characteristic and best-preserved feature is generally the parapet, with its cornice, or corbel-table, or *machecoulis*, and waterspouts: these are generally very numerous, not more than six feet apart, and often made like stone cannons projecting from the cornice under the battlement. The lower part of these peles is generally quite plain, and the original small windows, or loopholes, have commonly been replaced by larger modern windows. The tower of Kirk-Andrews-on-Eske, in Cumberland, is a fair average example, and shews the parapet and cornice, with the waterspouts, or gurgoyles, very distinctly.

In Ireland these tower-houses are extremely numerous in all parts of the country: in some parts they are called the Irish towers, in others merely the towers: they were, in fact, the manor-houses throughout the middle ages. From the fighting character of the people, every house was obliged to be fortified, even the abbeys. These towers are usually despised by the local antiquaries, and passed over as unworthy of notice, but they are really very interesting. They are of all periods, from the twelfth century to the seventeenth, and generally in good preservation so far as the stone-work is concerned; every scrap of wood has long been burnt. They are generally extremely plain and rude, and the windows in the lower part mere loopholes, but at the top of each is the state apartment, which generally has some pretension to ornament and comfort, and every dwelling-room has a fireplace and a garderobe. They differ from similar tower-houses in England and Scotland in several particulars, and have a distinct national character of their own. They almost always have bartizans projecting boldly out from the corners, carried on corbels forming *machecoulis*. These towers continued to be the usual dwelling-houses of the gentry, whether English or Irish, until the seventeenth century, when Cromwell shewed that these ancient defences were of no use against gunpowder; since which they have been deserted, but the walls and vaults left standing.

But of the MANOR-HOUSES in the interior of England— houses scarcely aspiring to the name of castle, although often fortified to a considerable extent—a few words must be said. It is impossible, however, in them to discover the same development as in the castles; the same rules and circumstances which governed their plans and designs from the earliest period of their existence appear to have influenced them now. We cannot discover, it is true, in the majority of instances, from the total absence of documents, the reasons for any particular design or plan; we can only suppose generally that the chances of attack weighed with the builder in deciding between civil and military arrangement, although, in some cases, other circumstances must have influenced the plans; for we sometimes find in the same district, and within a few miles of each other, one house bearing the stamp of the fortress, and another bearing that of the domestic mansion.

Besides the peles of Scotland and the border counties, and the towers of Ireland, in the more peaceful districts of England many houses were also built after the fashion of these towers. Square in plan and lofty, with turrets at the angles, *machecoulis* and battlements, and surrounded

DOMESTIC ARCHITECTURE: FIFTEENTH CENTURY.

TATTERSHALL CASTLE, LINCOLNSHIRE.

by a moat, they were well calculated to resist any sudden attack of marauders, but the large size of the windows shews that they were not intended for serious warfare. Tattershall Castle, Lincolnshire, is a fine example of this class of house: it is built of brick, and is a very noble and commanding structure. Middleton Tower, Norfolk, is another good house of the same class, not so lofty nor so rich, with smaller windows and more calculated for defence, but also of brick, and belonging to the same type.

In the peaceful districts the manor-houses, such as Great Chalfield and South Wraxall, in Wiltshire, are merely convenient dwelling-houses, with scarcely any attempt at fortifications; as also Ockwells, in Berkshire, and numerous others of the same class.

On the other hand, St. Donat's, on the borders of Wales, and therefore in a precarious, if not actually disturbed, district, is strongly fortified, with its moat and gatehouses, and outer and inner bailey, although of quite as late, if not of later, date than the other examples mentioned, and at the same time perfectly manorial in its character and purposes.

In Wingfield manor-house, Derbyshire, the massive turrets for defending the passage from the outer bailey to the inner court shew an intention of serious defence, while the more ornamental work in the porch to the hall, and the chapel window in the inner court, shew that it was not thought probable that an enemy would penetrate to that part of the building. Compton Castle, Devonshire, is a singular mixture of the two ideas: the large size of the windows shews that domestic comfort was not neglected, and that no great danger was apprehended; on the other hand, the parapets, and the number of bartizans, or projections for defending the walls, shew that it was intended to be able to resist any sudden attack.

Of Parsonage-houses the same remarks will apply as those on the manor-houses. They partook more of the civil character than of the military; and as we have in this century many more examples, they assume a greater importance than they have previously done. In themselves, however, there is scarcely a sufficient distinction of character from other buildings of the period to demand any notice in this introductory chapter.

The old Rectory-house at Chesterton, Cambridgeshire, is a good example of a parsonage-house of this period, partaking of the character of a tower, with a vaulted lower chamber, turrets at the angles, and a bartizan on one of them, while the windows are more of a domestic than of a warlike character.

The Town-houses at this period, no doubt, as the wealth of the country increased, underwent great improvement, but as far as we can judge, wood was still the chief material used in building them: for this reason especially we have few examples remaining; and it is only to some of the unfrequented streets of Coventry and the Butcher-row at Shrewsbury, that we can turn to gain any idea of the architectural details generally of the town-houses.

Doorways of the fifteenth and beginning of the sixteenth century, more especially of the Tudor era, have, however, been preserved in many of our older towns, of which a fine example remains in London-street, Norwich. Archways for horses to go into the court-yards, more frequently remain than the smaller doorways, and the spandrels are often ornamented with roses, or foliage, or other characteristic ornament. In the interior of town-houses the old fireplaces are often preserved,

DOMESTIC ARCHITECTURE: FIFTEENTH CENTURY.

RECTORY FARM, CHESTERTON, CAMBRIDGESHIRE.

and sometimes other ancient features, when the front has been entirely modernised.

In a large city like London many houses were, no doubt, built of stone; but partly from the ravaging effects of the Great Fire, and partly from the fact that wealth and progress are the greatest enemies with which the student of antiquities has to contend, excepting Crosby Hall, we have not a single example to refer to. The underground warehouse of Gerard's Hall, engraved in the second volume of this work, has, since the engraving was published, made way for a new street, and buildings more in accordance with the enlightened notions of the nineteenth century. There is little doubt that many a palace reared lofty walls on the banks of the Thames, where now nothing but coal-wharfs and warehouses overshadow the bed of mud, but not a single stone, that we are aware of, remains to tell the tale. The sources, then, whence the information is to be derived are few and meagre. The hand of the painter in the illuminated romances of the period, and records scattered here and there, must suffice,—existing buildings throwing little light upon the subject. The town-houses, however, are so intimately connected with the general appearance and history of the "towns," that more about them will be found in another chapter.

The developed type of the medieval mansion which we find existing in the fifteenth century, in its turn gave way to another, and, as many may consider, a more refined type. It would be beside the purpose in the present chapter to enter at any length upon the social position of the different classes of the people of England at the period; but in watching the change in the plans of buildings, the antiquary must to some extent consider the causes. In this way history becomes the key to architecture.

The progress of commerce, the success of English arms, and the increasing spirit of national enterprise, opened innumerable channels by which English society was enriched with luxuries, and purified by an acquaintance with the more refined manners of the continental nations. Glancing at the gorgeous illuminations with which the manuscripts of the fifteenth century are adorned, we are naturally struck with this evident fact.

Moreover, the increase of luxury and comfort was not solely confined to the abodes of royalty, but documents illustrative of the domestic manners of the humbler classes of society bear witness that the "hefd house" of the burgher, and the cottage home of the peasant, were alike rendered more cheerful by this national prosperity. Those luxuries which in a former age were found only in the halls of kings, had now become common in the households of the middle classes. Neither the lord nor the franklin now limited the requirements and elegancies of his home to the produce of his own estate. Merchant princes brought from over seas the riches and luxuries of those foreign countries, the names of which many of their fathers had only known in the romances of chivalry. India yielded her treasures, Alexandria her spices, Flanders and Brabant their warm cloth, and Arras the rich produce of her looms.

At home the industrial arts had made rapid progress. The institution of guilds and fraternities among the trades diffused a spirit of emulation into the commercial and working classes. Labour became divided; the "mysteries" of trade increased, and mechanics were no longer regarded as domestic servants. The sources whence we can readily obtain a clear insight into the every-day life of this century, if not numerous, are at least authentic. The genius of modern archæology has taught us to regard with attention many documents which for ages have been allowed to repose in security. Old wills, letters, wardrobe accounts, and household rolls, are, in the hands of the antiquary, as the dry bones of a past social being, which by skilful comparison are capable of realizing to the mind a true picture of that life of which they afford evidence.

Side by side with these we have the remains of the castles and mansions themselves, each illustrating the other: where the record fails, the structure often supplies its place, the style of architecture and the internal arrangements shewing the same social progress which the records would lead us to expect.

The most prominent and distinctive feature in the medieval house was the importance of the DINING-HALL. It was the chief room in the mansion, and on it the other buildings seemed mainly to depend, the offices and chambers being grouped around it. After the fifteenth century the great hall was almost lost. In it the lord of the manor had held his court; there daily his vassals and serfs had joined at the one large table for their evening meal: and with the importance of this hall seemed to decline that state and grandeur which had hitherto surrounded the hereditary landowner. It may be inferred that at this time his position was not so high in the social scale of society as it had been; rich and prosperous merchants were fast springing up in the now flourishing cities; and thus there was little necessity for his supporting the same state and dignity with which it had been the custom previously for those of his rank to surround themselves.

Again, in the decline of the hall may be traced a change in the position of the lower classes of society. Before, more as serfs, his labourers were entirely dependent on the lord of the manor for their food, and often shelter; but now they seem to have possessed homes for themselves, and to be no longer under the necessity of seeking their meals at the board of the lordly mansion. We have already noticed the absence of the band of armed retainers, without which the household of a castle was incomplete; and part of this band always accompanied their master in the event of a visit to a neighbouring lord. Thus we see that at the meals, when it was the custom for all to assemble together, the large hall was soon filled. But when the vassals and serfs dined at their own houses, when the household consisted but of a few retainers, and when, perhaps, from the better accommodation provided by inns and hostelries, it was not often incumbent upon the owner of a castle to entertain any large body of visitors, the hall at meal-time would but present empty benches; and so by degrees it was diminished in size, and brought more into accordance with the requirements of the proprietor.

Added to this, the necessity for a large number of dependants had ceased, in consequence of the rise of traders, shopkeepers, and independent workmen, in other words, that large portion of the population which we understand by the name of the "middle classes." It is in the fourteenth and fifteenth centuries that we trace the rise of this class, and the emerging of the great body of the people from serfdom to a state of comparative affluence and political importance. From the household accounts of that period we discover that many of those duties which in the preceding age were fulfilled by domestics, were now performed by traders. Carpenters, upholsterers, tailors, brewers, and bakers, usually formed part of the royal and baronial establishments of the thirteenth century. But with the increase of refinement and the progress of the domestic arts, these occupations ceased to be regarded as household duties. It is interesting to trace the cause of this change, and to watch the operation of those events which led to the gradual rise of the trading class.

It is well known that during the middle ages a great portion of the people existed in a state of vassalage. The stalwart body of English peasantry were slaves, and were so absolutely the property of their lord, that they were bought and sold as the live-stock of an estate. We might produce many instances from ancient records, did the question admit of doubt. Walter de Beauchamp, in the reign of Henry III., in granting certain land, conveyed with it "Richard and all his offspring[a];" and in 1314 Roger Felton assigned certain lands with all the serfs thereon, their chattels and progeny[b]. The miseries and poverty of these poor serfs is evident from the testimony of ancient annalists. They were taxed and imprisoned without mercy. Gradually and by slow degrees, however, they acquired some few privileges. The ancient custom of extorting from the serf the largest possible amount of manual labour, became from many causes partially relinquished for a stated tax in money.

The Norman baron was often the lord of several domains; he had castles and estates in many counties of England, all crowded with dependent serfs. It was frequently the case that the baron took up his abode in one of his castles, and there remained until he had consumed the fat of the land, and drained all vestiges of riches from his vassals. Power was on the side of the lord, the serf had no appeal. Having exhausted one domain, the lord would take up his abode at another, thus continually moving to collect his revenues in kind. This course was attended

---

[a] Madox, Formul. Angl., p. 188.   [b] Ibid., p. 315.

with many inconveniences; the baron might possess estates on which he did not care to reside, and thus the personal services which his serfs were bound to render, being unrequired, produced no absolute benefit. But by the substitution of a tax in money the revenue could be collected by his bailiff, and transmitted to him to any part at which he pleased to reside. This custom, without abolishing slavery, served greatly to modify it. It gave to the serf an independence in the pursuit of his calling; he could amass wealth, and although always liable to the rapacity of his lord, the possession of riches led to a great improvement in his social condition. It infused a spirit of emulation into trade, and developed the industrial talents of the people.

But this advancement of the commonalty was a work of time, and the social and domestic condition of the peasantry and trading classes for many ages appears to have been at the lowest ebb. National vices helped to retard their progress, and to render their homes barren of all comfort and refinement, making their condition for the moment little better, and in many cases worse, than when subject to serfdom they were dependent for their accommodation upon the will of their lord.

Chiefly, however, the decreased size of the hall was owing to the increased importance of other rooms in the house. At this time, there is little doubt, a considerable advance was made in the social, as well as in the moral, condition of the English as a nation. The hall, even where it existed, was now no longer employed at night as a general sleeping apartment, as had been the custom previously[c]. Chambers and dormitories were more plentifully

[c] The following extract from the Rolls in the time of Henry VIII. will illustrate the rapid change which was taking place at that time, but it had begun long before:—

"Makyng not only of a new wyndow

provided, and at the same time, the old solar was much enlarged, to which the ladies withdrew after dinner; the withdrawing-room, even in those days, assuming an importance scarcely inferior to that which we find attached to it in our own. The offices, perhaps, occupied nearly the same space as before, although they were ordinarily called upon to afford smaller supplies.

When, therefore, the drawing-room was enlarged, and other similar rooms probably added, such as a study for the lord, after the same manner as the boudoir for the lady; when the kitchen and offices generally occupied the greater part of the lower story of the house, instead of being erected apart, and when, above all, the number of the sleeping apartments was so considerably enlarged —we can easily understand that little room in proportion was left for that large hall which hitherto had been the boast of the country mansion.

It is true that large halls are found even in the Elizabethan period, but they are then rather the exception than the rule, and seldom do they occupy such a disproportionate space in regard to the rest of the house as they previously had done. When some landowner had many friends or relations to live with him, or thought it necessary to support a certain degree of state and dignity, he built a large dining-chamber; but though the

---

for the kynges chamber of Presence but also framyng and fynyshyng of iij new partysions wythin the galary, makyng of a newe partysion in the great chamber were the kynges warderobe of bedde and also new makynge of a great long shed in the utter court wyth vij new partycions in it for offycers to lye in, workyng in ye newe plankyng of the quens stabul and repayryng and mendyng of all the planke in the kynges stabil, and makyng of a new steer by the butte in the kynges gardyn and breckyng downe of a partycion in the quens warderobe, workynge also in the new makyng of a harber for the kynges grace to dyne and sope in, and makyng of a new seat in the kynges gardyn and makyng also of tabulls, ffornes, trestells and cobersse."—Extract from the Accounts of the Surveyor General, 34 Hen. VIII. MS. Additional, 10,109.

form was kept, the spirit and meaning of the old hall was lost.

We in these days find it difficult to picture to ourselves such a remnant of the old feudal times. We cannot bring before our mind the scene of a large household assembled together at the one common meal, the servants in the body of the hall, the master and his guests on the dais.

The nearest approach to the arrangement which we have described is to be found in the college-halls of our two Universities, which are left standing to us by the bounty of our ancestors as memorials of past manners and customs. In the hall, for instance, of William of Wykeham, as well in Winchester as in New College, is exhibited the perfect type: at one end the dais, on which was the high table, (called so to this day,) where the warden and senior fellows dined, while the juniors and scholars took up their position in the body of the hall. In other colleges it is the same—it was so in the first endowed colleges of Balliol and Merton, in Oxford; and such a hall has been built, within a few years, after the ancient model, in Pembroke College, in the same University. But these collegiate halls are, to a great extent, but large chambers arranged simply for the convenience of a large society presided over by superiors, and taking their origin, as is clear, in the earlier monastic institutions. It is true that a close similarity of plan existed in both, but there was a great principle which guided the arrangement of the feudal hall, and which was wanting in the other. The spirit of that hall has passed away with the system which gave it birth, never, perhaps, to be again revived.

At the beginning of the fifteenth century, as in the fourteenth, the HOUSES OF THE PEASANTRY were hovels of poverty and filth, and the villages were mere clusters of mud-built huts, covered with reeds or straw. They had no second room, and the single apartment served as a chamber in which all the family slept promiscuously, a circumstance which the Norman *trouvère* did not forget to make the subject of many a licentious jest. Longland, in "Piers the Plowman's Crede," gives us an uninviting description of a peasant's home[d]. The dank smoke from the turf fire could find no vent but through the window holes and the chinks of the door, and we are not surprised that the Plowman should complain that the

"Smoke and smothre smyt in his eyen."

The furniture of a medieval cottage was miserably scanty —a cupboard, a bench, and a few wooden platters and utensils for cooking, generally completed the household-stuff of the labouring man. His food was of the coarsest description, and he bitterly experienced the hardships of his condition in those times of scarcity and famine which so frequently occurred during the middle ages. The following lines from the "Nunns Priests Tale," will help us to form an idea of the domestic state of the lower classes in the fourteenth century. Chaucer is describing the lot of the widow :—

"Three large sowes she had, and no mo;
Three kine, and eke a sheep, that highte malle.
Full sooty was hire boure, and eke hire halle,
In whiche she ete many a slender mele.
Of poinant sauce, ne knew she never a dele.
No deintee morsel passed throughe hire throte;
Hire diete was accordant to hire cote."—l. 14,836.

In the fifteenth century there was a slight improvement; the cottages were somewhat increased in size, but

---

[d] The Irish cabins of the present day are often very much the same as here described, but they more commonly consist of two rooms separated by a large chimney-stack, and they are commonly built of stone, at least in many parts of the country where stone is abundant.

gradually and slowly. That we have hardly any remains of the humble habitations of this period is not surprising, as at best the material was wood. We meet with many small buildings, or remains of larger erections, now inhabited by the agricultural labourer, but in nearly all cases it will be found that the houses had originally been tenanted by those whose social position was far higher.

The timber-houses of the fifteenth century in the villages of Kent and some other parts are often little more than cottages. The house at Wingham, of which we give a view, is of rather higher pretensions, having an upper story overhanging, as usual, and an ornamented barge-board, and yet it is hardly large enough to have been a farm-house. It may be considered as a successor to the fisherman's house at Meare, in Somersetshire, described in our last volume.

The MATERIALS employed for building houses in the middle ages were always those which were cheapest and came most readily to hand; no money was spent in bringing materials from a distance. In those districts where stone was abundant it was employed in preference, and when it happened to be of good quality, as in great part of Somersetshire, Wiltshire, and Gloucestershire, the houses have come down to us in fine preservation, and are perhaps our best examples. In other districts, where no stone is to be had, and BRICK is the material of the country, as in the Eastern counties, we have very fine mansions of brick-work of the fifteenth and sixteenth centuries, whatever may have been the case at an earlier period. It is probable, indeed, that brick was never entirely disused from the time of the Romans downwards; but however that may have been, there is no dispute about the period we are now treating of. Norfolk and Suffolk abound with fine

DOMESTIC ARCHITECTURE: SIXTEENTH CENTURY.

PARAPET.
LAYER MARNEY, ESSEX.

brick mansions of the time of Henry VII. and Henry VIII., many of them in very perfect preservation, and the brick-work is made so ornamental that it may well be considered as competing with stone. Such houses as Compton Winyates, Warwickshire; Tattershall Castle, Lincolnshire; Layer Marney, Essex; Weston Hall, Suffolk, may well challenge comparison with any others of the same period, whatever the material may be. By using bricks of different colours also, and arranging them in patterns, a very happy effect is often produced, as at Layer Marney, and in the gatehouse of Jesus College, Cambridge. Sutton Place, near Guildford, in Surrey, is a very rich example of moulded brick-work, or terra-cotta, the dressings, and mouldings, and mullions being of a hard white brick, while the walls are of red brick, with patterns in black.

In the chalk districts the houses are frequently faced with flints, cut, and trimmed, and arranged with great skill and effect, of which there are fine examples at Norwich and Sandwich, and many others in different parts of Kent and Sussex.

In Ireland, where stone is very abundant and very hard, the houses are all built of that material, generally in its rough state, especially in the earlier houses, but in the fifteenth century they are frequently of cut stone.

TIMBER houses and half-timber[e] houses of this period are to be found everywhere, more or less perfect. Even where other materials were abundant, wood was so much more convenient, especially when a building was wanted to be erected in a hurry, that it was continually employed. It was shewn in a former volume how general

[e] Lydgate writes:—
"So eqully of tymbre and of stone,
Here housis were raised euerich on."
MS. Reg., 18 D. vi., fo. 18. b.

In the Romance of Amadas we read:—
"Betwene a forest and a citié,
He fonde a chapell of ston and tre."
Weber's Metrical Rom., iii. p. 246.

the use of wooden houses was even in London in the middle ages, and notwithstanding the danger from fire, hundreds of wooden houses still remain; and in country places timber houses are perhaps more common still than those of any other material. But the builders and architects of the fifteenth century knew how to make good use of their materials; and their timber houses are often as picturesque and effective as any others; such houses as Agecroft Hall, Lancashire, and the timber halls of Cheshire, are familiar to every one as favourite subjects for the artist's pencil.

The custom of making the upper stories of a house overhang the lower part was usual in the fifteenth century, both in town and in country houses. Sometimes this projecting upper story is carried upon an open arcade of wooden arches, forming a sort of cloister, as at Waltham, Essex. In other instances it is boldly corbelled out, as at Tamworth, and Wingham, Kent; and this occurs equally in towns: there are good examples in a genuine state in St. Mildred's, Canterbury, and Harrietsham, Kent. The timbers in the fronts of these wooden houses were often made very ornamental by panelling, either entirely carved on wood, of which there is a very rich example at Bury St. Edmunds, Suffolk, or the spaces be-between the timbers are filled with plaster[f], and the timbers left slightly projecting, and often painted black and white for effect, as is the general custom in Lancashire and Cheshire.

[f] A building scene is represented in a MS. of this century, in which the workmen are mixing mortar, and carrying it in buckets to the masons. One is plastering the *outside* of the walls of a tower with a trowel. MS. Harl. 2,278, fo. 28. b.

The medieval cement and mortar was remarkable for its durable qualities, as an old poet says :—

"The morter is maked so wel,
Se mai no man hit breke wiz no stele."
Hartshorne's Metrical Tales, p. 91.

DOMESTIC ARCHITECTURE: FIFTEENTH CENTURY.

AGECROFT HALL, LANCASHIRE.

CHAPTER II.

TOWNS AND TOWN HOUSES.

No great distinction can be drawn between the towns of the fifteenth century and those of the two previous centuries described in the second volume of this work (pp. 153—194). New towns were not required, a sufficient number being already provided; and although very many houses were rebuilt, they were for the most part on the same sites. The fortifications were still necessary, and these prevented, in a great degree, the enlargement of the towns by the throwing out of suburbs; although, from the increase of population, the old towns became more and more crowded, and the people were anxious to enlarge them, which they did rapidly in the following century, when leave was given to destroy the fortifications or outworks beyond them. Very few towns in England have retained their walls: York, Chester, and Conway are perhaps the most perfect, but in a great number of instances portions of the walls remain, and in still more the plan, and the names of the streets close within the wall for the purpose of manning it.

At first only houses of sufficient importance to be able to be fortified separately were built outside the walls. Even those colleges which were outside the city walls at Oxford were fortified: the embattled wall, with its bastions, enclosing the college and its grounds, still exists at Magdalen College as built in the fifteenth century, of which the builder's accounts are preserved in the college. The Tower of London is a miniature town in itself, with its

Norman keep, its walls of enceinte, its gate-houses, its courts or baileys, and streets; but it is more properly a castle, which has been greatly filled up with subsequent buildings. This, however, gives a good idea of the process which was going on in many towns silently during the fifteenth and sixteenth centuries: as wealth and population increased, the whole available space was gradually built over; even the market-place, which originally formed an important feature in the centre of each town, was very much encroached upon, and sometimes quite lost.

The internal arrangement and plan continued the same as before. In most cases the four principal streets meet in the centre of the town, in the market-place, where are situated the town-hall and the market-cross. The former have in almost all instances in England been rebuilt, but many very fine town-halls of this period remain on the Continent, more especially in the Low Countries, as at Bruges, Ghent, Louvain, Brussels, Antwerp, &c. Singularly enough, the market-crosses have more often been preserved in England, and we have many very fine ones remaining of this period, as at Malmesbury, Castle Combe, Chichester, Leighton-Buzzard, Winchester, and Bristol[a]. A series of engravings of them is given in the first volume of Britton's "Architectural Antiquities," and a complete set of them has been promised by Mr. Le Keux. Some of these market-crosses were carried upon arches and vaults, with a sufficient space under them for a butter-market. In

---

[a] There was the cross at Banbury, for instance, in the centre of the Horsefair, which gave rise to our nursery rhyme of

"Ride a-cockhorse to Banbury cross."
Leland, in describing "the fayrest streete" of that town, says, "In the west part is a large area invironed with meetly good buildinges, havinge a goodly crosse with many degrees (steps) about it. In this area is kept every Thursday a very celebrate markett. There runneth through this area a purle of fresh water."

some instances there is a fountain or reservoir of water, as at Lincoln; but fountains were never common in England. There were wells and cisterns for the supply of water, but these do not appear to have been often made into ornamental structures until a later period. One was erected in Oxford so late as the time of James I. by Otho Nicholson, and water to supply it was conveyed by pipes from Hincksey-hill, a distance of about two miles, where the small building for the conduit-head still remains. The conduit itself was removed about the end of the last century to Nuneham-park from its original position at Carfax, where the four streets meet, and where it must have been a considerable obstruction to the traffic when the market-place was built over: this must have occupied originally a considerable space, with St. Martin's Church in the north-west corner, and the old Town-hall in the south-east; the present Town-hall was built in front of the old one. The plan of Oxford has been already mentioned in our second volume as being that of the old Roman town, with the four ways meeting in the centre, where was the market-place. The gates are all now destroyed, but their sites are well known, and portions of the walls remain, especially the portion rebuilt by William of Wykeham, which is a very fine example of the walls of a town of the period.

Any nobleman's house, or monastery, or other establishment of importance, had its own separate fortifications in addition to those of the town; many of the cathedral closes still have their walls of enceinte, and their gate-houses remaining, as at Wells, Salisbury, and Canterbury: the bishop's palace also had its separate wall, and gate-house, and moat, as at Wells. Many noblemen's houses in London were fortified; of these, nothing now remains but the names, unless Northumberland House may be considered as a representation of the old type, being probably rebuilt on the old foundations. The houses of the merchant princes vied with those of the nobles, but do not appear to have been generally fortified. Crosby Hall, in Bishopsgate-street, London, is a very fine and perfect example, now threatened with destruction. The hall of John Halle at Salisbury shews that these merchant princes were not confined to London; it is as fine a hall as any nobleman's house of the period could exhibit. The guild-halls or club-houses of the fifteenth century were an important feature in the towns of that time. These were often converted into town-halls when the guilds were abolished by Henry VIII., as at Coventry and at Boston. St. Mary's Hall at Coventry is one of the most perfect town houses of the middle of the fifteenth century that we have remaining: every part is perfect; the gate-house, the cellars, the kitchen, the offices, the chambers, as well as the fine hall.

Many of the town walls and gates were rebuilt in this century, sometimes merely because the old ones were dilapidated, in other instances, as in London, for the purpose of enlargement. There were usually four principal gates at the extremities of the four principal streets, and many of the city gate-houses of this period have been preserved, as at Winchester, Southampton, Warwick, and Bristol; and many more have been destroyed within the last century, their sites being sometimes marked by their names only, as Ludgate, Bishopsgate, Billingsgate, and Aldgate[b].

---

[b] Leland, in describing Banbury, says, "There is another fayre street from south to north; and at each end of this street is a stone gate. There be also in the towne other gates besides these. Yet is there neither any certaine token or likelyhood, that ever the towne was diched or walled." These gates were built only for collecting tolls, as by themselves they would have been of little use for defence.

DOMESTIC ARCHITECTURE: FIFTEENTH CENTURY.

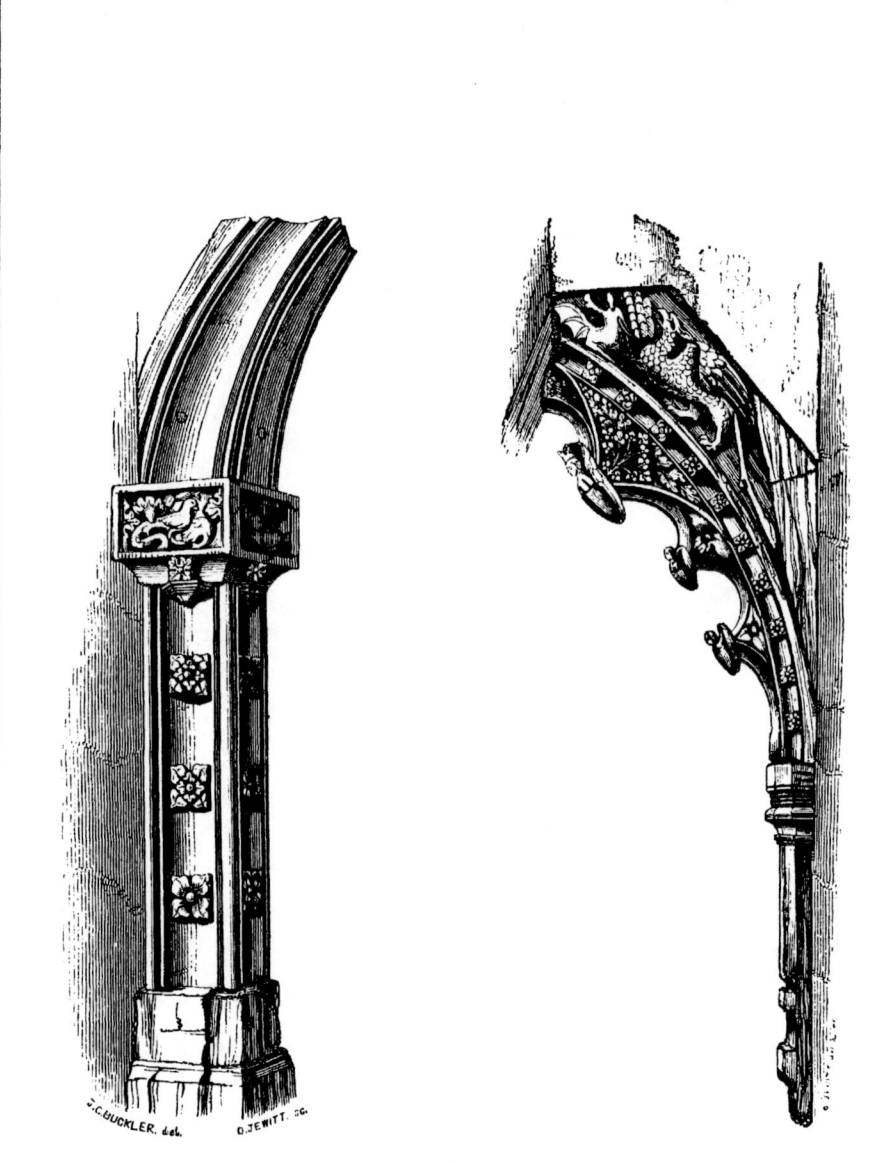

CORNER-POST,
GREAT CHESTERFORD, ESSEX.

BRACKET, PAVEMENT,
YORK.

DOMESTIC ARCHITECTURE: FIFTEENTH CENTURY.

DOORWAY, PAVEMENT, YORK.

DOORWAY, JUBBERGATE.

The principal streets were generally of a tolerable width, but the minor ones extremely narrow, and the houses, overhanging in successive stories, must sometimes have nearly met at the top; but this custom seems to have been carried further in the sixteenth and seventeenth centuries than in the fifteenth. These overhanging houses were necessarily of timber to a great extent, though instances do occur of stone fronts upon projecting beams, as at Sherborne, Dorsetshire; but in these cases the projection is comparatively slight. The lower story, or ground floor, is often of stone or brick, while the upper stories are of wood, as at Norton St. Philips, on the borders of Somersetshire and Wiltshire; the ground floor is often half underground, and protected by a vault, as in the previous century. The timber houses of this century have sometimes a very moderate projection, as at Canterbury, and in the Butcher-row at Shrewsbury: the upper projecting story is probably a later addition. The beautiful timber houses and hospitals of Coventry belong chiefly to the sixteenth and seventeenth centuries, as in most other towns: at Weobley, Herefordshire, there are a few of the fifteenth; the very beautiful and perfect one at Bishops-Cannings, Wiltshire, is probably of the sixteenth.

One very characteristic and ornamental feature of the timber houses in towns is the corner-post, which is enriched in various ways, frequently panelled, of which there is a good example in the churchyard of St. Peter's, Derby, the stem of which has a sort of fluted panelling, with a moulded base, and a capital with a row of Tudor flowers; the spandrel of the arch is carved with a sort of diaper pattern. At Great Chesterford, Essex, is a good one of remarkably square character, each face hollowed out, and the hollows filled at intervals with the square-leaved flower; the capital is also of square panels, enriched with foliage. At Salisbury is another very rich example, with panelling and mouldings with flowers, and the spandrels filled with flowing patterns; having, at first sight, an earlier look, but not really anterior to the time of Henry VII. At Bury St. Edmunds is a very curious example. Those in the Butcher-row at Shrewsbury are panelled only. In Northgate-street, Gloucester, is a remarkably rich one, with a figure of an angel in a niche, and smaller niches for other images by the side of it, the canopies richly carved with crockets and finials. Similar images in niches at the corners of streets are still common on the Continent, and were doubtless equally so in England before the Reformation, though they have been very generally destroyed, having been abused for superstitious uses.

The doorways of timber houses in towns were often richly ornamented with panelled or moulded doorposts, some with, others without capitals and bases, and spurs on each side supporting the overhanging upper story; of which there are good examples at Weobley, Herefordshire, a decayed town, full of good old timber houses, and Sherborne, Dorsetshire, which is also rich in old houses both of wood and stone. York was formerly celebrated for its rich timber houses, and though a large part of them have been destroyed within the last few years, there are still many remaining, the doorways and spurs of which are particularly fine. Some of these appear to have been the foot entrances to courts which were in common to several houses. They are chiefly remarkable from the enormous length of the spurs forming the two sides of the entrance, and supporting the projecting story, or rather supporting a projection beyond that projecting story. This taste in York con-

DOMESTIC ARCHITECTURE: FIFTEENTH CENTURY.

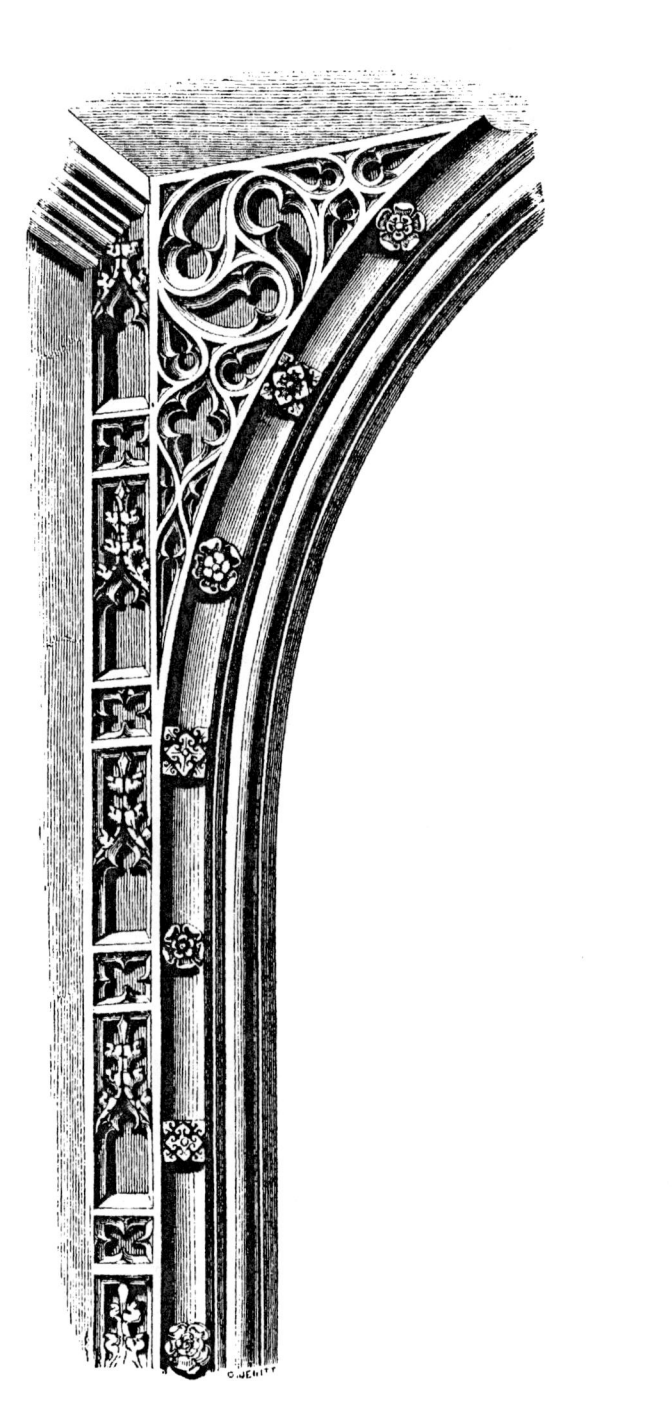

CORNER-POST,
SALISBURY.

DOMESTIC ARCHITECTURE: FIFTEENTH CENTURY.

PART OF A HOUSE IN EASTGATE STREET,
BURY ST. EDMUND'S, SUFFOLK.

tinued until late in the fifteenth century, and the spurs were then very richly carved.

Besides the corner-posts and doorways, the windows are also frequently enriched with mouldings and panelling, as at Saffron Walden, Essex, and the whole front of the house is often a continued series of panelling; sometimes plain, as at St. Mary le Wigford, Lincoln, and Tamworth, Staffordshire; in other instances the panelling is richly carved, of which a good example remains in a portion of a house in Eastgate-street, Bury St. Edmunds, and another fine one at Dunster, Somersetshire. The front of a house in the market-place at Newark is a mixture of timber and ornamental plaster, with a long series of niches and figures in plaster inserted in wooden panels; such examples are rare in England, though found in houses of the fifteenth and sixteenth centuries, of the Flamboyant style in France, as at Caen and Morlaix, and in Germany, as at Halberstadt and Brunswick. The upper part of this house at Newark affords also a good example of the long gallery, which became usual in the time of Elizabeth, but occurs also frequently in the latter part of the fifteenth century, as in the old hall of the De Burghs at Gainsborough, Lincolnshire, and is common in the time of Henry VIII.

The fronts of stone houses in towns were also frequently enriched with panelling over the whole surface of the wall, as in Colston's house in Small-street, Bristol, where the principal front towards the court is so ornamented. In London the great fire destroyed nearly every vestige of the houses of the middle ages; the Guildhall, being of stone, escaped its ravages; and Crosby Hall, being without the walls, and at that time a detached building, was not exposed to it. This was built about 1470, by Sir John Crosby, one of the merchant princes of his day, and affords us a noble example of the mansions of that period, although only the hall and a chamber adjoining have been preserved. The hall is one of the finest and most perfect that we have remaining; it has a very rich timber roof, and a bay window with a groined vault. The whole has been restored within a few years, but the original character is less damaged than is usually the case under that misnamed process. A fine set of engravings of this hall is given by Britton in the fourth volume of his "Architectural Antiquities."

Of the numerous other mansions with which London was adorned in the fifteenth century, we have now the names only to mark the sites, and these for the most part outside the walls, especially along the north bank of the Thames westward of the Temple. We may thus trace the sites of the once beautiful gardens and mansions of the Earls of Essex, Arundel, and Surrey, the Dukes of Norfolk and Somerset; beyond which we arrive at the Savoy Palace, the remains of which were destroyed in 1816 to make an opening to Waterloo-bridge, with the exception of the chapel of the palace, which, having been made parochial, has been preserved, and has a remarkably rich ceiling of the time of Henry VIII., worthy of more attention than it usually receives. Near this was the seat of the Duke of Beaufort; and beyond this those of the Earl of Craven, the Duke of Buckingham, and the Duke of Northumberland; this last, although rebuilt at a later period, is still continued as the town residence of the Duke, and preserves much of its medieval grandeur and dignity. We now arrive at the royal palaces of Whitehall and Westminster.

Whitehall was entirely rebuilt by Charles I. Of the palace of Westminster nothing remains but the great

DOMESTIC ARCHITECTURE: FIFTEENTH CENTURY.

HOUSE IN ST. MILDRED'S, CANTERBURY.

hall: of this the walls belong to the Norman period, but raised, and the character entirely altered, in the time of Richard II., when the present magnificent roof was put on; which still retains much of its original character, although one end has been destroyed to make way for Sir Charles Barry's improvements, and the louvre had been previously restored by Smirke.

To return to the more humble dwellings of the citizens and shop-keepers. These were, as has been said, chiefly of wood, and therefore have frequently disappeared; but in some parts of the country they are still frequently to be met with, as at Tamworth, Coventry, and Weobley. A timber house in St. Mildred's, Canterbury, is a fair example of a small tradesman's house of this period. In many towns on the Continent whole streets have been preserved of these wooden houses of the fifteenth century, as at Nuremberg, Hanover, Brunswick, Halberstadt, and Quedlingburgh, and several other towns in the north of Germany.

In all large cities some place was set apart as the recognised abode of thieves and other bad characters, and there were usually certain privileges of sanctuary belonging to it. In Paris it was called the *Cour des Miracles*[c]. The Jews also inhabited a separate quarter, and to a great extent still continue to do so, as about Houndsditch in London: at Frankfort-on-the-Maine the Jews' quarter is remarkable, the houses having been rebuilt in a regular street in the sixteenth century, and remain nearly intact.

Each shop was distinguished by a sign[d] hanging from

[c] Sauval, *Histoire et Recherches des Antiquités de la Ville de Paris*, vol. i. pp. 510, 511.

[d] There is a very amusing paper on the old signs of London in the "Spectator." Those of Paris in the fifteenth century are enumerated in a little tract published among the notes to the *Mystères inédits du quinzième Siècle*, (Paris, 1837, 8vo.,) vol. i. pp. 369—376.

a pole, which must have been a great obstruction, but at the same time extremely picturesque, as may be seen in many illuminations in manuscripts of this period. A few of these signs have been retained by particular trades; for instance, the barber's pole and basin may still be often seen in the back streets; though the basin is fast disappearing in England, it is still usual in France. The pawnbrokers continue to use the three golden balls, and sometimes the chequers, or money-changer's board. The bush, as the mark of a house of refreshment, may still be met with, though English landlords seem to be generally of opinion that their liquor is so good that it "needs no bush." In Brittany and other parts of France, where a small public-house is called a *bouchon*, this custom is still usual. Formerly every trade had its well-known signs, and several trades had a separate street or district assigned to each, as the leather-sellers in Leather-lane, the corn-dealers in Cornhill, &c.

In the principal streets there were shops for the display of goods, but these had not become common. In general there were store-rooms only, and the chief opportunity for displaying the goods was at the fairs, when the principal trade was carried on. The store-rooms were usually half underground, as in the previous century, (see vol. ii. p. 185,) and were still vaulted with stone, whether the upper structure was of wood or not.

The bedroom was sometimes at the back of the shop, more often in the upper chambers. The room on the first floor over the store-room was called the solar, and was the chief dwelling-room of the family of the merchant. There were also store-rooms in the roof, chiefly for corn and other provisions, which was hoisted up by means of a crane, the penthouse for which often remains,

DOMESTIC ARCHITECTURE: FIFTEENTH CENTURY.

HOUSE IN SMALL STREET, BRISTOL.

and has a picturesque effect. On the Continent these store-rooms in the roof, with their cranes, are still in common use. This formed the whole of the front of the building, as the erections were seldom of more than two stories high.

The kitchens of houses in the suburbs of London are built very much after the same fashion, half under ground; and in the same manner the principal floor, or solar, was commonly approached by an external flight of steps. There are several small houses on this plan remaining perfect at Kidwelly, in South Wales, and at Winchelsea; and a number of the cellars at Chester, where the upper part, having been of wood, has been destroyed by fire. Possibly the celebrated Rows owe their origin to this circumstance: in rebuilding the town after a great fire, it was found more convenient to make a footway and a sort of bazaar for shops upon the top of the vaults of the cellars, and by taking a passage out of the solars, than in the narrow roadway below, where the cellars would not generally make convenient shops; though some of them have lately been converted into show rooms. The cellars of houses of the fifteenth century remain in almost all old towns: there are several in Oxford, Shrewsbury, &c.

When the houses were of brick or stone, the street front did not overhang, but was carried up straight, and ornamented with panelling, as in the house in Small-street, Bristol, the inns at Glastonbury, and Sherborne and Grantham. When the material was wood, the upper story projected on corbels, but to a moderate extent; the custom of building lofty houses of wood with each successive story projecting one over the other, until in the narrow streets the upper windows almost meet, belongs, as we have said, to a later period, generally

36 DOMESTIC ARCHITECTURE: FIFTEENTH CENTURY.

to the time of Elizabeth and James I. A few instances remain of shops of the fifteenth century; perhaps the most perfect is the Butcher-row at Shrewsbury; but in general, the increase of wealth in England has swept them away, and we must seek in other countries for good examples: they abound in Brittany, and many other parts of France. In England, the general custom of having cellars such as we have described must have interfered with anything like shops, excepting in the market-places and rows specially built for that purpose. There was a butcher-row like that at Shrewsbury[e] in most towns.

TIMBER HOUSE. Douce MS 202.

[e] For further particulars respecting this butcher-row, see also under Shropshire, in chap. vii.

DOMESTIC ARCHITECTURE: FIFTEENTH CENTURY.

SHOPS IN THE
DOUBLE BUTCHER ROW, SHREWSBURY.

Numerous surveys of towns in the time of Elizabeth are extant, and these supply many details which it would lead us too far to enter upon; several of them are engraved in the maps of Agas and Speed, that of Winchester is also given by Mr. Smirke in the Proceedings of the Archæological Institute at Winchester, in 1845; the walls were perfect when these surveys were made.

Documentary material is also at hand to give us some idea of the towns and town-houses during the fifteenth century. One instance from a will is sufficient to shew the kind of evidence that is afforded from this source:—

"Item, I wil that my newe hous with the iij. tunys [f] of chemeneyis with in the yere aftir my disses be diseverid & partyd froom the hefd place vnder this forme folwyng: I wyl the entre with stoon wal be the strete syde longe to newe hous as ferre as the chymeneys stretchith, and a deseueraunce maad of ston wal ovir the entre to parte the litil botrie undir the gresys[g] to longe to the parlour wiche is redy maad and also deseverid with a walle of tymbyr fro the hefd place be an entre maad oute of the spynnynge hous. Item to close in a good walle ye dore y[t] is oute of ye parlour into ye spynnynge hous, whiche spynnynge hous I wille euer longe to my hefd place and the drawt chambyr above the spynnynge hous therto. Item: I wyl that ye newe prevy hous ovir the synke be the dore in to the yerde ward next the Facoun[h] wel closid & keverid to serue for the parlour and chambyr a lofte withe ye prevy & the closet a lofte to go overe togidre hool, vndir this forme as folowith in wryting: that is to say, I wille my feffees & my attornies put Seynt Marie priest of Seynt Marie Chirche in possession of my seid hous with the chemene of iij. tunys next the Facon.

"Item: I wil that Jenete Whitwelle my nece haue hir dwellynge in a part of my hefd place terme of hire lyffe, that is to say, I wil yt she chese if sche will haue the chambyr yt she hath loyn in w[t] the drawght chambyr therto, or ellys the chambyr abovyn the kechyne, with the draught chambyr longynge therto, with the esement of the prevy longynge therto. And I will she haue hire liberte at alle leffull tymes to go to the chapell to seye hire devocyons, in caas be yt she chese the seid

[f] Chimney shafts are still called *tuns* in some districts.

[g] The little buttery under the *stairs*. Gresys was a term used to signify the plural of *gre*, a step. In Norfolk, stairs are still called grissens.

[h] The Falcon inn.

chambyr aboue the kechene, and if she chese that she to haue the store hous thereto to leye in hire stuffe, and so alle that severall to hire selfe terme of hire liff, and she to leve the chambyr she hath loyn in, wich I wil doo remayne to the hafd place. Item, I wille the seid Janete terme of hire lyff haue hire liberte of fre owet goyng & in comyng at the gate be the strete syde, and as welle at the doore be the lane syde at alle lefull tymes, & easement of the kechene to make in hire mete, and esement of the welle in the yerde, and esement of the preuy in the same yeerd. And she to haue a keye of the grete gardyn gate to go in whan she wyll & hire sauth and what ffrende she wille calle to hire, and a place in the gardyn assigned to hire for herbis and for wood to lye in."—*From the will of John Baret of Bury,* 1463.

If, again, we refer to illuminations, we find an interesting representation of a town in a beautiful manuscript entitled *Le Tresor des Histoires*, from which the student may gain some valuable hints on the domestic architecture of that time[i], and in which he will see represented many of those details which we find mentioned by contemporary writers. Lydgate, in describing the city of Troy, as newly built by Priam, but delineates, in his graphic way, the aspect of the principal European cities of his own age. The " crafte of coryous masonyre" of which he speaks was the delight of the medieval architects, and the

> " Fresche alures withe lusty hye pynacles,
>   And monstrynge outwarde ryche tabernacles,
>   Vouted aboue lyke to reclynatoryes,
>   That called were deambulatoryes[j],
>   Men to walke to geder twayne & twayne,
>   To kepe them drye when it dyde rayne,"

were by no means of rare occurrence. It is curious to notice the sanitary arrangements of this period, and in-

[i] MS. Cottonian, Aug. v. fo. 142.

[j] Robert of Gloucester speaks of the " alures of the castle" where " the laydes thanne stode." Rob. of Glouc., p. 192. The alure is the passage behind the parapet on the top of a castle, which was frequently covered over, as at Warwick Castle, though more often with wood only: it is called by the French *chemin de ronde*.

teresting to find a reference to a system of drainage which would be creditable to a more enlightened age. Lydgate writes:—

> "And euery hous couerid was with leede,
> And gargoyle and many hydous heede,
> Withe spoutes thorugh, and pypes as they aughte,
> From the stoon werke to the canell rought,
> Voydynge fylthes lowe into the grounde,
> Thorugh grates perced of yron perced rounde,
> The stretes paued bothe in lengthe and brede,
> In cheker wyse with stones whyte & rede[k]."

And again, when speaking of the river which ran through the town:—

> "By archis stronge, his cours for to reflecte,
> Thorugh condyte pypis large and wyde withal,
> By certeyne meanes artyficiall
> That it made a ful purgacion,
> Of al odure and fylthes in the toun,
> Wasshynge the stretes as they stode arowe,
> And the gutters in the erthe lowe,
> That in the citie was no fylthe sene,
> For the canell scoured was so clene,
> And deuoyded into secrete wyse,
> That no man myght espye nor deuyse
> By what engyne the fylthes fer nor nere,
> Were borne awaye by cours of the ryuere.
> So couertly euery thynge was couered,
> Whereby the towne was utterly assured,
> From endengerynge of all corupcion,
> From wycked ayre and from inffexion[l]."

The paving of the streets of London and other large towns was common in the fifteenth century, as is proved by the frequent licenses granted by the crown for collecting the tax or rate for that purpose. The same evidence proves that sewers were commonly built and kept in

[k] MS. Cottonian, Aug. iv. fo. 28. a.   [l] Ibid., fo. 28. b.

repair by public rates at that period. The sewers in towns have often been destroyed in comparatively modern times in digging foundations for new houses, but those which remain of the monasteries, and sometimes other houses or castles of the middle ages, are so fine, large, and well built, that they are continually mistaken for subterraneous passages.

Bridges were also built and maintained at the public expense by means of rates in towns. These rates were collected by royal authority, and are therefore recorded in the public Rolls.

There were often sums of money left for the repair of bridges: e.g. in the will of Sir Robert Ogill, bearing the date of 1410, we find:—

"Item lego diversis pontibus infra Northumbriam, et precipue infra dominium meum fractis et emendandis, c. solidos."

In Count Neville's will, (1440,) we find:—

"Item do et lego at pontem faciendum apud Wynston, c. marcas; et ad pontem de Ulshawe juxta Middleham, xx*l*."

John Danby (1444) leaves in his will the following sums:

"Item lego ad emendacionem viæ circa pontem de Warleby. vj*s*. viij*d*. Item lego fabricæ pontis de Yagord, xl*d*. si velit extendere."

Roger Thornton, the opulent Newcastle merchant, leaves (1429) one hundred marks to the repairing of the Tyne bridge in that town, on condition the "mair and ye comyns" will release him from certain actions at law.

In the country, bridges were sometimes built and kept up at the public expense by taxes equivalent to our modern county rates, but they were comparatively rare. Fords were extensively used; and bridges were sometimes built by particular noblemen or monasteries. One at Culham, near Abingdon, is an instance of a free town bridge. It was built by the Abbot, and the opening celebrated with much pomp, as recorded in a cotemporary ballad, the original of which, or a copy, written on parchment in the fifteenth century, is still preserved in the hall of Christ's Hospital in the churchyard of St. Helen's, Abingdon:—

> "Henrici quinti regis quarto revoluto
> Anno, rex idem pontem fundavit utrumque,
> Supra locum binum Borford dictumque Culhamford;
> Inter eos namque via regia tendit alta.
> Annis adjunctis dat inter gradientibus amplum;
> Principium cujus Abendoniæ situatur.
> Annis tunc donum M. quater C. numeratis,
> Et sexto deno cum fecit opus pietatis.
> Vos qui transitis, hujus memores bene sitis,
> Et vestris precibus fundator sit relevatus.
>
> "Off alle Werkys in this Worlde that ever were wrought
> Holy chirche is chefe, there children been chersid[n].
> For be baptim these Barnes to blisse been i brought,
> Thorough the grace of God, and fayre refresshed.
> Another blissed besines is brigges to make,
> There that the pepul may not passe after greet showres.
> Dole[o] it is to drawe a deed body oute of a lake,
> That was fulled in a fount stoon[p], and a Felow of oures.
> Kyng Herry the fyft in his fourthe Yere,
> He hathe i founde for his folke a brige in Berkeschire.
> For cartis with cariage may goo and come clere,
> That many Wynters afore were mareed in the Myre.
> And som oute of her sadels flette[q] to the grounde,
> Wente forthe in the Water wist no man whare.
> Fyve Wekys after or they were i founde,
> Her kyn and her knowlech[r] caught hem uppe with care.
> Then the Commons of Abendon cryed on the kynge,
> Upon Dukes and lordes that were in this londe.
> The Kynge bad hem begynne apon Goddes blissing,
> And make it also stronge as they couthe with stone, lyme or sonde.

[n] Christened. [o] Grievous. [p] Washed in the font. [q] Fell. [r] Acquaintance.

Apon the day of seynt Albon they began this game,
And John Huchyns layde the firste stoon in the Kynges name.
Sir Peris Besillis, knyght curteys and keend,
For his fadir soule and his frendes he dyd as he scholde.
He gaf hem stonys i nowhe into the werkys ende,
Also mony as they nedid feche hem if they wolde.
Than crafti men for the querry made crowes of yre,
Weges, and wayes, and mony harde howys[s],
Jeffray Barbour bad pay hem her hyre.
Then must they have moolds to make on the bowys[t].
They cockid for cartes, and cast for her chisyng.
They founde oute the fundement, and layde in large stones;
They reysid up the archeys be gemeotre in rysyng,
With xi. laborers lavyng[u] at onys.
Ther was water i nowhe, stone, lyme and gravel,
Werkemen als wise as they coude fynde any.
And ever bad the barbour pay for her travel,
Til a M. Marke be spende eche a peny.
Then the strenghe of the streme astoned hem stronge,
In labor and lavyng moche money was lore[x].
Ther loved hem a ladde was a water man longe,
He helpe stop the streme til the werke were a fore.
It was a solace to see in a somer seson,
CCC. I wysse workyng at onys.
iiii. and iiii. reulyd be reson,
To wete who wrought best were set for the nonce[y].
The peple preved her power with the pecoyse[z].
The Mattok was man handeled right wele a whyle.
With spades and schovelis they made suche a noyse,
That men myght here hem thens a myle.
Wyves went oute to wite[a] how they wrought:
V. score in a flok it was a fayre syght.
In bord clothes bright white brede they brought,
Chees and chekenes clerelych A dyght[b].
These weren the dyches i diged in ful harde grounde,
And i cast up to arere with the wey,
Sethen they were i set with a quyk mownde
To holde in the bunkes for ever and ay.

[s] Hoes.   [t] Arch-stones.   [u] Baling.   [x] Lost.
[y] For this especial service.   [z] Pickaxe.   [a] Know.   [b] Prepared.

The gode lorde of Abendon left of his londe,
For the breed ^c of the brige xx iiii. fote large.
It was a greet socour of erthe and of sonde,
And yt he abated the rent of the barge.
An C. pownde, and xv^{li}. was truly payed
Be the hondes of John Huchyns and Banbery also,
For the waye and the barge thus it must be sayed.
Therto witnesse al Abendon, and many oon moo.
For now is Culham hithe i com to an ende,
An al the contre the better and no man the worse.
Few folke there were coude that wey wende,
But they waged a wed ^d or payed of her purse.
And if it were a begger had breed in his bagge,
He schulde be ryght soone i bid for to goo aboute,
And of the pore penyles the hiereward ^e wold habbe
A hood or a girdel, and let hem goo withoute.
Many moo myscheves there weren I say.
Culham hithe hath causid many a curse.
I blyssed be our helpers we have a better waye,
Withoute any peny for cart and for horse.
Thus acordid the kynge and the covent,
And the commones of Abendon as the Abbot wolde.
Thus they were cesed and set al in oon assent,
That al the brekynges of the brige the towne bere schulde.
This was preved acte also in the Perlement,
In perpetual pees to have and to holde.
This tale is i tolde in noon other entent
But for myrthe and in memory to yonge and to olde.
Now every good body that gothe on this brige,
Bid for the Barbour gentil Jeffray,
That clothed many a pore man to bed and to rige,
And hathe holpe to rentis to holde up this waye.
The wiche rentes right trewe men have i take on honde,
And graciously governed hem now a good while.
Who so have hem hereafter withe trewthe but he stonde,
It schal be knowen openly he dothe hymselfe begyle.
I councel every creature to kepe hym from the curse.
For of this tretys wil I no more telle.
And be not to covetous to youre owne purse,
For peril of the peynes in the pit of helle.

^c Breadth.   ^d Left something as a pledge.   ^e Take for the tolls.

Now God geve us grace to folowe treuthe even,
That we may have a place in the blysse of Heven. AMEN.

r. A. B. I. N. D. O. N. R. F. I.

"Take the ferst letter of youre foure fader with A, the worker of wex, and I and N, the colore of an asse; set them togeder, and tel me yf you can what it is than. Richard Fannande Iremonger hathe made this tabul, and set it here in the yere of Kyng Herry the sexte xxxvi[te]."

In France there was a society of brethren for the express purpose of building bridges, called *Fratres Pontis:* they wore a white dress, with the badge of a bridge and a cross on the breast, and they built the bridges at Avignon and St. Esprit over the Rhone in 1471[f].

Bridges frequently had gateway towers upon them[g], or at one end of them, to protect the passage, and the room over the gateway was sometimes a chapel, as at the west gate of Canterbury. There were also frequently wayside chapels upon them, for the convenience of pilgrims, who were the chief travellers of those days; a pilgrimage to Walsingham from distant parts of the country was as common then as an excursion to a watering-place is now. Many roads were formed for the especial use of pilgrims, and there were chapels at intervals along the way that led to any celebrated place of pilgrimage, as at Litcham, Norfolk, on the way to Walsingham. The ostensible object of these pilgrimages was to worship some particular image of the blessed Virgin, as the image of our lady of Walsingham, and the image was supposed to possess miraculous powers. The object of the pilgrimages being then considered as a religious one, it was natural to afford resting-places for the pilgrims in the form of

[f] Ex schedis D. Lancelot, ap. Ducange.

[g] The bridge at Cahors, in Aquitaine, is probably the most perfect remaining. It has three gateway towers upon it. At Carcassonne there is a chapel on a bridge of the beginning of the fifteenth century.

chapels by the wayside, and on a bridge was a favourite place for one of these chapels. There are still remains of several of them: perhaps the best is that on Wakefield bridge, Yorkshire, which is usually supposed to have been founded to commemorate the battle of Wakefield in 1460, on the spot where the young Earl of Rutland, second son of the Duke of York, was murdered by Lord Clifford[h], and it is certain that a chantry was then founded and endowed; but Mr. Buckler has shewn by the architectural character that the original structure of the chapel is as old as the time of Edward II., so that it must have been only altered and adapted for the purpose of the royal chantry, though it seems very singular, if the chapel was then standing and in use, that the boy and his tutor did not take shelter in it, and claim the privilege of sanctuary[i].

There was a celebrated chapel on the Ouse bridge, at York; another at Rotherham: the one at Bradford in Wiltshire has been rebuilt in the seventeenth century, or at least the upper part of it, with a sort of stone dome to it, and applied to some secular purpose. There are remains of one at St. Ives in Huntingdonshire[k].

We have before observed that the ALMSHOUSES or hospitals of the middle ages would alone afford ample materials for a separate work, and that a complete chronological series of them from the twelfth century to the sixteenth might be formed. Those remaining of the fifteenth century are naturally more numerous than at an earlier period, and those of the sixteenth abound everywhere. From the nature of these foundations, they have less frequently been rebuilt or altered than

[h] See Hall's "Chronicle."
[i] He was flying from the battle with Sir Robert Aspell, his chaplain and schoolmaster.
[k] For further information on this subject see Buckler's "Remarks on Wayside Chapels," 8vo., Oxford, 1843.

most other domestic buildings, and many remain quite intact, as Ford's Hospital at Coventry; the Alms-house at Sherborne, Dorsetshire; Ewelme Hospital, Oxfordshire; the Leicester Hospital at Warwick; the lepers' hospital of St. Bartholomew, near Oxford. In many instances, however, when the funds have increased sufficiently, they have been rebuilt in modern times.

There are said to have been upwards of twenty-two thousand hospitals for lepers in Europe, of which above two thousand were in France; they were of a religious character, and were priories. Since the mode of curing this disease was discovered, these hospitals have been devoted to other purposes, and the buildings have generally disappeared. At Beauvais they remain nearly perfect, and are very extensive, now used for farm-buildings. There are fine hospitals remaining also at Bourges, at Compiègne, and at Le Mans; in Belgium at Ghent, and in Rhenish Prussia at Cues; in the north of Germany at Lubeck, and in Italy a very magnificent one at Milan. These few are selected merely because engravings of them are readily accessible: to pursue this subject would lead us much too far for our limits.

INNS AND TAVERNS[1] may claim a venerable antiquity, and are mentioned at a very early period; but when previous to the fifteenth century did they offer to the weary traveller and the pleasure-seeking knight such luxuries and such accommodation as they then afforded? In 1463 Sir John Howard dined with a friend, and paid six-shillings and eight-pence "for the tondi off

---

[1] The subject of the inns and taverns of the middle ages is alone sufficient for a separate work, and in French there is such a work by M. Francisque-Michel, to whom we have so frequently occasion to refer: *Histoire des Cabarets et des Hôtelleries*, &c., par MM. Francisque-Michel et Edouard Fournier. Paris, 1854, 2 vols. 8vo. It is impossible in the present work to do more than indicate the sources of information on the various subjects connected with it.

DOMESTIC ARCHITECTURE: FIFTEENTH CENTURY.

INN
NORTON ST. PHILIP'S, SOMERSETSHIRE.

the dynere at the Mermayde[m]." At the "Bible" in Fish-street he paid two shillings for his dinner. He drank his wine at the "Sone in Lumbart Street," and supped with Lord Audley at "Wekesonys" in Southwark. Doubtless the same inconveniences on the road were experienced as had for ages annoyed the traveller. Such oft-repeated entries as "my lord gaf his gudes ij*s.* iiij*d.*" do not indicate much improvement in the public thoroughfares. Four-pence[n] was paid "ffor a horse hyre." This was the usual rate at which hackneys were hired at this period:—

> "ffor cariage the porter hors schall hyre,
> ffoure pens a pece withinne the shyre,
> Be statut he schall take that on ʒe day,
> That is kynges crye in faye[o]."

There are many inns of the fifteenth century still remaining in different parts of England, as at Glastonbury and Norton St. Philip's, Somersetshire. The George Inn at Salisbury remains nearly perfect, and has some good barge-boards in the yard. Chaucer's Pilgrim's Inn, the "Tabard," Southwark, was entirely destroyed by a fire in the time of Charles II., but rebuilt on the old plan: the building of that period still exists, and is a curious and interesting example. The Christopher, at Eton, with its open galleries round the court-yard for passages after the ancient fashion, will be remembered by many of our readers, and has only recently been closed. The Star at Oxford has a similar gallery, and had until quite recently some very good barge-boards over the coach-office, which were probably of the fifteenth century.

The Belle Sauvage on Ludgate-hill is mentioned in the

[m] Manners and Household Expences, p. 151.
[n] Equal to about seven shillings of our money.   [o] MS. Sloane, 1,986, p. 29.

31st Henry VI., in the will of John Frensh, gentleman, late citizen and goldsmith of London:—

"Know ye that I have granted, and by this my present writing confirmed to Joan Frensh, widow, my mother, all that tenement or inn, with its appurtenances, called *Savage's Inn*, otherwise called the *Bell on the hoop*, in the parish of St. Bridget, in Fleet Street, London."

The *Bolt-in-ton* appears also, from an entry in the Patent Roll 21 Henry VI., to have been an inn at that time. In a licence of alienation to the Friars Carmelites of London of certain premises in the parish of St. Dunstan, Fleet-street, "Hospicium vocatum *le Boltenton*" is mentioned as a boundary[p].

In the *Archæologia*, vol. xviii. p. 421, is an engraving of two ancient figures in wood, supposed to represent itinerant masons, which were then fixed against a public-house opposite Wooburn Church, Buckinghamshire, in 1804: the figures were of the size of life. The younger of the persons represented holds in one hand a pair of compasses, and in the other a rule; the elder person has a quadrant in his right hand, and in his left a walking staff. These figures appear from the costume to be of the sixteenth century, and were probably the original sign of a house of call for masons.

[p] See *Archæologia*, vol. xviii. p. 197.

DOMESTIC ARCHITECTURE: FIFTEENTH CENTURY.

BRAZIER AND LOUVRE,
HALL OF WESTMINSTER SCHOOL.

CHAPTER III.

THE HALL.

THE ARRANGEMENTS of the hall were so fully described in our last volume that comparatively little remains to be said here, since there is little change of plan in this respect between the fourteenth and the fifteenth century. When the hall is retained at all, as it most commonly is, the features of it continue the same, the dais at the upper end, the screens at the lower end, a reredos in the centre, with an open louvre over it to carry off the smoke, or sometimes a large fireplace on one side, or two fireplaces if the hall is large.

The entrance porch of the hall is an important feature. It is usually at the end of the screens, over the state entrance, and has a small room over it connected with the music-gallery. There is often a groined vault over the entrance and under this small chamber, as at Kenilworth and Penshurst and Wingfield Manor. The porches at South Wraxall, Norrington House, and Woodland, all in Wiltshire, may be mentioned as good examples, but this feature is almost universal.

At Great Chalfield, and in other instances, there is a sort of squint or oblique opening through a slit in the wall, from the kitchen or some other servants' office to the porch, to enable the servants to see who was at the door. At Wanswell Court there is a small window for the same purpose. There is also frequently a grating provided in the wicket, as at Cothele, Cornwall, and in so many other instances, that this may be considered a general custom to guard against surprise, and to prevent the intrusion of importunate beggars. In the Irish towers there is generally a small inner porch, which formed part of the defences; a person entering would find himself in a small square space, with doors barred on their sides, one in front opening to the lower chamber, on one side to a porter's lodge, or small guard-chamber, and on the other to the staircase; behind him the portcullis might be let down, and over his head was a small opening through the vault, for the purpose of throwing down stones or other missiles in case of need: this opening is appropriately called " the murthering hole." These rude and rough contrivances belong to the same period as the elaborate and handsome porch, with its groined vault, in England, and this difference in the principal entrance to a manor-house in the two countries strikingly illustrates the different condition and character of the people.

To return to our English halls. There is frequently a second porch, of a plainer and smaller kind, over the back door of the hall, in the servants' court, and the staircase to the music-gallery is sometimes placed there in a turret, as at Norton St. Philip, Somersetshire.

We occasionally meet with a sort of internal porch over the door of a room, especially when the door is in a corner and this porch is placed across the angle, as at Thame Park, Oxfordshire.

> " A porche bylte of square stons,
> Full myghtly inarched evury owne [a]."

Behind the screens, or in the screens, as it was called, which was the servants' part of the hall, a great deal of work had to be carried on, and various conveniences were required, of which traces often remain in the walls, such

[a] Lydgate's Story of Thebes, sign. d. i.

DOMESTIC ARCHITECTURE: FIFTEENTH CENTURY.

NICHE IN THE HALL.

IRON IN THE NICHE.

LITTLE WENHAM HALL, SUFFOLK.

as a buttery-hatch, still used in our college halls: a similar small opening for passing dishes through from the kitchen, when the situation made it convenient, is frequently met with, as at Canon's Ashby, Northamptonshire; also a lavatory for washing hands and dishes, with a water-drain from it, as at Lincoln, and Appleby, Leicestershire. In the Irish towers, where the state room at the top answered the purpose of a hall, there is usually a water-drain at the servants' end of the room, near the top of the stairs which led from the kitchen. In Little Wenham Hall, Suffolk, there is a remarkable niche of the fifteenth century, with good panelling, and in it is a twisted iron hook, apparently for a towel to hang upon in connection with a lavatory.

It has been mentioned that at the lower end of the hall, behind the screen, there were usually three doorways, one to the pantry, one to the buttery, and the central one to a passage between these two apartments leading to the kitchen, whether on a level, as at Penshurst, or approached by a straight flight of stairs, when the kitchen is on a lower level, as at Chepstow and Coventry[b]. But in the smaller houses[c] there are frequently only two doorways, and in some cases there are none, the communication with the offices being by a stair-

[b] In an old romance it is said that Fulke Fitz-Warine, an English baron of the thirteenth century, caused the highway to pass through his hall, in order that nobody should escape his hospitality. "Cesti Fouke fust bon viandour e large; e fesoit turner le real chemin par mi sa sale à soun maner de Alleston, pur ce que nul estrange y dust passer s'il n'avoit viaunde ou herbergage ou autre honour ou bien du suen."— *Histoire de Foulques Fitz-Warin*, publ. par Francisque-Michel, p. 97. Paris, 1840. 8vo.

[c] The hall of the manor-house of the Fettiplace family, at Childrey, Berkshire, was remaining perfect until the year 1852, and was a curious and valuable specimen of a timber hall of the fifteenth century; it was wantonly destroyed to make some modern improvements. Fortunately, a careful drawing of it has been preserved by the Messrs. Buckler, and an engraving of it appeared in the "Illustrated London News" for Feb. 21, 1857.

case at the opposite end of the screens to the state entrance, as at the bishop's palace, St. David's, and Linlithgow Palace, Scotland. Sometimes the communication is by a back door at the end of the screens across the servants' court, as at Martock, Somersetshire.

Over the screens was the music-gallery, or loft for the minstrels, which had usually a separate entrance by a small staircase from the porch; this gallery was an important feature of the hall, and its occupants contributed greatly to the amusement of the guests assembled below: the musicians or minstrels, and the bag-pipers, were here assembled. There is frequently a doorway at the back of the music-gallery opening into a chamber of some importance, which seems to have been sometimes called the "oriel," and which has often a rich window at one end of it, as at Great Chalfield, Wiltshire, and South Wingfield Manor-house, Derbyshire; in the latter instance, and some others, it seems to have been the chapel. In other cases it was probably only a room for the use of the minstrels.

The music-gallery, with the screens and doorways under it, at Great Chalfield, Wilts, was perfect a few years since, when the drawing, of which we give an engraving, was made by Mr. Buckler: it has unfortunately since been destroyed.

In some instances, when the hall was lofty, there was also a gallery round the upper part of the wall, immediately under the roof; this is said to have been a general practice in Scotland, but it is often difficult to decide whether there was a gallery or a low upper chamber separated by a floor; the wood-work has always been destroyed, and the corbels, the upper windows, and doorways, would be the same in either case; in many of the Scotch towers the hall is so small and narrow that

CHESTERFIELD CHURCH.

it does not seem probable there was a gallery; on the other hand, in the larger castles, where the hall is on a grand scale, it is very probable that there was such an arrangement. This appears to have been the case in the great hall at Durham, where the roof was evidently intended to be seen from below, while the clerestory windows and corbels seem to shew that there was originally a gallery, where a floor has since been introduced.

The halls of the different colleges in Oxford and Cambridge are among the best-preserved examples of halls of the fifteenth century, and continue in use with the same arrangements as in a nobleman's house of that period,—the dais at the upper end for the high table raised a step or two, with the bay window at the end, in which stands the sideboard, the screen at the lower end, and the offices communicating with it, the open timber roof, and the wainscoting upon the walls. In New College and Magdalen College, Oxford, the wainscoting is ornamented with the linen panel of the time of Henry VIII. Christ Church hall is another well-known example of that period, with a fine roof, and a rich piece of fan-tracery vaulting to the recess of the bay window; the staircase is of the time of Charles I.

The halls of Hampton Court, Eltham Palace, and Crosby Hall may also be mentioned. The hall of Trinity College, Cambridge, with its roof and louvre, is another fine example; but they are far too numerous to be mentioned in detail. The hall of St. Mary's Guild at Coventry is another very fine one, and very perfect, with part of the screen at the lower end, and the tapestry at the upper end, behind the dais, a remarkable specimen of the time of Henry VI., and painted glass over it, connected with the same subject.

The DAIS, although a very general feature, is not an

invariable one. At Hampton Court there is none, and from the levels of the doorways it does not appear that there ever could have been one. There is a large chamber behind the upper end of the hall, which is still hung with the original tapestry of the time of Henry VIII.; and though this is called the withdrawing-room, it may have been used as a dining-room for the high table, otherwise there was no distinction for the high table. In smaller halls there was often no dais.

In the centre of the high table, on the dais, stood the throne or chair of state, with a canopy over it, to which the name of dais is also sometimes applied.

Furniture of the middle ages, even of the fifteenth century, is extremely scarce, and it is difficult to find enough to describe accurately what it has been; our chief reliance must therefore be in the illuminations of manuscripts of the period, and in these banquets are often represented, and the state chair is a prominent object, as in the specimen we have selected from Douce's Collection of MSS. in the Bodleian Library, Nos. 202 and 208. In St. Mary's Hall at Coventry the state chair remains tolerably perfect, and richly panelled, with the back to it, but without the canopy over it.

In some instances the sideboard, instead of being merely a piece of furniture placed in the recess of the bay window, is placed at the end of the hall, behind the dais, in a recess provided for it in the wall; these recesses are sometimes plain, merely to receive the wood-work, as in Kidwelly Castle, South Wales; in other cases the stone-work is enriched with ornament, as at Dirleton Castle, Scotland.

The BAY WINDOW is a very important feature in the hall of the fifteenth century. It seems to have been introduced towards the end of the fourteenth, and rapidly

DOMESTIC ARCHITECTURE: SIXTEENTH CENTURY.

THORNBURY CASTLE GLOUCESTERSHIRE.

THE HALL.

increased in size and importance until the time of Henry VIII., when it becomes one of the most conspicuous features of the house, as at Cowdray and Compton Winyate. The usual position for it is at one end of the dais, and there are sometimes two, one at each end. In some instances, as at Fawsley, Northants, it is in the middle of one side of the hall, and has a separate raised platform to itself, but this is an exceptional arrangement. It is sometimes formed in the inside of a sort of turret, and has a small chamber over the vaulted ceiling, as at Great Chalfield, Wilts, and Fawsley.

Sometimes the groined vault over the bay is at a considerably lower level than the roof of the hall, the space being divided into two stories, and the bay window is thus made to correspond with the porch and the room over it, as at Kingston Seymour, Somerset. In some of the later houses of the time of Henry VIII., where the lofty hall was divided into a dining-room below and a drawing-room above, the grand feature of the bay window could not be dispensed with for external effect, and it was carried up through both stories, as at Thornbury Castle, Gloucestershire. The bay window frequently occupies one corner of the inner court, as in the house at Salisbury, now known as the Work-house, and at Compton Winyate, Warwickshire.

In the recess formed by the bay window there was also usually a cupboard for the plate and porcelain, fitted with shelves, and so arranged that the contents could be displayed when the doors were thrown open; this was a piece of furniture, of which numerous examples may be seen in the illuminations of MSS. of this period[d].

---

[d] As in Douce's Collection of MSS., Nos. 219 and 311. By an inventory attached to the will of this period (1412,) we find in the hall "unum copperburd," valued at vis. viiid.

It will be seen that the contents of this cupboard were not only gold and silver plate in great profusion, but also ornamental glass and porcelain. These form the subjects for separate works, and can only be mentioned here. Respecting the pottery and porcelain of the middle ages, a good deal of information will be found in Mr. Marryatt's valuable work, "Collections towards a History of Pottery and Porcelain in the Fifteenth, Sixteenth, Seventeenth, and Eighteenth Centuries[e]." The glass manufacture equally affords matter for a separate book, as does the metalwork, especially in the precious metals. There are many scattered notices of these, but we believe they have not been collected. Every inventory contains a number of cups and vessels of gold and silver. As shewing the ornamentation of cups, the *Testamentum Alani de Newark* mentions:—

Burette, Bibl. du Roi, Paris.

"Item lego Conventui Monast. B. M. Ebor. unum ciphum deauratum, habentem formam calicis coopertum, in cujus summitate ymago Leonis fixa est, et habet vasas de Leonibus."

John Baron Graystock leaves the following (1436):—

[e] Second Edition, 1858, 8vo. See also *Traité des arts céramiques ou des poteries*, &c., by Alexandre Brongniart, (Paris, 1844, 2 vols. 8vo., with an atlas, 4to.); *Description méthodique du Musée céramique de la manufacture royale de Sèvres*, by the same and D. Riocreux, (Paris, 1845, 4to.); and "A Guide to the Knowledge of Pottery and Porcelain," by Henry G. Bohn, 12mo., 1857.

"Maximum ciphum argenti cum coopertorio vocatum Le Chartre de Morpath,—unum ciphum argenti et deauratum cum coopertorio ex dono mihi datum per Rectorem de Weme, vi. ciphos argenti, single, —xii. cocliaria (spoons) argenti, ij. pelves cum duobus lavacris argenti, vi. discos, vi. salsaria (salt-cellars) et j. chargior argenti sen' factur'," &c.

The reredos, or brazier for the fire of logs, in the centre of the hall, continued in use, but in addition to this large fireplaces were introduced into the walls. These became much more common in the fifteenth century than they had been before; although fireplaces and chimneys were used at all periods in the other chambers, they were not so common in the hall, where the reredos was probably thought sufficient in earlier days, but at this period the fireplace becomes an important feature in the hall, and one of its chief ornaments; the hood and mantel-piece being enriched with panelling, and painted with shields of arms and other ornaments, although less elaborate than the sumptuous fireplaces of the time of Elizabeth and James I.

The situation of the fireplace in the hall varies extremely. In the larger halls there are frequently two, as at Kenilworth, where there is one on each side. The most usual situation is near the steps of the dais, and on the side opposite the bay window, but there is no general rule: at Haddon Hall it is between the windows. More usually, when there are windows on one side only, the fireplace is on the opposite side, in the blank wall, as at the Mote, Ightham, Kent. In Linlithgow Palace the arrangement is peculiar: there are two large fireplaces side by side, occupying the whole of the upper end of the hall; this was probably as a remedy for the coldness and humidity of the climate. In Yanwath Hall, Westmoreland, there is one large fireplace at the end of the hall, and a passage by the side of it leading into a tower at the back. The reredos, or large brazier, in the centre of the hall, continued in use in some of the colleges of Oxford and Cambridge until within the present century; in Lincoln College the reredos was used within the memory of some of the present Fellows of the college, and the louvre still remains. In the hall of Westminster School it was in use as late as 1850[f]. The reredos was always accompanied by dogs, on which to place the logs of wood for the fire.

The arch of the fireplace is often flat, and formed by joggling the stones in a very ingenious manner: in other instances it is a low Tudor arch. Sometimes there is a projecting hood, but at this period that is frequently dispensed with, and the arch of the fireplace is flush with the face of the wall, which is ornamented with panelling, and a battlement over it, as at Southwell Palace, Notts. The fireplaces in Scotland are generally large and fine, and resemble the French Flamboyant fireplaces, with their magnificent hoods[g].

The open timber ROOFS of the halls of houses of the fifteenth century are often quite as fine and as rich as those of the churches, and with this advantage over them, that there is generally a louvre in the centre, which lights up the hall, and enables the tracery to be seen, which in churches is often lost in the gloom. The hall of Trinity College, Cambridge, is a fine example of this kind. Christ Church hall, in Oxford, has lost its louvre, which is to be regretted. Westminster Hall is celebrated for the wide span of its fine roof, erected in

[f] It was only removed during the improvements in the time of Dean Buckland, and at his suggestion Mr. Jewitt was employed to take a drawing of the hall, with the reredos, before it was removed, being, probably, the last instance of this ancient usage being continued to our own day.

[g] Of the finest French fireplaces of our neighbours, the reader will find an account in Sauval's *Histoire et Recherches des Antiquités de la Ville de Paris*, vol. ii. p. 279. (*Le dedans des maison royales*).

DOMESTIC ARCHITECTURE: FIFTEENTH CENTURY.

FIREPLACE,

SOUTHWELL PALACE, NOTTINGHAMSHIRE.

THE HALL.

the time of Richard II., and taking the place of the nave and two side aisles of the original Norman hall[h]. The roof, however, has a great thrust against the side walls, and requires enormous buttresses to support it. The hall of Westminster School is a simple and good example, with its louvre perfect. The louvre of the great hall was restored by Smirke, and there is some doubt as to its exact accuracy, although it was intended to be a faithful restoration. It is generally observed that pendants are more commonly used in the roofs of halls than in those of churches[i].

At one end of the hall, over the dais, there is frequently a window in the gable, which lights up the roof with great advantage, as in St. Mary's Hall, Coventry, and in most of Wolsey's halls. Sometimes there is a window of this kind at each end, as at Fawsley Court; this arrangement of course depends on the general plan of the house, and whether the hall roof is sufficiently high to allow of a window over the chambers attached to the end of it. Where the bed-chambers are in several stories in a sort of tower at the end of the hall, there can be no window. There is frequently a small opening for looking into the hall from the solar or lord's chamber over the cellar at the back of the dais, and this opening appears to have been partially concealed. At Great Chalfield there is a chamber of equal importance at the lower end of the hall, over the offices, and behind the music-gallery; and in this instance there was an open-

[h] According to Sauval, the two finest halls in France were that of the Petit-Bourbon, at Paris, and that of the castle of Montargis. "Sa largeur est," adds Sauval, speaking of the former, "de dix-huit pas communs sur trente-cinq toises de longueur, et la couverture si rehaussée, que le comble paraît aussi élevé que ceux des églises de St. Gervais et de St. Eustache," &c.—*Histoire et Recherches des Antiquités de la Ville de Paris*, vol. ii, p. 209.

[i] The roofs of Athelhampton Hall, Dorsetshire, and Wear Gifford, Devonshire, engraved in the "Glossary of Architecture," are fine examples.

ing from each of these chambers at either end of th[e] hall, and they were concealed in the form of stone mask[s] through the eyes and mouth of which a full view of th[e] hall could be obtained. These masks have been pr[e]served, although unfortunately removed from their or[i]ginal position in some modern *improvements*. One [of] them is shewn in its proper position in our view [of] the interior of this hall, for which we are indebted [to] Mr. Buckler, who had fortunately made a careful draw[ing] of it previous to the recent alterations.

Openings in the Hall, Great Chalfield.

In the fifteenth century, and more especially in t[he] beginning of the sixteenth, the CEILINGS are often v[ery] richly ornamented; the earlier examples are more co[m]monly of wood only, divided into square panels by r[ibs] of bold projection, and often well moulded; and at [the] intersection of these ribs are square bosses, carved w[ith] foliage, or with shields of arms, or other ornamen[ts], much in the same manner as we often find in the ai[sles] of churches of the same period.

In the time of Henry VIII. the ceilings are m[ore]

commonly of plaster, with a great variety of patterns stamped in them; sometimes with pendants in the place of the bosses, in other cases merely panelling, of which there is a rich example in the ceiling of the chapel of the Savoy Palace in the Strand.

As to the external covering of the roof, tiles or slates were made use of, as found convenient, as the following extracts shew.

In the Household Book of Henry VII. we have these items:—

"9 Hen. VII. Carpenter for making the hall roofe xlix[li].
17 Hen. VII. Item to Adrian Berne for 34000 ardois (slates) xxviii[li]. vj[s]. viij[d].[k]"

In the Surveyor-General's account in 34 Henry VIII. :—

"Serchyng vnryppyng, new tylyng and poyntyng ouer the west syde of the Quenes pallet chambre[l]."

In the Romance of Sir Degrevant a chamber roof is thus described:—

"There was a royall rooffe,
In a chambre of loffe,
Hyt was busked above,
With besaunts full bright[m]."

Tiles appear to have been scarce at times. A writer of one of the Paston letters complains that about 1475 there "is none to get for no money," and Master Stoley begs the loan or "almes of tylle," to roof one of his "fayrest chambres," which "standyth halfe uncouerd for defaulte of tylle[n]."

Of the DECORATIONS of the hall it will be necessary now to speak. Considerable improvements had been made in this respect. The rich displayed their

[k] MS. Additional, 7,099 ff. 13, 68.
[l] Ibid., 10,109, fo. 84. a.
[m] Thornton Romances, p. 236.
[n] Paston Letters, vol. v. p. 136.

wealth, not so much in the acquisition of household comforts as in the splendour and profusion of their plate, and the stuffs with which they decorated their walls. The most lucrative trade of the fifteenth century was that of a "tapister." In old charters of the time he is generally designated as a "Merchaunt de tappicerie." Our own merchant-princes acquired their marvellous wealth by their commerce in baudekin and arras. The purchase of a "chamber," or "halling," that is, the necessary hangings for those apartments[o], was a transaction of considerable importance, and usually ratified by a deed, signed and sealed with great formality. They were treasures deemed worthy of being bequeathed by royalty. Heavy subsidies were laid upon its importation. The king, however, sometimes exercised his royal prerogative. In 1441 Henry VII. granted to a mercer of London the privilege of bringing into this country cloth of arras, "suche as that he schal by byonde see *for lordes*, withoute paying of custome or subsidie[p]." The rich hangings in the great hall of Henry VI. would have exhausted the fortune of a country squire. Among the additional charters in the British Museum are many curious documents illustrative of the extravagant prices given for these domestic luxuries. Eight hundred golden francs, *francs d'or*, were paid by the Duc de Touraine for "un tappis sarrazinois," embroidered with the history of Charlemagne, bought for l'Hotel de Beauté[q]. The Duc d'Orleans

[o] The term "hall," "chamber," or "bed," was often applied to the tapestry. A curious document, date 1398, records the purchase by the Duc d'Orleans of a portable chamber, "une chambre portative," consisting of a seler, dosser, curtains and counterpoint. *Additional Chart.*, No. 2,771. We have also a payment of 158*l*. 6*s*. 8*d*. in the wardrobe accounts of Henry VII., for "browdryng of two chambres."—MS. Additional, 7,099, fo. 36.

[p] MS. Cotton. Cleopat. F. v. fo. 24 b.

[q] Additional Chart., No. 2,696. See Francisque-Michel, *Recherches sur ... les étoffes de Soie*, &c., vol. ii. p. 391.

THE HALL.

paid 2,220 francs for "a chamber" of three pieces of tapestry[r]. The interior was thus richly decorated, even when the building itself was poor. When Cardinal Beaufort, who was sent as ambassador to make peace with France in 1439, arrived in the marshes of Calais, there was a handsome hall erected there, upwards of a hundred feet in length, and made to accommodate three hundred persons at table. It contained at the north end all necessary offices — a pantry, buttery, wine and other cellars, and two chambers, and at the south end a passage led into the kitchen. The hall was beautifully hung with crimson tapestry. A short distance from the cardinal's was the hall of the Duchess of Burgundy, which was built of old rotten timber, and covered with dirty sails, but the interior was richly adorned with arras[s].

Edward IV. in 1480 bought of Piers de Vraulx, of Gascoigne, stuffs to the amount of 238*l*. 15*s*. 6*d*., a sum which, when compared with its value in modern currency, appears enormous[t]. Henry VII., however, exceeded him in his taste for such ornaments. We may take as examples three entries from the wardrobe accounts of that monarch:—

"To a merchaunt of Flandres for 52 elles of arras, 265*l*. 6*s*. 8*d*.
For a cloth of estate 47 yerds di xi*li*. the yerd, 522*l*. 10*s*.
To Lewas de ffava for a pece of cloth of gold, and vii. peces of baudekyn, 286*l*. 9*s*."[u]

These sums in the aggregate would be equivalent to about 12,000*l*. of our present currency.

[r] Ibid., No. 2,733.
[s] Proceedings of the Privy Council, vol. v. p. 341.
[t] MS. Harl., 4,780, fo. 3. a. Twenty pieces of arras, some pieces of velvet, and valances for a bed, were purchased for Edward IV. at a cost of 984*l*. 8*s*. 8*d*. Devon's Issue Rolls of the Exchequer, p. 491. On the arras were representations of the Passion, and of the history of "Nabugodonoser" and of Alexander.
[u] MS. Additional, 7,099, ff. 44, 52, 66.

The use of TAPESTRY had thus become general among the nobility and gentry, and such entries as "My lorde payd to Capeldyk, mayster Pekerynges man, for iiij. peses of aras of the story of Suzan ix*li*. iij*s*. iiij*d*.[x]," are of frequent occurrence. In a splendid manuscript of Froissart's Chronicles, written for Philip de Comines[y] at the latter end of the fifteenth century, we have many views of royal and noble halls. Almost without exception they are represented as being hung with gorgeous tapestry. Scenes of romance and war are skilfully depicted. In Bradshaw's "Lyfe of Saynt Werburge[z]" we have the following passage:—

"Clothes of gold and arras were hanged in the hall,
Depaynted with pyctures and hystoryes many folde,
Well wraughte and craftely with precyous stones all,
Glyterynge as Phebus, and the beten golde[a]."

The subjects of tapestry before the Reformation are more usually historical, after that time generally either scriptural or pagan; the Renaissance had the same influence on all the arts. In the historical tapestry real events were displayed as accurately as the skill of the artist would allow, and before the general use of oil-paintings the most accurate portraits were executed either in tapestry or in painted glass. The original tapestry of the hall of Hampton Court Palace has been preserved in those parts which are under the music-gallery and in the withdrawing-room at the upper end, and the subjects of these are historical; that in the body of the hall, with Scripture subjects, is Elizabethan, and has been brought from some other place. The very fine original tapestry of the time of Henry VII., preserved in Magda-

[x] Howard's Household Book, p. 288.
[y] De Comines was born 1445, and died 1509.
[z] 8vo., 1521, printed by Pinson.
[a] Chapter xvi.

len College, Oxford[b], represents the marriage of Prince Arthur, the elder brother of Henry VIII., with Catherine of Arragon, which afterwards formed the pretext for the divorce.

As an instance of the quantity of tapestry employed, the inventory of St. Mary's Guild at Boston affords the following:—

"IN THE HALL.—A hangynge at the *deyte* (?) [deyse or dais], 11 yards long, 2½ yards wide. Another steyned hangynge, contaynyng, in lynth 9⅓ yardes, and in deepnes 2 yards and ½."

A great deal of curious information respecting tapestry will be found in the valuable work of M. Francisque-Michel, *Recherches sur le commerce, la fabrication et l'usage des Etoffes de soie, d'or et d'argent et autres tissus précieux en Occident, principalement en France, pendant le moyen âge.* As this work occupies two quarto volumes, it is obvious that we can do no more than refer to it here. We observe that he makes frequent mention of *damas* amongst the usual fabrics of this period, worked with gold and silver, and woven of various colours, red, blue, green, violet, yellow, and grey. This was the same as our word damask, a fabric imported from Damascus, and which when mentioned in English inventories is usually of a red or plum colour.

There is much more ancient tapestry remaining than is generally supposed; it has been very often rolled up and put aside as lumber, and forgotten, but is now frequently brought to light again. The pegs on which the tapestry was hung often remain where the tapestry

---

[b] This tapestry is now preserved in what are called the Founder's Chambers, over the principal gateway, but does not seem to have been made for the place which it occupies, and one piece is in duplicate; it was probably intended for the hall, though perhaps never placed there.

itself has disappeared, as in the hall of Sudeley, and of the Prior's house at Wenlock[c].

As an instance of the barbarity exercised towards the vestiges of antiquities, a letter printed in the "Gentleman's Magazine" in 1784 may be quoted. A "Constant Reader" recommends Mr. Urban's inspection of an old tapestry that hangs in the shop of Mr. Walker, a broker in Harp Alley. It represented the history of Haman and Mordecai, expressed in the habits, &c., of the fifteenth or sixteenth century. It formed part of the hangings of the chapel at Somerset House, whence it was sold to Mr. Walker, who "*had sold several portions*, and asked a guinea and a-half for the remainder[d]."

The inscription ran as follows:—

"Prudome Merdoci ✠ le roy kaist ceste nuet insompne ✠ pour ce fist ses anales lire ✠ an naidgers celleu ✠ volt cruce Aman demanda.

"qst sa pensee ✠ et ainsi que adventier adoune ✠ ut con'vient on le volt ocire ✠ quel duc eust hen'e mig'l ✠ Aocour celuy qui sancta tourna ✠ et comment ce fait lui fist dire ✠ Merdoce que fust leal ✠ son s're et de mirt le garda ✠ aman respondit haultemant.

"povoir nea ✠ lement pour le bien luy sire ✠ laux demandez nul doy real ✠ honeur real servi a ✠ le roy dist sai le prestement."

The walls of the hall were hung with tapestry to the height of eight or ten feet from the ground, above which they were painted. When the nobles travelled from one part of the country to another, they carried their carpets and tapestry with them, and frequently the glass casements also.

The subjects worked in the tapestry, painted on the walls and on the glass, were usually the same, and formed a continuation one of the other; and when the colours were all fresh, probably one part was nearly as brilliant as the other. These subjects were generally taken from

[c] Buckler's "History of Magdalen College, Oxford," p. 85.
[d] Gent. Mag., vol. liv. p. 268.

THE HALL.

the popular romances of the day, or hunting-scenes, with abundance of foliage and numerous figures.

The old castle of Tamworth, described in Dugdale's "Warwickshire," had, according to a correspondent of the "Gentleman's Magazine," gigantic figures painted in fresco upon the wall of the hall, with the inscription beneath,—Sir Lancelot de Lake and Sir Tarquin,—the *Morte d'Arthur* evidently having been the subject of the painter's pencil.

Historical subjects were also frequently employed: a good example of this remains in the end wall of St. Mary's Hall, Coventry, representing the entry of Henry VI. into that city, the same subject being continued in the tapestry and in the painted glass over it.

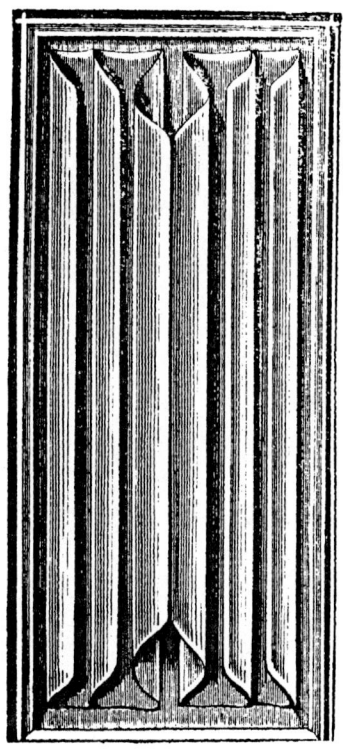

The Linen Panel,
Layer Marney House, Essex.

Towards the close of the fifteenth century tapestry began to be disused, and its place supplied by wainscoting or stamped leather. Wainscot of the time of Henry VIII. may generally be distinguished by the pattern called the "linen panel," being an exact imitation of the folds of a linen napkin, sometimes with a representation of the fringe, as in the abbot's house at Beaulieu, Hampshire.

There is some very rich stamped leather in place of tapestry for hangings in one of the founder's chambers at Magdalen College, Oxford, which have been recently restored in a very careful manner as faithfully as possible to what they were originally; and the effect is extremely rich and gorgeous, without being at all tawdry. The tapestry has been carefully repaired only; the stamped leather was too far gone, and has been exactly copied.

The FLOORING of the hall was usually paved with tiles of various colours, and so laid down as to form ingenious patterns[e]. In Piers the Plowman's Crede we read of—

"Cloisters y paved with poyntile, ich point after other;"

that is, with square tiles one after the other. In the accounts of the Surveyor-General of Henry VIII. we find frequent mention of paving tiles[f]; and about the same time the refectory of Christ Church, Oxford, was paved with green and yellow tiles. The hearths before the chimney were also paved with coloured tiles. A sum of money was paid in the time of Henry VIII. to John Brasey of London, for "c. pavyng tyle for pavyng before the chymneys[g];" and on the reparation of the manor of Greenwich, Edmund Cardysh supplied "c. pavyng tiles of kynd gode, for the pavyng of halparys[h] before the chymneys[i]."

We also read,—

"And of this halle forther to diffine,
With stons square be level or by line,
It paued was at grete diligens[k]."

The FURNITURE of the hall was still of the rudest form. In a curious manuscript of this period the duties of the

[e] See MS. Harleian, No. 4,380.
[f] MS. Additional, Brit. Mus., No. 10,109.
[g] Ibid., fo. 49. We often find paving tiles mentioned in wills and other documents of the period under the name of "flaundrestyll," as most of the coloured tiles were imported from Flanders at that date, as well as at a later period.
[h] Or Halpace, see "Glossary of Architecture," p. 246.
[i] MS. Additional, 10,109, fo. 89.
[k] MS. Reg. 18, D., vol. i. fol. 24. a.

DOMESTIC ARCHITECTURE: SIXTEENTH CENTURY.

THE HALL,

YANWATH HALL, WESTMORELAND.

marshal of the hall are thus described. He was to bring in the fuel, and

> "In halle make fyre at eyche a mele,
> Borde trestuls and formes also;
> Ye cupborde in his warde schall go,
> The desurs, cortines, and henge in halle[1]."

These few lines enumerate the usual garniture of the chief apartment in this century.

The REFECTORY of one of the larger abbeys would contain much the same furniture as that of a nobleman's of the same period, and that of one of the smaller religious houses or of the abbot the same as those of the smaller gentry, as may be seen by the following example in the inventory of the priory of Durham, (1446), which is chiefly remarkable for the large quantity of plate carefully described, and giving an insight into the names and uses of the cups and bowls of the period:—

"REFECTORIUM. In Refectorio sunt, xiij. Cuppæ deauratæ, quarum, xij. cum cooperculis, et una sine cooperculo.

ij. Cuppæ non deauratæ, cum uno cooperculo.

una Pecia cum pede, habens cooperculum cum aquilâ in summitate ejusdem.

j. Pecia cum cooperculo, stans super iiij. angelis deauratis.

iiij. Peciæ planæ, quondam Ricardi Hessewell, cum cooperculo habente nodum latum cum nomine ejusdem in eodem insculpto.

ij. Peciæ planæ cum ij. cooperculis.

vj. Peciæ planæ sine cooperculis, nuper Johannis Fissheburn.

viij. Peciæ planæ, diversarum sectarum.

vj. Bikkez[m] diversarum sectarum.

xiij. Bikkes cum ij. cooperculis.

j. Pecia magna et profunda, quondam Thomæ Gretham.

xij. Bikkez antiqua in custodiâ Johannis Dale.

iij. Nuces[n] cum iij. pedibus argenteis et deauratis, quarum una cum cooperculo.

x^{xx}xj. Coclearia argenti diversorum operum et ponderis.

duæ Ollæ[o] argenteæ, utraque continente unum potellum.

duæ Fiolæ argenteæ et deauratæ.

---

[1] MS. Sloane, No. 1,986, p. 30.
[m] A large cup called a beaker.
[n] Cocoa-nut cups.

[o] Ollæ, Fiolæ, and Murræ are different kinds of cups and bowls, which it is not necessary here to describe.

70 DOMESTIC ARCHITECTURE: FIFTEENTH CENTURY.

iij. Salsaria cum cooperculis pro eisdem.
xj. Salsaria argentea unius sectæ, pro sale.
iiij. Salsaria argentea diversarum sectarum.
xij. Disci argenti cum literis R e. ff.[p] supra borduram.
v. Doblers argenti.
xj. Salsaria diversorum operum.
xij. Platers et ij. Chargeours argenti cum literis R coronatis et armis Walteri Skirlawe, ex dono Ricardi Hessewell.

j. Murra cum pede deaurato, vocata Herdewyke, cum cooperculo.
alia Murra larga et magna vocata Abell, sine cooperculo.
una alia Murra pro altâ mensâ in Refectorio, cum cooperculo.
unus Ciphus vocatus Beda.
xij. Murræ magnæ et largæ cum uno cooperculo; quorum iij. cum pedibus.
xxxiij. Murræ usuales, et una Nux cum ij. cooperculis."

In the hall of the prior's house, at the same date:—

"In Aula. j. Dorsale continens sex pecias cum Avibus Sancti Cuthberti et armis Ecclesiæ.
iij. Peciæ de blodeo brodrato cum sertis et Deo gr'as, et duæ Peciæ non brodratæ.

vi. Qwisshons cum leonibus coronatis, et scripturâ De la Roi.
iij. Pelves de auricalco cum iij. lavacris, quorum ij. apud Bearepayr."

And in an inventory of 1498, taken in the college at Bishop's Auckland, we read of—

"i. Almery (cupboard).
i. Bord with trests (trestles).
j. choppyng knyfe.
i. Ymage of o^r Ladye.
iij. mete bords, *remouable*.
iij. payre trests.

"iiij. fourmys (forms).
j. cobbord.
i. hangyng of grene say [q].
iij. old latyne Basyngs.
ij. ewers to ye same.
x. old standis of tre (wood)."

The hall of a vicar of this period, we learn by an inventory attached to his will (1412), contained—

"ij. Dorsoria cum uno Banwher (dorsars and bankers were explained in our last volume), xxiij*s*. iv*d*.
xii. whysshynes (cushions), xii*d*.

ij. mensæ cum trestellis (sets of planks with trestles,) xii*s*.
Duæ pelves cum lavacris (basins with jugs), iiij*s*."

[p] Probably belonging to the refectorium.

[q] "Say" is a kind of cloth, called also "shag." It is often found in inventories under the Latin *de sago*.

Again, in the inventory of John Danby we find he had—

"In culsidr' (in cushions), j. dos et j. bankor (one dorser and banker), iiij*d*."

A brass eagle remained till recently in Magdalen College hall, Oxford, from which Scripture was read during meals. When the custom ceased, the piece of furniture was discarded.

Although CHAIRS[r] and buffet stools were, during this period, in more general use, and were often very beautifully decorated with needle-work, benches and forms were still the seats in the hall. The tables were of the rudest make. The poets of the age, faithful in their delineations, describe them as mere "bordes" and trestles. The high table at which the lord sat was moveable, but the side tables were generally fixtures of coarse materials and workmanship, and made by carpenters; these were the tables "dormant." Lydgate writes:—

> "Eke in the halle it was cournable,
> On ech party was a dormant table[s]."

Even as late as the reign of Henry VIII., the great halls in the palaces of that monarch contained little else but "tables dormaunte" and "fformes dormaunte[t]." These were a part of the usual hall "fittings," and were sometimes included in the builder's contract, and repaired by the landlord. A tenement belonging to Edward IV., and let for the support of the great wardrobe, was repaired in 1480, and "a quarter of tymbre" was

---

[r] The Duchess of Orleans bought of Jehan de Troies "a chair for her chamber, the four legs of which were *painted* vermillion, with a cover on which were depicted dogs and birds, and other devices, garnished with a fringe of soy." Addit. Chart., No. 2,776. MS. illuminations would lead us to the supposition that the chamber furniture was usually *painted*.

[s] MS. Reg. 18 D. vi. fo. 24. a.

[t] MS. Harl. 1,419, fo. 417. b.

purchased "for the benches in the all[u]." It was specified in the contract for Hengrave that "the same hall was to be benched aboute[x]."

In an inventory of goods belonging to the monastery of Peterborough at the time of the dissolution, we find in the abbot's hall, "Four fixed tables, four forms, one table[y] with two trestles at the high bench, some old tapestry hangings, one cupboard, one chair, and one chaffer[z]." In the Guildhall of Boston we learn by an inventory that there were eight tables on the north side of the hall, joined and nailed to the trestles, and seven on the south side, similarly arranged, with twelve forms placed by the sides of the tables, and three tables and three forms in the chapel chamber. There was also, it seems, a smaller table covered with parchment, "noted with Antems of our Lady, with 3 collecs," and covered with linen cloth. By the same inventory we also learn that the hall was lighted by "five candlestykes hyngynge like potts," whereof the highest had five branches, and each of the others three. Six table-cloths are stated to have been renewed in the time of Mr. Tomlynson, alderman. A great quantity of other table-linen is mentioned in this part of the roll: the table-cloths are of great length,—six, seven, and even nine yards long[a].

A manuscript in the British Museum of 13 Henry VI. gives a list of the royal furniture; we find, however, but little except tables, moveable and "dormant," cupboards,

---

[u] MS. Harl. 4,780, fo. 23. a.

[x] Gage's Hengrave, p. 42.

[y] The word "table" had then the same signification as the Latin word *tabula*, and did not include the frame and legs on which it rests, as in modern usage. In most cases, as above, the table, or board, was detached and rested on trestles.

[z] Stevens' Continuation to Dugdale's Monasticon Anglicanum, vol. i. p. 487.

[a] It is not certain that all the furniture mentioned was in use in the hall in the fifteenth century, as the inventory bears the date of 1534, but it is very probable that no material change took place.

DOMESTIC ARCHITECTURE: FIFTEENTH CENTURY.

LOCKER.

HOUSE IN THE CLOSE, LINCOLN.

WATER-DRAIN.

MOAT-HOUSE, APPLEBY, LEICESTERSHIRE.

THE HALL.

forms, and stools, but the catalogue is rich in cloth, damask, and satin coverings for these articles[b]. The cupboard was an important item in the furniture of the hall. It was sometimes called an ambry, or almery[c], and used for displaying the plate:—

"The cupborde with plate shynyng fayre and clere[d]."

The almery, however, not being confined to the hall, will be treated of more at length in a subsequent chapter.

The plate was also frequently kept in a LOCKER, or cupboard, in the wall, and this was made ornamental, as at Little Wenham Hall. A good example also remained in a house in the close at Lincoln so recently as 1848, but has lately been destroyed. It was ornamented with shields of armorial bearings, the two on the sides represented as hanging from pegs.

The furniture of the royal manors as late as the reign of Henry VIII. was of a meagre description, it required no greater skill than that of a common carpenter to make it[e]. The high bench or principal seat, however, was sometimes elaborately carved and ornamented, and the dorsers and bankers were exquisitely worked. Interesting specimens of state chairs of this period may be seen in a beautiful manuscript in the Cottonian collection[f]. The common forms upon which the guests sat were also covered with rich bankers:—

"The bankers on the binkes lay and fayre lordes yfonde[g]."

A list of the tapestry and arras belonging to Henry V. is preserved among the Rolls of Parliament; many of

---

[b] MS. Additional, No. 17,721, ff. 45, 48.
[c] Archæological Journal, vol. v. p. 319.
[d] Lyfe of Saynt Werburge.
[e] Additional MS. 10,109, fo. 83. See Appendix of Illustrations.
[f] Marked Aug. A. v. ff. 103, 116.
[g] MS. Cottonian Julius v. fo. 175.

the pieces intended for the decoration of the hall were worked with Scriptural and emblematical histories[h].

The LAVERS, *lavacra*, so frequently mentioned in the inventories, require some further notice. They were small basins of silver or metal richly enamelled, about the size, and not very unlike, a modern soup-plate or hot-water-plate, with a spout to pour the water out of. A very rich one was exhibited in 1857 to the Society of Antiquaries and to the Archæological Institute by Mr. Franks, and is engraved in the Journal of the Institute: it is now, we believe, preserved in the British Museum. These lavers were used for the guests at the high table only; the people in the body of the hall were expected to wash at the fixed lavatory near the entrance, usually behind the screen, where they were often attached by means of a chain. In the hall of St. Mary's Guild at Boston, already referred to, the inventory mentions—

"A laver of laten, hangynge with a chayne of yron."

Connected with the lavatory there was usually a water-drain behind the screen, near the entrance, remains of which may frequently be found, as at South Wingfield Manor-house, and Dacre Castle. It is often of the same form as the piscina in a church: more frequently it was a plain square block of stone, with a basin hollowed out, and a pipe from it, as at the Moat-house, Appleby, Leicestershire. In the Irish tower-houses the water-drain is near the entrance of the upper room, or principal chamber. Water-drains are also found in other CHAMBERS, and will be further described under that head.

The custom of DINING IN THE HALL, which in the fourteenth century had begun to decline, now became more often relinquished, not, however, without an effort on the

[h] Rot. Parl., vol. iv. p. 214.

part of many lovers of time-honoured customs to retain this usage of a chivalric age. In a curious transcript made in this century of some statutes for the ordering of a family, originally framed by Grosteste, Bishop of Lincoln, the lord is admonished—

"As muche as ȝe may withoute peril of sykenes and weryneys ete ȝe in the halle afore youre meyny ffor that schal be to youre profyte and worschippe[j]."

But in spite of this admonition, which it had been found necessary to promulgate, dining in chambers was, to the scandal of all lovers of right government, fast growing into favour with the rich, whose increased luxuries rendered a too close sociability with their dependants inconvenient and expensive. In addition to the instances already cited, we find in the rules made for the royal household in 1458, that the marshal of the hall was to see "That the order of settynge in the halle be kepte aftir the olde custome[k];" and even in the early days of Queen Elizabeth it was considered a good household precept that "all eatinge in chambers should be prohibited other than suche as are ordynarely allowed to kepe chambers[l]." Many years before this, however, we find distinct directions, among "Certen Artycles for Regulatyng the Householde" of Henry VII., for the ceremonies to be observed in "settyng the kynges borde" in his bed-chamber:—

"Also if the kyng sytt in the chamber, than the borde must be on the lyft hand; for ever where as the bedds hede ys, and the chymney, that must be the upper ende off the borde, and at that end must the bisshopp sytt, and the quene on the othyr hand of the kyng: ther ys no odyr choyse, and ther as the bisshoppe sytteth shall he lay the surnap for the kyng to wasche with[m], and hit plese the kyng, he may

[j] MS. Sloane, 1,986, p. 197.
[k] MS. Lansdowne, No. 1, fo. 73, a.
[l] Ibid., No. 86, fo. 102.

[m] The surnape appears to have answered the purpose of the modern table napkin. Its arrangement on the table

comand that day, ij persons, that is to say ij lords and ladyes, ij or elles a lord and a lady, *if so be the roome be large ynough* n."

This must have been an inconvenient custom, and the great chamber became a necessary apartment, not only as a dining-parlour, but as a reception-room in which to entertain guests whilst the tables were being laid in the hall. In an English version of the Romance of "Melusine," of the fifteenth century, the hall is described as "hanged nobly withe riche clothes;" from the hall the guests were led into another chamber, "moche noble and riche." Here they were entertained until "there came the styward and enclyned hym, said, My lady ye may wesche whan it playse ye, for al thyng is redy to dyner. . . . And then they toke eche other by the hand and wessche o."

Of the interior, when used for the purpose of receiving

was attended with much ceremony. See MS. Additional, 4,712, fo. 9, b, and MS. Harl. 305, fo. 3. "The maner of drawynge the surnape at the coronacon of Quene Anne" (Boleyn) is minutely described by John Stevens, "marshall of the seid halle," in MS. Additional, 6,113, fo. 34, a. On that occasion the surnape was carried by the Earl of Rutland. At the royal table it was sometimes placed before the bishop: "The kynge made a bek unto the bysshoppe when he schal wasch." MS. Add. 4,712, fo. 4, a. The surnape was of rich diaper damask, and often handsomely adorned with a fringe. Among the stuff in the great wardrobe in the Tower in 12 Hen. VIII., was "a surnape clothe of launde, embrandered withe golde at bothe ends and fringes at endes withe golde," valued at lx s. MS. Harl. 4,217, sect. 10. They were used when the lavers, filled with rosewater, were brought round after dinner. Although Le Grand d'Aussy affirms that the English did not use table-napkins at this period, we find "Napkyns de Reyns," or linen of Reims in Champagne, among the effects of Henry V. Rot. Parl. iv. p. 228. And in a MS. written 1452 we have this line:—

"Youre sponys and napkyns fayre folde woulde be."

Also,

"Lay thy soueraynes napkyn clenely."
MS. Sloane, 1,315, fo. 5.

In the sixteenth century notices of them are common enough. They were manufactured in France and Flanders, with the royal arms and initials for our sovereigns. See *Archæologia*, xxvii. p. 421.

n MS. Additional, 4,712, fo. 9, a. In an account of the reception of the ambassador from Charles of Burgoigne by Edward IV. and his Queen, we read, "The quene dyd to be ordeined a grete bankette in her owne chambre." MS. Additional, 6,113, fo. 105, a.

o MS. Reg. 18. B. ii. fo. 119, h. Brit. Mus.

DOMESTIC ARCHITECTURE: FIFTEENTH CENTURY.

ILLUSTRATIONS FROM MSS. IN THE BODLEIAN LIBRARY.

INTERIOR OF A HALL.

Shewing the Dais, the Plate-cupboard, the Minstrels' Gallery, &c.

From a MS. of Quintus Curtius.

guests, we find a very faithful delineation in a MS. of Quintus Curtius, of the date of the fifteenth century, preserved in the Bodleian. It will be seen by the engraving that the tables and trestles have been removed. Attention should be paid to the buffet, with the plates, cups, and bowls, &c., on one side of the dais, and the minstrels' gallery at the end of the hall. Many guests have already arrived, and it will be seen that the servants are handing refreshments. The jester, also, occupies a prominent position, and throughout the costumes are very characteristic.

No serious innovation took place, however, until the beginning of the sixteenth century, when the introduction of the banqueting-room, or dining-parlour, led the upper classes gradually to abandon the custom of eating with their retainers in the hall, and we find an allusion to it in the Ordinances of Eltham, made in 1526, where it is stated that "Sundrie noblemen and gentlemen and others doe muche delighte and use to dyne in corners and secret places, not repayring to the kinges chamber or hall[p]." This is also evident by the fact that few domestic buildings were without dining-rooms entirely detached from the hall. In the accounts of the Surveyor-General to Henry VIII., before referred to, we find a statement of the repairs done to the "kynges dynyng chamber," and also to the "quenys dynyng chamber," at the manor of Greenwich[q].

The partial disuse of the great hall led to many architectural innovations. A good example of this occurs at Wanswell Court, Gloucestershire, where the space that would usually have been allotted for the dais and the high table is parted off from the rest of the hall by a

[p] Collection of Ordinances for the Government of the Royal Household. 4to., 1790, p. 153.
[q] MS. Additional 10,109, fo. 89.

solid screen, and so made into a separate dining-room; a lath-and-plaster partition has since been carried from the top of the screen, which was finished with an ornamental battlement, up to the roof, but it is evident that this upper part was originally open. In Hampton Court Palace there is a dining-chamber at the upper end of the hall, and no dais; and although the present floor is not original, the levels of the different doors shew that the original arrangement has been followed.

Chambers were sometimes built above it; the fine high timber roofs, so characteristic of the old halls, were not now an invariable feature. Instead of the lord's solar or chamber being built over a cellar at one end of the hall, it was sometimes over the hall itself. Among the "raparacons maade and doon" in a tenement appertaining to the Great Wardrobe of Edward IV., money was "payd to William Rorton for borde, naill, and lome, for cering and amendyng of the chambre flore, that duste shoulde not falle downe vppon them that sittes and occupies his halle[r];" and in the contract for Hengrave the builder was to "seal ye ij. grett chambers above ye deysshe[s]." Among the Rymer MSS. in the British Museum there is a petition presented to Henry VI. in 1445, by William Clebe, clerk of the works, which may serve to illustrate the history of the royal hall at Eltham. It is addressed to the king, as follows:—

"Sheweth unto Your Hyghness youre poure chapelyn Willyam Clebe, clerk of youre werks, that late of newe hath made by your commaundment at your Tour of London a kechen with al other maner of offices, with loggings thereto belonging and a new draght brygge, and as yet recyved never in money xld., and now late there is appoynted by your counsail to make in all hast possible for the plesir of Your Highnes and necessary resort of straingers to come in likely hast to your manoir of Eltham, for a new halle with a squillery, saucery and surveyng place,

[r] MS. Harl. 4,780, fo. 24. a.   [s] Gage's Hengrave, p. 43.

DOMESTIC ARCHITECTURE: FIFTEENTH CENTURY.

THE HALL,

WANSWELL COURT, GLOUCESTERSHIRE.

al of new and reformacon honourable for the Quenes loggyng there as now desolated, & at Shene the waterbrigge, the great quadrangle with a gatehous, all of new to be made for necessary logging of your worshipfull houshould, with closer of brike toured aboute your gardein ther, and at Westminster the Grete chamboure for your graciouse personne, and the Quenes logging, with the Parlement chambre and Paynted chambre, with reformation of your conduyts there, and ordinance for the scaffold to be made in Westm. Chirch for the estate of the coronation. Plese it therefore your highnesse to commaunde youre Tresorer onward for puryance & hasty expedition of the necessities aforsaide unto your saide clerk good assignment of M$li.$ to be receyvd of the first payment of the dismes granted vnto your highnes by the clergy, and he therefor to answer you in his account byfore youre barons in your escheker, consideryng that the said Willyam hath & most payne hym for to purvey money the mene v^c. marc or more to pay wekely pouer workemen, laborers stuff and cariage, to goddys plesir and profit, as hit shall appeare by Gods grace for Gods love and for pile of your said places[t]."

The CUSTOMS and the etiquette observed at the feasts were similar to those of the previous age. The guests washed before and after meals, but the usage was attended with more ceremony than formerly, and when the ewerer brought water

"He schal knele down upon his kne,
Ellys he forgetes his curtasé[u]."

It was also the duty of the ewerer to lay the cloth upon the table, and "much lore y wys" was required on his part to fulfil this portion of his duty to perfection:—

"The ewerer schal hele his lordes borde,
Withe dowbull napere at on bare worde,
The seluage to the lordes syde withe wine,
And doune schal henge that other way wynne.
The overe nape schal dowbull be layde,
To the ottur syde ye seluage brade,
The other seluage he schal replye,
As towell hit were fayrest in hye[x]."

The "borde clothes" were not always white, but ap-

[t] MS. Additional, 4,609, p. 409.   [u] MS. Sloane, 1,986, p. 40.   [x] Ibid.

pear from many passages in old romances to have been embroidered with various materials:—

> "The tables were covered with cloths of dyaper
> Richly enlarged with siluer and withe golde[y]."

The cloth being laid, the panterer brought forth the bread, wrapped in a white napkin, the salt, the knives, and the spoons, all of which were to be placed on the table with much ceremony and form. The

> "Saller y coveryd and sett in route,"

was placed at the top of the table, and a large loaf at the side of it. This was at the high seat, and it was there that three knives and a spoon were usually laid:—

> "Of the two the haftes schynne outwarde be,
> Of the thrydde the hafte inwarde lays he,
> The spony stele therby schall be layde[z]."

The carver then entered the hall, and took his place at the table:—

> "Smal towell aboute his neck schall bene
> To clens his knyfys that ben so kene[a],"

and at once commenced the cautious process of assaying. He cut a slice off the loaf and gave it to the paneter, who, kneeling, immediately tasted it. The squire who happened to perform the office of carver then went to the kitchen, and cutting a piece off the meat, gave it to the master cook, who assayed it in a similar manner. The sewer and his assistants then placed the covers upon the dishes, and as the clarions and trumpets of the waits struck up a joyous tune, they were carried into the great hall[b]. The men whom the sewer employed to carry the

[y] Lyfe of Saynte Werburge.
[z] MS. Sloane, 1,986, fo. 41.
[a] Ibid., p. 42.
[b] See a good illustration of the carver and his assistants, from the Luttrell Psalter, in a former part of this work, vol. ii. p. 124. The name of the office of sewer is derived from the old French *esculier*, or the *scutellarius*, i.e. the person who had to arrange the dishes, in the same way as the *scutellery* (scullery) was by rights the place where the dishes were kept.

meat were strictly enjoined never to raise the covers, lest they should excite suspicion of treason:—

> "Whosoever he takes that mete to bere
> Schal not so hardy the coverture rere,
> ffor colde ne hote I warne you alle,
> ffor suspecyone of treson as may befalle."

The process of assaying again commenced:—

> "When the sewer comys unto the borde,
> All the mete he sayes at on bare worde,
> The potage fyrst withe brede ycorvyn,
> Couerys hom agayn lest they ben storvyn.
> With fysshe or flesshe yf he be serued,
> A morsell thereof schall he be kervyd.
> And touche the messe over alle aboute,
> The sewer hit etes withouten doubte.
> Withe baken mete yf he servyd be tho,
> The laydes up rered or he fyr go,
> The paste or pye he sayes withinne,
> Dippes brede in gravé no more ne myne[c]."

The wines were also tasted in a like manner by the butler, and even a cup of water was not given to the lord without being carefully assayed. The guests, now being satisfied as to the flavour and wholesomeness of the fare, commenced their gastronomic operations, and the carver found ample opportunity for the exercise of his skill. Upon the nature of the entertainment, of the "subtilties" of the "arte of cury" laid before the guests, of the delicious mortrews, and of the poignant sauces, we have not space to dilate, but must say with Lydgate, in one of his pieces,—

> "The dynere coursis eke at euery feste,
> The large plente done unto ye leste,
> The straunge metis ye maner of ye seruyse,
> Y passe over ffor y was not yere[d]."

Before a trenchour was raised, however, grace was said

[c] MS. Sloane, 1,986, p. 44.   [d] MS. Cottonian, Aug. A. iv. fo. 46. a.

with a loud voice, and the aumenere placed the almsdish upon the board, into which a good "chet lofe" was put before bread was distributed to any of the guests. This was one of those pleasing and benevolent customs which our forefathers of old most readily approved, and which Churchmen loved to introduce into domestic life. The aumenere, or elemosinario, was usually the chaplain of the lord, and by virtue of his office he carried a rod or staff in his hand:—

> "All the broken mete he kepys y wate,
> To dole to pore men at ye gate.
> And drynke yt leves serued in halle,
> Of ryche and pore, bothe grete & smalle,
> He is sworne to overse the servis well,
> And dele it to the pore euery dele[e]."

It is to be feared that this good custom, founded in charity and love, was sometimes abused, and that which was designed for the "pore men at ye gate" went too often into the scullery and the kitchen, to form a riotous repast for the grooms and knaves of the household. "Commande ʒe," says Bishop Grosteste, in his rules for the ordering of a family, "that youre almys be kepyd, and sende not to boys and knafis, nother in the halle, nother outh of ye halle, ne be wasted in soperys ne dyners of gromys, but wysely, temperately, and withoute bate or letyng be hit distributed & deportyd to poure men, beggers, syke folke & febull[f]." It was probably in consequence of this pilfering of the poor man's fare that Lord Howard was induced in 1482 to pay twopence "for a lok for the alms tobbe[g]." The almsdish was sometimes a beautiful ornament to the table, being enriched with chasings and encircled with mottoes. At the feasts of

[e] MS. Sloane, No. 1,986, fo. 43.
[f] Ibid., p. 194.
[g] Household Book, p. 228. Not only tubs, but also baskets, were used for the alms.

Henry VI. a most magnificent almsdish was displayed, which was called the "Tiger;" and an indenture is still in existence testifying that it had been duly received into the custody of the royal treasurer[h].

At the conclusion of the meal, the usher brought in the basins and towels, and

> "Whenne they have waschen and grace is sayde,
> Away he takes at a brade,
> Awoydes the borde unto the flore,
> Tase away the trestes that ben so store[i]."

Perhaps there is no class of books more illustrative of domestic manners than those which treat of etiquette. They display the usages of the polite society of their respective ages, present to us faithful portraitures of the man of fashion and of the gentleman, and serve as landmarks by which to distinguish the various stages of our social refinement. Several curious and interesting relics of this nature, appertaining to the period we are now considering, have been preserved, and from a comparison of them we are enabled to lay down the rules which "a man of curtasye" was to observe "atte borde," from his first arrival at the gate to the close of the repast:—

> "When thou comes to a lordis gate,
> The porter thou schall fynde theratte."

And he was to

> "Aske hym leve in to go
> To speke with lorde, lady, squyer or grome."

According to the etiquette of the day, if the party sought or visited "be of logh degre," it was usual for him to leave the hall and meet his visitor, but

> "Yf he be gentylmen of kyn,
> The porter wille lede the to hym."

[h] Ancient Kalenders and Inventories, vol. iii. p. 370.
[i] MS. Sloane, 1,986, p. 46.

On arriving at the hall door he was to take off his hood and gloves, and if the company "be at the first mete," he was to make his obeisance to the host:—

> "And sithen byfore the strenè thou stonde
> In myddys ye halle upon ye flore,
> Whille marshale or ussher come fro ye dore
> And bydde the sitt or to the borde the lade."

Before taking his seat, however, he washed his hands in the lavatory; and whilst "atte borde" he was to be careful of his personal demeanour, above all to be "stabull of chere," and "lyttull of worde." The way he cut and eat his bread was one of the tests and indications of good manners, and the rule of etiquette upon this point is detailed with much minuteness. On sitting down to meat, the man of "curtasy" cut his bread in two, dividing the crumb from the crust:—

> "In forme then kutt the over dole,
> Sett horn togedur as hit were hole,
> Sithen kutt the nether crust in thre."

He was not to bite his bread, for he is told—

> "That is no curtesye to use in toun,
> But breke as much as thou wylle ete,
> The remelant to pore thou schalt lete."

Having achieved this with becoming dexterity, he was to lay his trenchorn before him, to "sitte up ryghte," and to be careful to give no indication of an inordinate appetite. If any spoke to him whilst he was engaged in eating, he was to tarry until he had finished his morsel before he replied. It was a mark of ill-breeding to eat on both sides of the mouth, and was one which was apt to excite the contempt of those better informed in the usages of polite society:—

> "On bothe halfe thy mouthe yf that thou ete,
> Mony a skorne schall thou gete,

> Thou shalt not laughe, ne speke no thyng,
> While thi mouthe be full of mete ne drinke,
> Ne snipe not with grete sowndyng,
> Nother potage ne other thyng,
> Let not thei spone stond in thy dysshe,
> Whether thou be serued with flesshe or fysshe,
> No lay hit not on thy dysshe syde,
> But clense hit honestly with outen pride."

He was to look that his fingers disclosed no signs of pollution, and to see that his "nayles were clene and blythe," lest he should foul the white cloth before him. One would have thought an admonition such as this unnecessary to a frequenter of baronial halls, did we not find other indications of a still greater coarseness of manners. "Whoso woulde of curtasye lere" is gravely told that if he spits over the table he will be "holden an uncurtasye man;" and our ideas of the refinement of the manners of the age will not be increased by reading that—

> "Yf thi nose thou clene, as may befalle,
> Take thy honde thou clene wythalle,
> Priuely wyth skyrt do hit awaye,
> Or ellis thrugh thi tepit that is so gaye."

He was not so far to forget his good breeding as to pick his teeth at meals,—

> "Withe knyfe, ne stre styk, ne wand;"

nor to wipe them with the "borde clothe," but observe at all times a becoming delicacy of manners. He was not to lean his elbows on the table, nor "atte wine" to take the principal seat, unless especially invited to do so; and he was to observe, in quaffing his wine, that he held the cup with due gentility:—

> "Dip not thi thombe thy drinke into,
> Thou art uncurtasye yf thou hit do."

And further on he is warned of losing all claim to good manners if he dipped his food into the salt-cellar:—

"In salt saler yf that thou pit,
Either fysshe or flesshe that men may wyt,
Yt is a vyce as men me telles,
And gret wonder hit most he ellis."

In addition to all these rules of etiquette, he was to be careful when he washed after meat, that he did not spit about the floor, or before any one to whom respect was due; and finally, we are told that—

"Who so dispyse this lesson ryzt,
At borde to sitt he hase no myzt [j]."

The customs of France and England were so much the same, that the following description of a hall in the fifteenth century is equally applicable to either country. It contains several curious pieces of information relating to the manners of the time:—

"Dedans la sale du logis (car en avoir deux cela tient du grand) la corne de cerf ferrée et attachée au plancher, où pendoient bonnets, chapeaux, gresliers[k], couples[l] et lesses[m] pour les chiens, et le gros chapelet de patenostres pour le commun. Et sur le dressoüer, ou buffet à deux estages, la saincte Bible de la traduction commandée par le roy Charles le Quint[n], y a plus de deux cens ans, les quatre Fils Aymon, Oger le Danois, Melusine, le Calendrier des Bergiers, la Legende dorée, ou le Romant de la Roze. Derriere la grand' porte, force longues et grandes gaules de gibier[o], et au bas de la sale, sur bois cousus et entravez dans la muraille, demie-douzaine d'arcs, avec leurs carquois et flesches, deux bonnes et grandes rondeles[p], avec deux espées courtes et larges, deux halebardes, deux piques de vingt-deux pieds de long, deux ou trois cottes ou chemises de mailles dans le petit coffret plein de son, deux fortes arbalestes de passe, avec leurs bandages et garrots dedens, et en la grand' fenestre, sur la cheminée, trois hacquebutes… et au joignant la perche pour l'espervier, et plus bas à costé les ton-

[j] MS. Sloane, No. 1,986, p. 21.
[k] Hunting-horns.
[l] Coplings.
[m] Cords; Fr. *laisses*.
[n] Charles V. of France, called "the Wise."
[o] Pegs to hang game upon.
[p] Bucklers.

nelles, esclotoueres, rets, filets, pantieres, et autres engins de chasse. Et sous le grand banc de la sale, large de trois pieds, la belle paille fresche pour coucher les chiens, lesquels, pour ouyr et sentir leurs maistre près d'eux, en sont meilleurs et vigoureux. Au demeurant, deux assez bonnes chambres pour les survenans et estrangers, et, en la cheminée, de beau gros bois verd, lardé d'un ou deux fagots secs, qui rendent un feu de longue durée [q]."

There were the stag's antlers for hanging the hats and caps upon, and to which were attached the hunting-horns and the coupling-cords of the dogs, as also the rosaries for the use of the common people. Upon the "dresser," or sideboard, was placed the translation of the Bible as authorized by Charles v. of France a hundred years previously, beside various "romance" books of the period. Behind the great door were the pegs to hang the game upon. Upon the boarding at the end of the hall, and over the chimney, were hung weapons, both offensive and defensive, while on one side were the nets and other instruments connected with hunting. It is curious to notice, too, that beneath the large bench, which was three feet wide, was strewed fresh straw for the hounds to lie upon, that they might be close to their master; while for strangers and guests two good chambers were provided in addition, and in the fireplace layers of green and dry fagots, by which arrangement the fire burnt more slowly.

[q] *Les Contes et Discours d'Eutrapel*, par Noel du Fail, 1732, 12mo., vol. ii. pp. 45, 46. (Du temps present et passé.)

CHAPTER IV.

THE CHAMBERS AND OFFICES. GENERAL ARRANGEMENT.

THE gradual change from the strong castle to the manor-house slightly fortified, and in which the fortifications appear to have been often as much for show as for use, has been already mentioned: but something more should be said about the usual plan and arrangement of the house and the outbuildings; for although these present infinite variety, there are still certain general principles of arrangement which were adhered to in all cases where the nature of the ground would admit of it. The space enclosed by the outer wall and surrounded by the moat was frequently of considerable extent, and divided into several courts, corresponding to the baileys of the earlier castles. The entrance was over a bridge, originally a draw-bridge, with an outer fortification or barbican; but as time drew on, and the country became more peaceful, the bridge became generally of stone or brick, and was protected by a gate-house on the inner side only, with, at first, a portcullis, as at Warwick, where it is still continued in use to add to the grandeur of the whole effect; but in the later houses the portcullis generally disappears, and the gate-house itself assumes a more peaceful and ornamental character, and becomes of more importance[a]; sometimes quite a separate dwelling-house, as at Saltwood Castle, Kent, and Athelhampton, Dorsetshire; and the room over the gateway is sometimes the chapel.

[a] See chapter vi.

DOMESTIC ARCHITECTURE: FIFTEENTH CENTURY.

PORCH AND WINDOW OF THE CHAPEL.

GATEWAY OF INNER COURT.

WINGFIELD MANOR, DERBYSHIRE.

Passing through the gateway, we enter the outer court or bailey, which was generally of considerable extent, and contained the farm buildings and the stables, or a part of them, as there were sometimes stables in the inner court also. The large barn and the farm buildings of the fifteenth century often remain nearly perfect, when the house itself has been destroyed; and in a few instances both have been preserved, as at Place House, Tisbury, Wiltshire, which is one of the most perfect houses of the fifteenth century that we have remaining, and at Great Chalfield manor-house, also in Wiltshire, and St. Donats Castle in Glamorganshire, another very perfect example. At Great Chalfield the outer court or farm-yard is on one side of the principal court, and separated from it by the range of stables: the inner gate-house forms a part of this range, and is not a distinct building; the outer gate-house has disappeared: at South Wraxall the plan is nearly the same.

At South Wingfield manor-house the outer and inner courts are also separated by a range of buildings, which are to some extent fortified. The windows of the principal apartments look into the inner court, as usual, and the entrance to the hall is through a porch from this court, with a small room over it, and a richly panelled parapet and battlement. By the side of the porch, as shewn in the upper part of our engraving, is a rich window to an upper chamber, supposed to have been the chapel, as it is the only rich window about the building, and there is no other trace of a chapel: it is, however, an unusual situation for one, being at the lower end of the hall, over the buttery and pantry; it is called the drawing-room, but apparently without authority. In most of the castles of South Wales there is a large outer bailey, in which the farm buildings are situated; and in the greater part of the castles and houses of this period the principal entrance must always have been through the farm-yard.

The inner bailey, or principal court, was also entered by an archway under the inner gate-house, whether this was detached or formed part of a range of buildings. The court was frequently surrounded by buildings on all sides, forming a quadrangle, as in the colleges of Oxford and Cambridge, generally the most perfect types we have remaining of the larger houses of the fifteenth century, and at Penshurst and Knole, Kent. Sometimes this court is of irregular shape, from the nature of the ground, as at St. Donats, which stands upon a cliff overlooking the Bristol Channel. At Cothele House, Cornwall, the inner quadrangle is perfect, the outer court has almost disappeared, the farm buildings are destroyed, and the gate-house turned into a stable.

This principal court was, however, not always surrounded by buildings on all sides; the side facing the principal front of the house has often a boundary wall only, as at Chalfield, Tisbury, South Wraxall. At Tisbury, which is a smaller house than the others, the inner gate-house forms one side of the court, the offices the opposite one, with the principal front between them, connected at the angles only.

At the back of the house was the servants' court, the usual entrance to which was by the back door of the hall, at the end of the screens. The kitchen often forms one side of this court, and it is sometimes entirely surrounded by the various offices, especially in the larger houses, as at Fawsley, Northamptonshire. Sometimes the courts are surrounded by walls, with detached buildings at irregular intervals, as at Dudley Castle, Staffordshire. There were frequently also wooden buildings attached to the inside of the walls, sometimes with a lean-to roof only, of which the corbels often remain, and sometimes the put-log holes, and the weather-moulding; in other instances they seem to have been of a more important and permanent character, as chimneys are provided for them in the walls; but these wooden structures have almost entirely disappeared.

Before describing the general arrangement of the interior of the house, it should be observed that it was very common in the fifteenth century, as well as in earlier periods, to raise the whole of the habitable portion of the house upon a VAULTED SUBSTRUCTURE, divided into a series of cellars or store-rooms, very substantially built, as a security against fire. These were sometimes half under ground, and in other instances merely built upon the surface, and forming what may be called the ground-floor of the house, although not usually consisting of habitable rooms, and often used as stables. These vaults often remain when the whole of the superstructure has been swept away, the upper part having frequently been of wood only; and such vaults are often very puzzling to tyros in the study, who mistake them for the inhabited rooms. Such vaults or cellars occur in houses of all descriptions, in monasteries, in castles, in fortified towns. Nearly the whole city of Chester is built upon a series of them, with the Rows or passages made on the top of the vaults. The whole town of Winchelsea also was built upon them, and the upper parts of the houses were almost entirely of wood[b].

In a few instances the vaults are built on a larger

[b] The whole of the habitable apartments in the castle of Beaumaris stand upon such vaults, and a long series of these vaults were only the pits of the *garderobes*, and had no opening into them except from above: such pits are often erroneously called dungeons; they are sometimes partially under ground, sometimes entirely so: at Beaumaris they are merely built on the surface, and the same is the case in several of the castles of South Wales.

scale, and more lofty, and are used for the servants' apartments. Of this arrangement Warwick Castle affords a fine example of the time of Richard II.: the kitchen is one of this series of vaulted chambers, and remains perfect and in use; the other usual servants' chambers follow in suite, and there are also the wine-cellar, the beer-cellar, and the wood-cellar; one of these contains a lavatory and water-drain. These chambers are partially under ground on the side next the court, but on the other side, next the river, where the windows are, they are far above it, on the cliff. These apartments remain nearly in their original state, and are the most perfect and interesting part of the house.

The ARRANGEMENT of the principal apartments did not differ materially at the beginning of this century from that of the two preceding. The hall continues to occupy the centre of the house, and is lofty, generally reaching from the ground or the top of the vaults to the roof; but sometimes there was a room over it, as at Chepstow and at Great Chalfield. At the lower end of the hall were the servants' apartments, and at the upper end the family apartments: in these two wings the rooms are comparatively small and low, each wing being commonly divided into two or three stories; and sometimes the wings assume the form of towers, and are four or five stories high. In general the number of these small chambers increases as the building gets later in date, and as these were chiefly bed-rooms, they shew an increased degree of comfort and refinement; and the custom of sleeping in the hall seems to have been generally discontinued, unless on special occasions when the house was much crowded. The hall is sometimes almost detached from the other buildings, having windows in the gables at each end as well as on both sides, and is

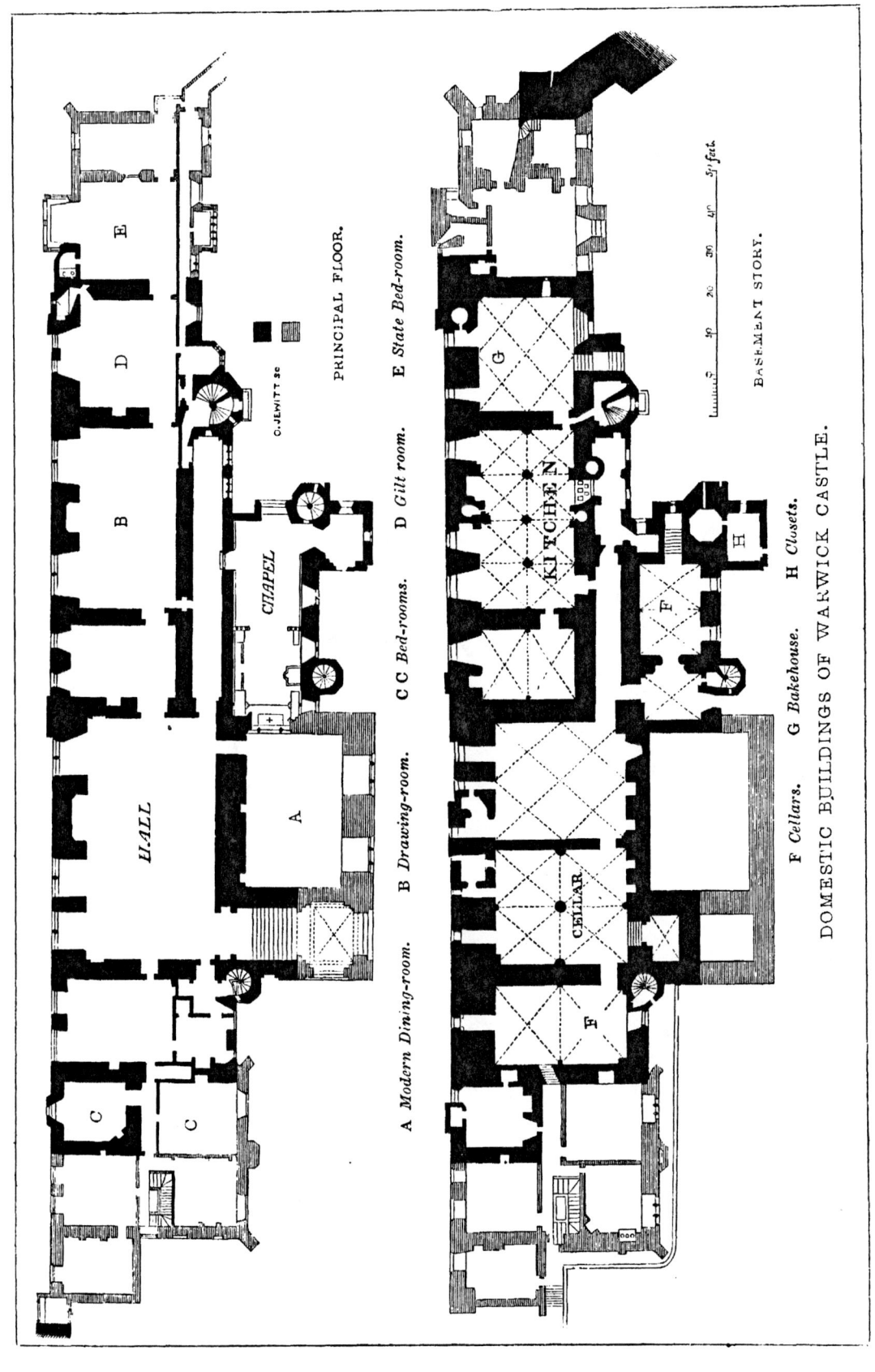

DOMESTIC BUILDINGS OF WARWICK CASTLE.

connected with the other buildings by low rooms or passages only, as at Fawsley, Northamptonshire, and St. Mary's Hall, Coventry. But in most cases the buildings at either end are two stories high, and the roof is the same height as that of the hall; sometimes the gable end still stands clear above the two low stories attached on the outside of it.—The arrangement of the offices and the position of the kitchen continued much the same as in the previous century, described in our last volume.— The position of the chapel varies extremely, and there seems to be no rule for it, excepting that it is always near to the dais, and connected with it by a short passage or staircase.

At the upper end of the hall, at the back of the dais, in the earlier period is generally the cellar, with the solar or lord's chamber over it; in the later period these become the dining-room, and the drawing-room over it. In some cases, as we have mentioned, the dais itself is separated from the hall by a solid wall, and becomes a distinct dining-room. In the time of Henry VII. and VIII. in the smaller houses the hall sometimes disappears altogether, and its place is supplied by the dining-room and drawing-room; and this arrangement became almost universal in the time of Elizabeth. The old halls have also very frequently been divided by a floor into two low rooms at a later time, while the old roof is still preserved.

It is exceedingly difficult to apply the names of the chambers which are entered in the inventories to the different parts of a house, because as the change in the arrangements of the rooms took place, sometimes new names were adopted, at others the old names were retained with a different signification. The *Aula* may, perhaps, to the end of the century be considered as the chief or largest room in the building, but while at the commencement of the century it was more especially the dining-chamber, towards the end, when the habit of dining in separate rooms crept in, it was more frequently employed as an audience-chamber, perhaps serving for the dinner only on a few state occasions. The name of most frequent occurrence is the *camera*. We find, for instance, the "camera superior" and the "camera inferior" in the inventories, but as the contents of the one resemble exactly the contents of the other, we must apply the superior and inferior simply to their position, and take "camera" as the generic term for any apartment of the house excepting the hall, chapel, and offices.

In the will of William Esyngton of Newcastle, (1415,) we find the apartments summed up as follows:—

"Item do et lego omnia principalia mea tam in camera, aula, penore[c], coquina, brasiatorio (brewhouse), pandoxatorio (malthouse), stabulo," &c.

We have thus his chamber, hall, cellar, kitchen, malthouse, brewhouse, and stable.

Robert Conyers of Sockburn describes his goods in his will thus, (1431):—

"Omnia utensilia tam in camerâ, quam in aulâ, pincernâ[d], (another name for the cellarium or buttery), panetria (pantry), pistrina (bakehouse), una cum plaustris et carucis (waggons and carts), cum toto apparatu," &c.

The camera usually contained a bed, and the ordinary furniture of a bed-chamber; but it must be remembered

[c] *Penore*, from *penus*. Probably the "cellar" where the wine is kept, not the place where it is decanted, which is the "buttery." The word *cellarium* is applied both to buttery and cellar. "Quod vinum refectorarius dicti monasterii recipere debet et tenetur in penore domini abbatis."—*Transactio inter Abbat et Monachos Crassenses*, anno 1351, ap. du Cange.

[d] *Pincerna* is derived from the Greek πινειν κιρνα, and is rather the place where the wine was mixed or decanted, not the place where it was stored, which is our meaning of the word cellar.

that it still answered the purpose of a parlour or sitting-room, the bed being covered over during the daytime with a handsome coverlid, as is still the custom in France and other foreign countries to this day.

The following inventory of the goods belonging to the Vicar of Gainford, and attached to his will made in 1412, shews the usual amount of furniture in the chambers at the period:—

"Duo lecti rubei coloris, viz. cooperti cum tapetiis, xxs.
Duo lecti de blodio (blood-colour), xs.[e]
Unus parvus lectus de blodio worstett, vis. viiid.
Unus lectus albus, iiis. iiijd.
Duo coopercla (coverlids), vis.
Unum whylt (quilt) cum iiij. matresse, vis. viiid.
xiiij. Lodices (blankets[f]), xivs.
xix. paria Linthiaminum (pairs of sheets), xxxjs. viiid.
Unum mantellum de rubeo fresed (a coarse kind of cloth), xxxs.
Tres Togæ furruratæ (lined with fur), xls.
Unum pylche[g] de stranlion, xxs.
Tres Togæ singulæ, xiijs. iiiid.
Quatuor ulnæ panni lanei de sendry coloris (colour of ashes?) cum una tela (web) de russet, xxvis. viiid.
Armatura (armour, &c.), xxvis. viijd.
viij. Libræ ceræ (candles), iiijs.
Unum par de Trussyngcofers[h] (packing-chests?) iiijd.
Unum wyrehatte (.....) vs."

In the inventory of his goods taken on the death of John Danby, (1444,) are found:—

"In CAMERA.—x. coopertoria (coverlets), xjs.
j. fed-bed (feather-bed) et iij. materes, vijs.
iij. lodices (blankets), iijs.
v. Linthiamina, iijs. iiiid.
j. web de sac, xxd.
v. bowsturs (bolsters), xxd.
v. ulni de russet, iijs. ixd.
In mappis et manutergiis (in cloths and towels), xvd.
j. magna cista (chest), xld.
Alia parva cista, xijd.
Aliæ duæ cistæ, ijs."

[e] *Blodius* is considered by the best antiquaries to be "blood" colour, (Sax., *blot.*) At the same time, we have seen it translated in some works as if for *bloius*, i.e. blue colour.

[f] The "lodex" was not made of the same material as our modern blanket, but it answered the same purpose in the bed-coverings.

[g] *Pylch* is given by Bailey as a flannel night-garment or clout for an infant. What material *stranlion* was we cannot tell, there is probably some error of the scribe.

[h] To truss is to pack up; hence, probably, trussing cofers were boxes for packing up chattels for travelling. Similar to our word 'trunk.'

While, however, the camera in the private house served the purpose of a bed-chamber, there were also other names in use, such as the *cubiculum, dormitorium,* &c.; the latter more especially when any large number of persons slept in the same room.

There was often a smaller room attached to the larger, which served as a closet for keeping clothes, &c., which went by the name of *wardrobe*. Thus we find in the inventory of the Prior of Durham, (1446):—

"Garderoba.—In primis j. par de Gardevyaunce[i], cum Armis Thomæ Langton.
ij. Clothesekkez (clothes-horse?).
j. mantica (mantle).
Una larga *Cista* (chest) de opere Flaundrensi[k].
iiij. Costeræ paleatæ de viridi et blodio (striped alternately with green and red), cum diversis animalibus intextis in eisdem, pro aulâ de Pyttyngton.
iij. paria del Cofors (chests).
ij. Barehidez" (bearskins, used probably as saddle-cloths.)

The inventory taken at Ewelme in 1466, after mentioning the great chamber, containing the bed and the coverings belonging to it, goes on to mention the hangings, &c., in "my lady's closet," and in "the gentlewoman's closet." And further on we read of "tapits of red worsted" distributed in "the lord's chamber," "in my lord's outer closet," in the chamber of the "ewearye" (washing-closet), and in "the norserye."

The names of the lower rooms of the house and the offices are in general more carefully expressed. As we have shewn in the previous volume, the pantry and the buttery may be clearly defined, though their use now was gradually changed, one room at the end of the century serving much the purposes which originally required two chambers. The *panetrium* in some instances was used as

---

[i] Literally, we expect, meat safes; afterwards safes or cupboards of any description.

[k] These chests were generally of wood, and imported from Flanders, though perhaps in some cases the Flemish work was imitated in England.

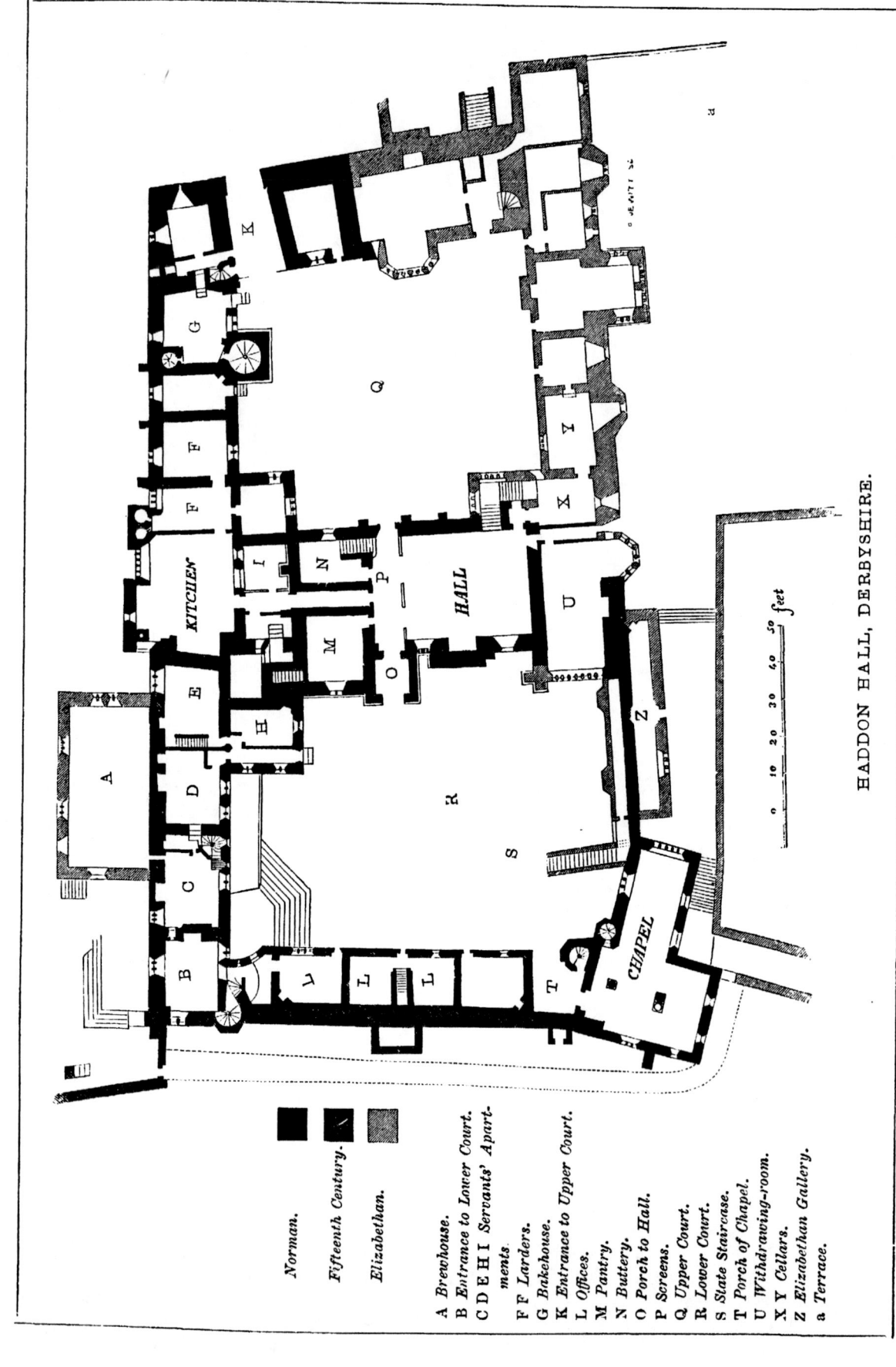

the larder (*lardarium salsarium*), and the *botellarium*, or *pincerna*, as a cellar (*celarium* or *penus*). The kitchen (*coquina*) remained the same. The *scutellarium* (scullery) in a few instances is noticed, as also the minor offices of bakehouse (*pistrina*), brewhouse and malthouse (*brassinium* and *pandoxatorium*). We might increase the list by adding the stables, granaries, and such like, but the above catalogue is sufficient to shew the usual requirements which the architect took into consideration when erecting a fifteenth-century house[1].

Considerable obscurity still exists concerning the habitual SLEEPING APARTMENTS of the middle ages. There is no doubt that the domestics and retainers occasionally slept upon straw laid down for the purpose in the hall, but this was on particular occasions, when the house or castle was over-crowded, and does not appear to have been the usual habit for any part of the establishment, at least not in the fifteenth century, when the chambers had become much more numerous, both at the higher end of the hall for the family and guests, and at the lower end for the domestics. The usual sleeping apartment for the lord and lady, or master and mistress of the family, appears to have been on the ground floor, either in the withdrawing-room behind the dais, which seems to have been the case in the smaller houses, or in other apartments further removed from the hall, when space

---

[1] On the continent at the same period the following list serves as an illustration of the usual arrangement of a house:—"Chacun (étage de l'hôtel de Soissons) consistoit en une grande salle, une chambre de parade, une grande chambre, une garde-robe, des cabinets et une chapelle; les salles recevoient jour par des croisées hautes de 13 pieds et demi, et larges de 4 et demi; les chambres de parade portoient 8 toises 2 pieds et demi de longueur; les chambres, tant du duc que de la duchesse (d'Orléans), avoient six toises de long, et trois de large; les autres, 7 et demi en quarré; le tout éclair de croisées longues, étroites et fermées de fil d'archal, avec un treillis de fer percé, de lambris et de plat-fonds de bois d'Irlande, ouvré de la même façon que j'ai décrit en parlant des appartemens du roi et de la reine au Louvre."—Sauval.

allowed. There is often a tower near the end of the hall, as at Lympne, Kent, containing a number of chambers, many of which were bed-rooms. Chaucer's "Miller's Tale" shews that the chief bed-room in a house in the street of a town was on the ground-floor, or probably a little above the level of the street, over the cellar, which was half underground, according to the usual fashion of town-houses of the period.

In monastic establishments it was usual for the monks to sleep in a common dormitory[m], which was divided into a number of small cells ranged down both sides, separated either by boarded partitions or by curtains, but open at the top, with a small window at one end of each cell, and a door at the other opening into a central passage, at one end of which was the bed of the abbot, or other chief officer. Each cell contained a bed, and a shelf for books over the head of it.

There is reason to believe that in the larger houses and castles there was commonly a chamber at the top of the house, near the roof, which served for a dormitory[m], very much after the same fashion as in the monasteries, or the long room at Eton College. There is a room of this kind, called the dormitory, at Layer Marney, Essex. In some cases the dormitory seems to have been over the hall, and it is not improbable that the upper range of smaller windows over the large windows of the hall at Chepstow may have belonged to a dormitory. The cor-

---

[m] "Upon the west syde of the cloyster there was a faire large house called the DORTER, where all the monuks and the novices did lye, every monncke having a litle chamber of wainscott, verie close, severall by themselves, and their wyndowes towards the cloyster, every windowe servinge for one chambre, by reasonne the particion betwixt every chamber was close wainscotted, one from another, and in every of their windowes a deske to supporte there bookes for there studdie. In the west syde of the said dorter was the like chambers, and in like sorte placed, with there wyndowes and desks towardes the Fermery and the water, the chambers beinge all well boarded under foute."—Antient Rites of Durham.

DOMESTIC ARCHITECTURE: SIXTEENTH CENTURY.

DORMITORY, LAYER MARNEY, ESSEX.

W. Twopeny, del. O. Jewitt, sc.

bels in the upper part of the walls of several halls in Scotland have been already mentioned as rather indicating a floor than a gallery, and this upper room was probably appropriated to the purpose of a sleeping apartment. In the later houses, in which the hall becomes a less important feature, the bed-chambers become more numerous and more important in proportion, marking the gradual progress of civilization, until in Elizabethan houses they become almost as numerous and as important as in modern times.

The FURNITURE of the sleeping apartments was also during this century considerably improved. The rude wooden bench was discarded for a bedstead of somewhat elegant construction, and the legs and cornices displayed the ingenuity of the carver, whose craft was now in much request. Four-post bedsteads were first introduced in this century. Richard, Earl of Arundel, left to his son Richard a standing bed (*estandard*), that is, one the tester of which was supported by pillars[n]. As in the previous century, the bed-hangings were of the richest texture. Thomas de Mussendum, in 1402, bequeathed to his wife a bed and coverlet made of velvet and satin[o]. Sentences and mottos were often embroidered upon the coverlids: thus the Duke of Exeter, in 1447, bequeathed to "Anne my wyff yat now is, a bed of arras, with the scriptur of honnor, with all the costers[p]." The beds were well supplied with linen and pillows. In 1434, Joan Bergavenny left by will—

"A bed of gold swans, the tapestry of green, with bunches of flowers of divers kinds, two pairs of sheets of Raynes[q], a pair of fustaynes, six

---

[n] Nichols' Royal Wills, p. 131.
[o] Ibid.
[p] Ibid., p. 284. The costers (*costerys—costeræ*) were the side pieces of the bed-hangings, answering to our bed-curtains.
[q] Reims in Champagne, where there was a celebrated manufactory.

pair of other sheets, six pair of blankets, six mattresses, six pillows, and the cushions and bancoves that belonged to the bed [r]."

The bedchamber of the English yeoman was furnished with a proportionate degree of comfort. John Baret left his niece his

"Grene hangyd bedde steyned with my armys therin that hanggith in the chambyr ovir the kechene, with the cortynes; the grene kevering longgyng therto, another coverlyte, ij. blankets, ij. pere of good shets, the transpson (?), the costerys (curtains) of the chambyr and of ye draugh chambyr that be of the same sorte, a gret piloe and a sma'l piloe—the federbed is her owne, y[t] hire maistresse gaf hire at London [s]."

An inventory made in 30 Henry VIII., of "Suche warderobe stuffe of the beddis as remayneth within the standyng warderobe in Wyndsour Castell," contains the particulars of eight beds, some of which are described as "sore worne," or "nede to be amended." They were of satin, Tartar hanging, crape, tawney silk, and silk of baudekyn [t].

In houses of a less important class the bed was made up on the floor, the chambers were seldom furnished with bedsteads, except perhaps of the commonest description. In the regulations of Bishop Waynflete for the lodging of the scholars, it was ordered that each of the rooms on the ground floor should hold two principal beds and one truckle bed; the chambers over them each two truckle beds: and even when Waynflete entertained royalty, the nobles slept on truckle beds, two or three in a room [u]. It was usual, on engaging a servant, to stipulate that he was to find his own bed.

[r] *Test. Vetusta.*

[s] Wills and Inventories of the Register of Bury St. Edmunds, 4to., p. 22.

[t] MS. Additional in Brit. Mus., No. 10,602, fo. 2. The word "baudekyn" is often met with in inventories, signifying some kind of material. It was probably the stuff of which a "baldequin," or canopy that was carried over kings and bishops on state occasions, was made, and hence the origin of the term.

[u] Chandler's Life of Waynflete, p. 204.

THE CHAMBERS AND OFFICES. 101

In 1465, Sir John Howard engaged a servant who agreed to find himself in bedding[x].

The sleeping apartments[y] were given in charge of the usher of the bedchamber, whose duty it was to see to the providing of all things necessary for comfort and convenience, and under his orders, in royal households at least, were usually two grooms and a page. It was the duty of the grooms of the chamber to procure a regular supply of tallwood[z] and fuel for the fire:—

> "And fuel to chymne hym falles to gete,
> And strens in cros to seue the hete."

They were also to provide clean rushes and straw for the floors and palets. According to the Household Book of Edward IV., the groom of the chamber was to bring daily "rushes and litter for the paylettes all the yere; of the sergeaunts of the hall and this yeoman or this groom berith up nyghtly stuffe for the kynges bed, and bydeth therby till it be made, and on the mornynge they sette it doun to their office ageyne saufly and clenely that no stranger schall touche it[a]." In the summer season they were to gather sweet herbs and flowers

---

[x] Manners and Household Expenses, p. 204.

[y] In a manuscript in the British Museum, (MS. Harleian, No. 4,431, fo. 2,) of the early part of the fifteenth century, there is a beautiful representation of the interior of a bedroom. The illuminated drawing is interesting, as shewing the architectural and domestic arrangements of a chamber of this period. The apartment is high and spacious. A large window at the end is approached by stone steps, which form capacious seats at the side. In addition to the lattice-work, there are inside shutters for the purpose of keeping out the wind and rain. The walls are covered with richly embroidered tapestry hung upon tenter-hooks. The bedstead has a tester, and the rich arras hangings are worked with *fleur de lis*. A chair, displaying much taste in its construction, with the back and cushions embroidered, is at the bedside, and a couch well cushioned and covered with arras gives an air of comfort and refinement to the chamber.

[z] "A long sort of shive (splinter) riven out of trees, which is cut shorter into billets."—Bailey.

[a] Liber Niger, Domus Regis Aug. Ed. IV., printed by the Society of Antiquaries, p. 40.

with which to decorate and perfume the royal chamber. "The gromes schall gadyr for the kinges gowns and shetes and othyr cloths the swete floures, herbis, rotes, and thynges to make them breathe most holesomely and delectable[b]." In the Sloane manuscript the office of the groom is set forth in detail. We give the following curious passage, descriptive of the art of bed-making in the early part of the fifteenth century:—

> "Gromes paletts shyn fyle and make litter,
> Six fote on lengthe withouten diswer,
> Un fote y wys hit schall be brode,
> Wele watered y wythen be craft y trode,
> Uyspes drawen out at fote and syde,
> Wele wrethyn and thyd agaȝne that tyde."

The arrangement of the bed-clothes and hangings are next described:—

> "To the grosdyl stode hegh on lengthe and brade,
> ffor lordys two beddys schall be made,
> Bothe utter and inner so God me glade.
> That henges shall be with hole sylor,
> Wyth crochetts and loupys set on lyver.
> The valance on sylour shall henge withinne,
> That reche schall even to grounde aboute,
> Nother more nother less with outen doute.
> He strykes hom up with forket wande,
> And lappes up faste aboute the lyfte hande.
> The knop up turnes and closes on syȝt,
> As holde by nek that henges full lyȝt.
> The counterpynt he lays on beddys fete,
> And wysshenes on sydes shyn lye full mete[c]."

As the progress of refinement and morals in domestic life is evidenced by minute details, we may look with interest to points of household economy and manners which otherwise might appear trifling. During the middle ages it was the prevailing custom to sleep entirely

[b] Ibid.
[c] MS. Sloane, No. 1,986, fo. 32. *With-* *outen diswere*, without doubt; *uyspes*, wisps of straw; *wrethyn*, wreathed.

DOMESTIC ARCHITECTURE: FIFTEENTH CENTURY.

BEDS, FROM MSS. IN THE BODLEIAN LIBRARY.

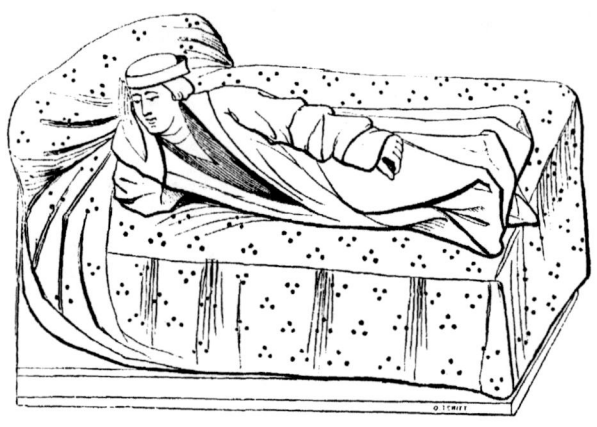

COUCH, OR BED. Douce. 195.

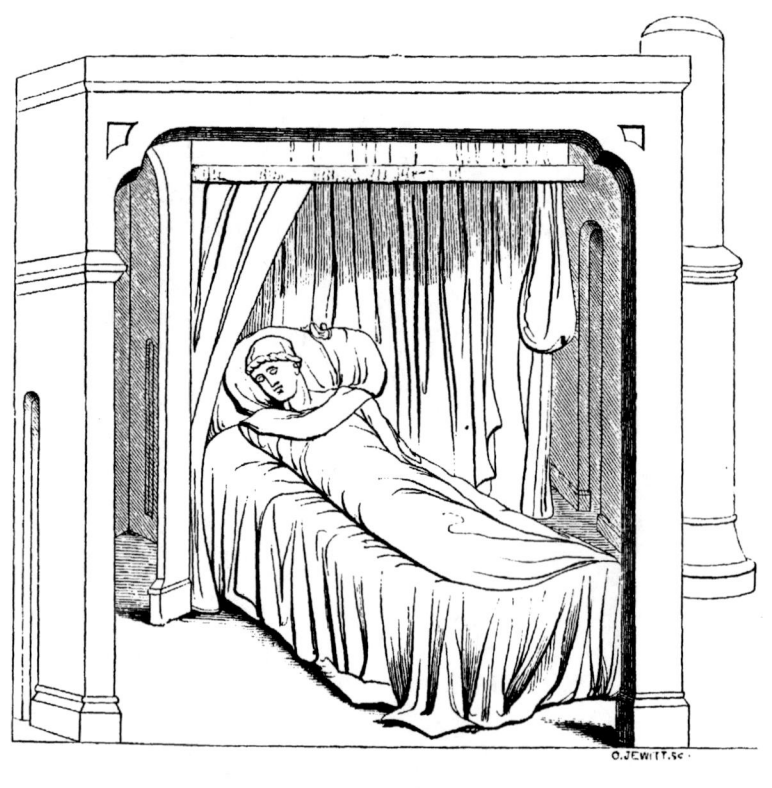

naked, and it would be difficult to refer to manuscript illuminations previous to the fifteenth century in which persons are depicted in bed as wearing night-dresses. In the fifteenth century, however, it became the custom to wear night-gowns, and in the curious manuscript to which we have often referred, we read:—

"The lorde schall shyft his gowne at nyȝt,
Syttand on fote shete tyl he be dyȝt [d]."

Before we proceed to speak of the other chambers, it may not be out of place to say a few more words on the BEDS, as documentary evidence on this subject is very abundant. Of these there are different kinds[e], and they were generally supplied with very rich coverings, as the inventories following testify.

A curious document is preserved[f], illustrating, not only the material of which the beds of this period were made, but as shewing the value attached to this article of domestic furniture. It is a writ of 1 Henry VI., (1423,) to the keeper of the royal wardrobe, for the delivery of a complete "bed of hawkyng" to the Duke of Exeter, which the "late king" (Henry V.) had given to him, with a proviso that he died possessed of sufficient property to fulfil all the bequests of his will without it, but if his executors found that there was not sufficient, the Duke was to have it in preference to others on paying its value. A schedule attached gives a minute description of the various pieces which formed the "bed;"

[d] MS. Sloane, No. 1,986, p. 33.

[e] "Les lits, que l'on nommoit couches et couchettes, étoient extraordinairement grands; quand ils ne portoient que 6 pieds de long sur autant de large, ou leur dormoit simplement le nom de couchettes; mais lorsqu'ils étoint de 8 pieds et demi sur 7 et demi, ou bien de 11 sur 10, ou de 12 sur 11, en ce cas-là on les appeloit des couches. Toutes au reste étoient montées sur des marches qui avoient deux pieds de largeur plus que les couches. On paroit les marches des plus beaux tapis, et les lits d'étoffes les plus exquises," &c.—Sauval, *Hist. et Rech. des Antiquités de la Ville de Paris.*

[f] MS. Additional, No. 4,603, fo. 337.

it consisted of a selour, a testor, a counterpoint, six tapits of arras, with figures of hunting and hawking worked in gold, two curtains, and one traverse of "tartaryn." The whole was estimated at 139*l.* 11*s.* 8*d* [g].

In the inventory of the prior of Durham (1446), we have the furniture of the bed very minutely described; and the extract is also interesting as shewing the usual contents of the bed-chambers of a house:—

"CAMERA SUPERIOR.—Unus Lectus pendens cum riddellis (curtains), tapetâ (quilt), silours (valance?) et ij. coopertoriis de blodio sago[h] ejusdem coloris, et costeræ paleatæ (striped curtains) pro ornatu murorum ejusdem Cameræ, paleatæ de blodio sago intenso et remisso[i]: j. Canobium (counterpane[k]?); j. Dormonde (pillow?) cujus superior pars de blodio, cum rosis in corneris; j. par Lodicum (blankets) novorum; j. par Lintheaminum (sheets); j. Culcitrum[l] (bolster?) cum iiij. Evangelistis in corneris; j. Lectus blodius cum tapetâ cum leopardis et pellicanis ac arboribus in eodem intextis.

Duo panni de blodio pro sedili sive cancello.

iij. Bankquerez paleat, de blodio intenso et remisso.

x. Quisshons (cushions) de blodio sago.

j. par (sel) Cultellorum magnorum continens iiij. pecias, quorum manubria (handles) sunt argentea et deaurata.

Aliud par continens tres Cultellos, quorum Manubria de ebore et in parte argentea et deaurata.

CAMERA INFERIOR. — Lectus pendens, de blodio sago intenso et remisso, cum riddellis tapetâ, silour et coopertorio paleato, ejusdem sectæ; iiij Costeræ pro ornatu murorum, de blodio, intenso et remisso.

j. Canobium, j. Dormonde novum et largum cum 𝔥𝔢 insculpt' in corneris.

j. par Lodicum de fustian.

[g] Equal to about 2,800*l.* of modern money.

[h] *Saye*, a stuff made of silk and wool mixed. See F. Michel, *Etoffes de Soie*, ii. 246.

[i] "De blodio intenso et remisso" probably refers to the red being alternately light and dark. It occurs constantly in the same inventory.

[k] *Chalons* is also a word used for bed-coverings, though it does not appear of what precise use. "Pannos pictos qui vocantur Chaluns" occur in an inventory, Mon. Ang. ii. 720. The word may, perhaps, only refer to the material, and that it was made at Chalons.

[l] *Culcitrum* literally is nothing more than a cushion, but here it seems to be used as a pillow or bolster.

THE CHAMBERS AND OFFICES.

Aliud par Lodicum.
j. par Lintheaminum.
Unum Culcitrum cujus superior pars de glauco serico.
Aliud culcitrum cum aquilâ duo habente capita.
Unus Lectus bonus, blodeus, cum tapetâ cum arboribus et pellicanis diversorum colorum intextis.
v. Qwysshons de blodio sago.
Unus blodeus Pannus pro Cuppborde, de sago.
Una Mensa de Prusiâ cum foliis.

Pro alio Lecto ibidem, imprimis, j. fethirbede, j dormonde, j. par lodicum, j. par lintheaminum, j. lectus albus cum tapetâ cum arboribus et sertis intextis.
j. Coopertorium de blodio sago.
In Camera sub Volta j. canobium, j. dormonde, j. par lodicum, j. par lintheaminum, j. culcitrum, j. lectus cum papilionibus intextis.
j. Pannus blodeus pro coopertorio Cathedræ."

Count Ralph de Neville, in his will, leaves to his son, among other goods,—

"Unum lectum de arras, cum costeris paled de colore rubeo, viridi et albo qui solebant penderere in magna Camerâ infra Castrum de Sherefhoton."

This piece of tapestry, therefore, it seems, with its edges striped with red, green, and white, had once hung in the principal chamber of another castle, but had been transferred thence for a covering to his bed. We conclude with one more document relating to the king's bed:—

"Herafter folowith the reckenyng of the Kinges greate bedde of Walnutte tree at Yorke place, and of the stuf provided for the same.

"ffirst. Received of the Master of the Horse twoo peces of Walnuttree whiche he gave unto the Kinges grace, and never had more stuf.
Also I, William Kendall, paide for the cariage thereof from Croydon to London, iijs. iiijd.
And also provided xviij. waynescottes at xd. the pece, xvs.
Provided for the bottom of the bedde iij. deale bordes, at iijs. iiijd. the pece, sum xs.

For cariage of the same, vjd.
For iron worke to the same, iijs. iiijd.
For glewe, xx^{ti}d.
For lye to season the walnuttree, xs.
For vj. men, being carvers, for tenne monethes, at xxs. every moneth, fyndyng theym self, lxli.
.... monethes, at xxs. the moneth, vjli.
.... rewe wryght for gilding of

P

the . . . . (wherof I have a ac-
quytaunce), xvj*li*.
Paide to the Master of Saint
Laurence pountcny in London
for the hire of a house wheryn
the same was wrought, xl*s*.

"Summa totalis, lxxxvj*li*. iij*s*. x*d*.

"Wherof I have received of Mr. Alford at iij. sundry tymes, xxx^{ti}*li*., as apperith by his boke, that is to sey, v*li*. at one tyme; and by Mr. Hennages letter, x*li*.; and by the Kinges commaundement, xv*li*., all the residue of the said xxx*li*.

"And where as I the said William for the devise and also embocyng and clensyng of a quarter of every piece of theyre worke, for the better instruccions of theym, and for provision of money, besides daily attendaunce (as alwaies I have ben redy by commaundment) as yet never had no peny nor none other rewarde; Whiche I wille submytte to youre wysedom and discresion."

(Endorsed) "The charge of the Kynges bedd made of Walnottree." (temp. Henry VIII.)

CRADLES also were not things unknown, as the annexed illustration, from one of the Douce MSS. of the period, testifies. We 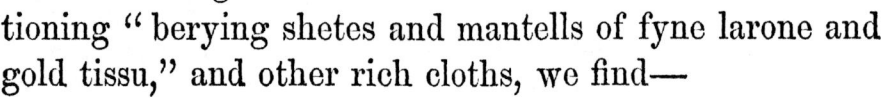 see that they were made for rocking, much the same as in modern days. They are also mentioned in inventories of this period, as in that of Reginald de la Pole: after mentioning "berying shetes and mantells of fyne larone and gold tissu," and other rich cloths, we find—

"Item, a pane^m and a head-shete for ye Cradell of the same sute, bothe furred with mynever."

The APPAREL of the state chamber, or "Chamber of Pleasaunce," was in keeping with the splendour of the bedding, and surpassed in richness of texture and gorgeousness of colouring anything that had been produced in the preceding century. When the ambassador from

---

^m A piece of cloth. We still retain the word in "counter-pane."

DOMESTIC ARCHITECTURE: FIFTEENTH AND SIXTEENTH CENTURY.

WOODEN PANEL, SYON HOUSE, MIDDLESEX.

COLCHESTER ESSEX.

Charles of Burgundy was entertained by Edward IV., there were prepared for his reception—

" iij. chambres of Pleasaunce, all hanged with whyte silke and lynnen clothe, and all the floures covered withe carpettes. There was ordeined a bedde for hym selue of as good doune as coulde be gotton, the shetes of Raynys, also fyne fustyns, the counterpoynte clothe of golde furred w^t armyn, the tester and the celer also shyninge clothe of golde, the curteyns of whyte Sarcenette, as for his hede sute and pillowes were of the Quenes owne ordonnance[n]."

When Philip of Castile was entertained by Henry VII. at Windsor, the apartments appropriated for his use are thus described in one of the Paston letters:—

"They were the rychestly hanged that ewer I sawe, vii. chambers togeder hangyd withe clothe of Arras wroght with gold as thyk as cowd be, and as for iij. beddes of astate, no kyng crystyned can shewe sych iij.[o]"

It is difficult to outstep by any conception of the imagination an idea of decorative splendour of silk and arras, that is not warranted by the historic evidences of the time.

Unfortunately, as we have before had occasion to observe in describing the hall, these hangings have almost entirely disappeared, and very frequently nothing remains but the pegs that they hung upon. The wooden panels which formed the usual decoration of the lower part of the walls more frequently remain, and being enriched with carving, give some idea of the lavish expenditure bestowed upon such decorations. We must bear in mind that in these, as in all other decorations in the work of the middle ages, colour was an essential feature; the carver and the colourer were called upon to assist each other, and each to heighten the effect of the other's work in producing the richest and most splendid orna-

[n] MS. Additional, No. 6,113, fo. 106. a.   [o] Paston Letters, vol. v. p. 448.

mentation that their skill and their means would allow. Such panels as those at Colchester, when further enriched by painting and gilding, must have been very beautiful articles of decoration, and when these were accompanied by equally rich hangings, and the windows filled with painted glass, the magnificence of these Gothic chambers could hardly be surpassed by the height of modern luxury.

The panels, whether of stone, wood, or plaster, were often ornamented with scrolls bearing inscriptions, or with inscriptions or the initials of the owners without any scroll. At first these had an heraldic character, and the inscription was often the motto of the family, as the word Esperance on a panel at Sion House, Middlesex. The initials of husband and wife united by a true-lover's knot frequently occur, as at South Wraxall, Wilts, or ornamented by the crest or badge of the family. These inscriptions commonly occur over the fireplace, but are not at all confined to that situation. They occur also in external work, as in the front of an oriel window, or on the spandrels of the arch of a doorway, or over the entrance gateway. This custom was continued in Elizabethan and Jacobean work, and is then frequently accompanied by the date. Texts of Scripture or moral axioms were often used in the later examples, a custom still continued in parts of Switzerland.

In a descriptive passage belonging to the earlier part of this century, we have an allusion to the decoration of walls with statuettes, and gable-shaped canopies over them:—

> "All the wallus of geete,
> Withe gaye gablettus and grete,
> Kyngges settyng in ther seteᴾ."

[p] Romance of Sir Degrevant, Thornton Romances, p. 238.

THE CHAMBERS AND OFFICES.

The walls of the principal apartments were usually cased with wainscot to the height of about eight feet, above which were sometimes hangings of tapestry, or other cloth, as at the upper end of St. Mary's Hall, Coventry. In a letter written by Sir John Howard to one of his bailiffs in 1469, we have the following interesting passage:—

" I pray you take the measure of the hall, and of the length and of the *deepness as much as must be hanged*, and likewise of the parlor, and the chamber over the parlor, and the chamber where that I lay in, and of the chamber over the pantry and buttery; of all these I pray you send me the measure in haste, and I trust before long ye shall see the chambers better hanged than ever ye saw them[q]."

In the time of Henry VIII. the most common pattern for the wainscot was an imitation of folds of linen, called the "linen pattern," as in Thame Park, Oxfordshire, and in the hall of Magdalen College, Oxford. This last is said to have been brought from Reading Abbey; it is, however, a good example of this style of ornament, which abounds everywhere in houses of this period. Over the wainscot at this time also it was usual to introduce ornamental plaster-work, called "pargetting," in place of the tapestry, especially where the room was low and afforded little space between the wainscot and the ceiling. Of this kind of ornament the room in Thame Park affords also a good example, of which an engraving is annexed from a drawing by Mr. Twopeny.

The CORNICE of the chamber is often enriched with the usual ornaments of the period, most commonly executed in plaster only, but sometimes of wood. The ornaments of the latest Gothic period, in the beginning

[q] Manners and Household Expences of England in the Thirteenth and Fifteenth Centuries, p. xci.

of the seventeenth century, are often imitations of the earlier styles, such as the zigzag at Rochester and the billet at the Mote, Ightham, Kent. The barge-boards, or verge-boards, on the exterior often have a similar character to a cornice, as at the Mote, Ightham, and at Winchester. In the later examples of the time of Henry VIII. the heads of the Cæsars and other heads are frequently introduced in panelling, either on the exterior in terra-cotta, or in the interior in the plaster-work either of the cornice or on the surface of the wall immediately under the cornice, as in the illustration already referred to from Thame Park. At this period other classical ornaments began to be used, such as small figures of Cupids or other allegorical figures intermixed with foliage, this being the last period of Gothic art, and the transition to the Roman or Italian. The struggle was of long continuance; throughout the reign of Elizabeth there was a constant mixture of Gothic and Italian details. In the time of James I. a strong effort was made to revive the pure Gothic, but under Charles I. it entirely succumbed to its rival, the Italian, under the influence of the genius of Inigo Jones, although a few instances are met with of very good Gothic style even at this late period, as the celebrated staircase to the hall at Christ Church, Oxford, which is of later date than the handsome Jacobean staircase at Crewe Hall, Cheshire. In the specimens we have given in the accompanying engraving this mixture of styles will be observed.

The parlours of the fifteenth century were sometimes CARPETED. In an inventory of the wardrobe of Henry V. we find carpets enumerated[r]. These carpets, however, were ever regarded as indications of luxury and pomp. Thus we read of—

[r] Rot. Parl., vol. iv. p. 214.

DOMESTIC ARCHITECTURE: FIFTEENTH AND SIXTEENTH CENTURY.

CORNICE, ROCHESTER, KENT.

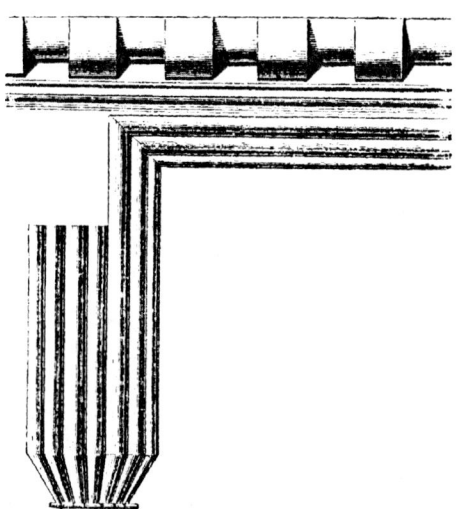

THE MOTE, IGHTHAM, KENT.

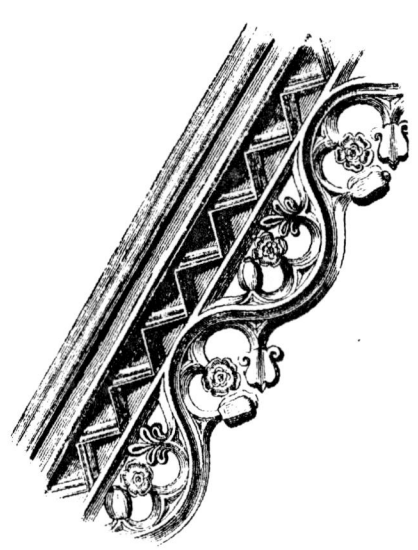
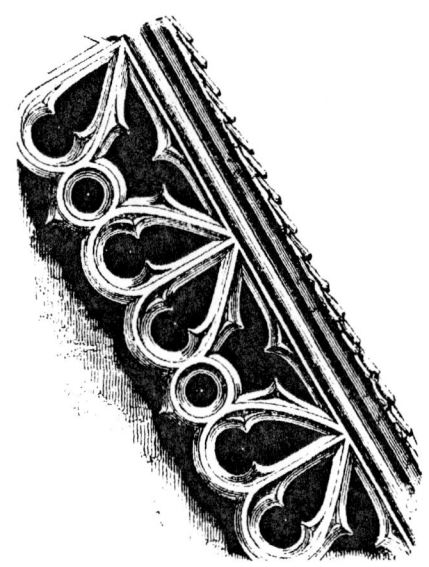

THE MOTE, IGHTHAM, KENT.   WINCHESTER.

> "Tapets of Spayne on flor by syde,
> That sprad shyn be for pompe & pryde,
> The chamber sydes ryzt to the dore,
> He henges with tapets that ben ful store[s]."

In the "Story of Thebes" we have also the following allusion to the use of carpets:—

> "To a chamber she led him vp alofte
> Ful wel beseine, there in a bed ryȝt softe
> Rychly abouten apparrailed
> *Withe clothe of golde all the floure irailed*
> Of the same, bothe in lengthe & brede[t]."

But these were luxuries by no means in general use; rushes were still employed as the usual covering of the floors. In 1464 Sir John Howard paid sixteen-pence "to the gromys off chambre ffor rushis" for his parlour[u]. In the household of Edward IV. the serjeant of the hall was to see that sufficient quantity of rushes were provided for the royal apartments[x]. Straw and rushes were used for covering the floors as late as the time of Henry VIII.[y] Matting was also sometimes used for that purpose. One of the items in the accounts of the Surveyor-General of Henry VIII. was for "workyng in the newe mattyng of the quens bed chamber, and newe mattynge of the quens closet & the galary by the kynges closet, & mendyng of the mattyng in the kynges closett[z]."

The COUCH appears to have been an elegant introduction of this period. It is of foreign origin, and was in use on the Continent at the beginning of the fifteenth, if not at the end of the preceding century. We have representations of it in MSS.[a] Early examples were but an improvement upon the primitive bench, or form

---

[s] MS. Sloane, No. 1,986, p. 33.

[t] *Wel beseine*, very becoming; *floure irailed*, floor spread or covered.

[u] Manners and Household Expences, p. 155.

[x] Liber Niger, p. 22.

[y] *Archæologia*, vol. iv. p. 312.

[z] MS. Additional, No. 10,109, fo. 196.

[a] MS. Additional, 12,228, fo. 140, 142; MS. Harl., 4,431.

with a "bink[b]." According to *Les Honneurs de la Cour* of Alienor de Poitiers, the position of a couch in the chamber of a lady was a matter of courtly privilege. None but a royal lady ought to place her couch opposite the fire; the place for the couch of one of inferior rank was in the corner of the room. The Lady Alienor is shocked at the conduct of some of the ladies of Flanders, who had so disregarded the rules of etiquette as to place their couches before the fire; but " dequoy l'on s'est bien mocque," says our fair authority[c].

The bench, bank, or bink, was distinguished from the form by having a back[d], over which a banker was thrown when the room was "kept." Sometimes these benches were supplied with lockers, and the table-linen, &c., was kept in them. Lockers and settles, generally placed under the win-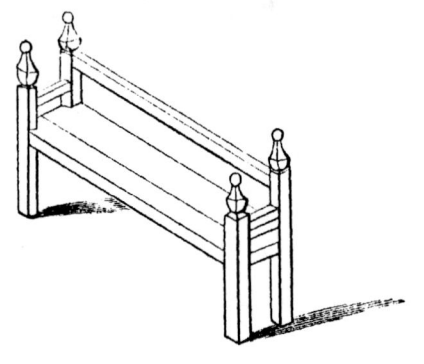

BENCH. Douce MS., 202.

dows or at the sides of the recess, formed both a chest and a seat. In a mansion of the sixteenth century, "tilles," or settles, are described in almost every room[e]. A good example remains at Combe St. Nicholas, Somersetshire.

The plate, dresses, and linen in the royal wardrobes were kept in large chests, called standards. In 1421, Sir Henry Moon petitioned to be allowed iron-bound "standardes" and sackclothes for keeping the necessary articles belonging to his office[f]. In the reign of Henry VIII. carts

---

[b] See example in MS. Cottonian, Aug. v. fo. 334. b.

[c] St. Palaye, *Memoires sur l'ancienne Chevalerie*, tom. ii. p. 242.

[d] Among the goods of John Baron of Mappleton, in 1534, we find "a fyrme with a *bynk* bord;" also a "cupbord w^t a *dysbink*." Surtees' *Wills and Invent.*

[e] Rot. Add., 16,128.

[f] MS. Cottonian, Vesp., F. xiii. fo. 30.

DOMESTIC ARCHITECTURE: SIXTEENTH CENTURY.

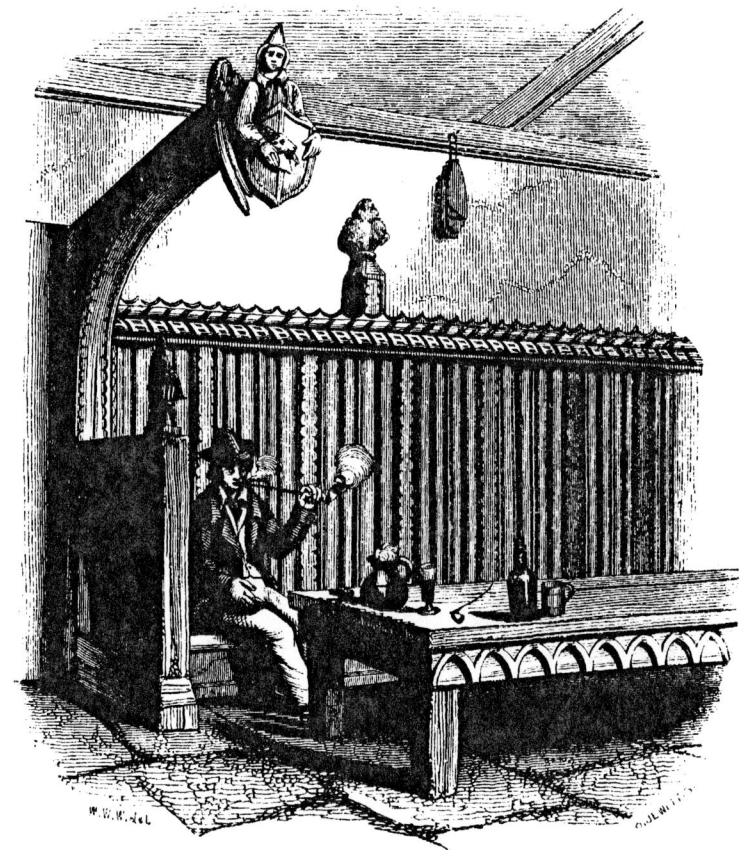

SETTLE,

COMBE ST. NICHOLAS, SOMERSETSHIRE.

THE CHAMBERS AND OFFICES. 113

were hired to convey the standards when the king moved from one palace to another. On two occasions carts were hired "to bring the greate standards, w^t the riche cootes of the garde, from london to hampton courte." The king hired a house in London "for the standyng of the greate standardes, withe the riche cootes of the garde," at a rental of one pound fourteen shillings and eight-pence per annum [g].

In fact, the standard was employed simply as a large packing chest, and when families were moving once or twice each year from one estate to another, they were brought into constant requisition. For instance, in the inventories of the family of Reginald de la Pole, Duke of Suffolk, relating to their journeys between Wingfield Manor in Suffolk, and Ewelme in Oxfordshire, the standards are frequently mentioned:—

"A square standarde, and covered with blaakletheir, and bowden with yrne (iron), with 2 lokys, the oon lokke broken, and the key with my lady.
A grete red standerd full of stuff, locked with 2 lockes, and sealed with Stanley's seall, ye keyes in my ladies keping.
A gret standard of the Chapell bounde wth ierne with 2 lokks."

In another part we find a list of the

"Stuff brought from Wingefeld to Ewelme in a standard,"

which consists chiefly of the hangings of the altar, tapestry, vestments, cushions, &c.

As an instance of elaborate ornament, we may give the accompanying chest from Rockingham Castle, Northamptonshire, which is enriched with sunk panels, painted with the shields of arms of the royal family of England, and of Lord Hastings, Constable of the castle in

[g] MS. Arundel, No. 97. fo. 169, 176.

114   DOMESTIC ARCHITECTURE: FIFTEENTH CENTURY.

the time of Edward IV., together with foliage and other ornament.

Standard-Chest, Rockingham Castle, Northants.

Smaller CHESTS were used for preserving treasure. We meet with these constantly delineated in the illuminated manuscripts of this period. An engraving is given from a manuscript in the Bodleian Library, which shews not only the money-chest, but affords a good example of the settle also. Another treasure-chest is here engraved from the Douce collection.

Treasure-Chest, Douce, 371.

Such small chests or coffins, both of iron and of wood, may frequently be met with belonging to this period. Those of iron are commonly round at the top, with bands round them, and richly worked locks.

A few words should also be added on the CHAIRS in use in the chambers, which do not appear to have been very commonly used, as we find frequent mention in the old romances of sitting on beds or couches. Most of the chairs which we have remaining, and they are very rare, belong rather to state occasions and to the hall than to ordinary use in the chambers. A fine series of bishops'

DOMESTIC ARCHITECTURE: FIFTEENTH CENTURY.

FURNITURE, &c., FROM MSS. IN THE BODLEIAN LIBRARY.

LONG SETTLE, TABLE, AND MONEY-CHEST.

Bodley, 283. "Avarice."

chairs or thrones might be formed from the twelfth century downwards, and the coronation chair has been described in a former volume. The chief seat on the dais had usually a canopy over it, as shewn in the accompanying illustration from the illuminations in manuscripts from Douce's collection, now in the Bodleian. These canopies were often richly ornamented with panelling and pinnacles, and the backs of the seats were carved. Cushions were placed on the seats, and dorsers at the back. In the inventory taken at Ewelme in 1466 we find—

Seat. Douce, 371.

"A chaire of tymbre of astate, covered w^t blu cloth of gold, and 4 pomells of coper, and gilt, enamyled with 99 K.[h]
A case of lether thereto.
A chaire of astate of yren[i], covered with purpell satyn fur[d], and a case of lether therto.

2 long cushions stuff'd of fethers, covered with lether, each 1 yard 1 quarter long, and 3 quarters brode.
A square cushon stuffed of fethers, covered w^t lether of 3 quarters square."

"On the 16th of July, A.D. 1444, Henry gave audience to the ambassadors of France and Sicily, at Westminster Palace, seated on a very high chair of state, called a salette[k], covered with tapestry of blue diaper, the livery of Henry the fifth. . . . The following day the king gave them an audience in his privy chamber[l]."

John Baret of Bury, in 1463, left to his niece "a

---

[h] A state chair of wood.
[i] An iron chair, probably similar to the one called Queen Mary's chair in Winchester cathedral.

[k] In French they have retained the word *sellette* for the judge's seat.
[l] Strickland's Queens of England, vol. iii. p. 203.

116 DOMESTIC ARCHITECTURE: FIFTEENTH CENTURY.

chayer, iij. footys-stolys, iij. cusshonges," in his parlour, and among other things " a rounde table [m]."

We find entries also of the "bofet- or buffett-stool[n]." This probably referred to a small stool which was usually placed beneath the buffet or sideboard; probably in many cases used for standing upon to reach the vessels or platters which were lodged upon the uppermost shelves[n].

Table, Douce, 271.

The CHIMNEY-PIECE was not always a fixture, but merely screwed or hung over the fireplace, and, like the hangings of the walls, taken down when the owner was absent from the mansion. It was sometimes a tablet of wood, upon which some fabulous scene or armorial insignia was carved or painted[o]. Mottoes were frequently introduced, alluding to the builder or owner of the mansion. A curious chimney-piece, probably of this century, was found in an old mansion in Kent. It had the words "Wass heil," and "Dinc hule," carved on it, with a wassail bowl in the centre, on which were two hawks, intended as a rebus of the builder's name, Henry Hawkes[p]. In a beautifully illuminated copy of Lydgate's "Life of St. Edmund," we have a representation of a fireplace with little recesses above it, (instead of an ornamental chimney-piece,) in which cups are arranged[q]. In 1482, Lord Howard "paid to Burton of Cornhill at

[m] Wills and Inventories from the Registers of Bury St. Edmunds.—See MS. Harleian, No. 4,431, fo. 60 and 181 for circular chairs. Also for a large Gothic chair see MS. Cottonian, A. v. fo. 94. For stools and couches see Additional MSS., No. 12,228, fo. 140, 142, 147.

[n] In Sir John Cullum's History of Hanstead, a bequest occurs (1553) of a "buffed stool," which is explained to be an oval stool without a back, and having a hole in the seat for the convenience of lifting it.

[o] A painting in MS. Harl., 4,380, represents a chimney-piece decorated with a shield with a *fleur-de-lis*.

[p] Antiq. Repertory, vol. iii. p. 155.

[q] MS. Harl., 2,278, fo. 13. b.

DOMESTIC ARCHITECTURE: FIFTEENTH CENTURY.

FIREPLACE,

SHERBORNE ABBEY.

FIREPLACE,

BARRACKS, SALISBURY

DOMESTIC ARCHITECTURE: FIFTEENTH CENTURY.

FIREPLACE.

CERNE ABBAS, DORSETSHIRE.

THE CHAMBERS AND OFFICES. 117

London for the apparayll of a chymeny, cont. xi. pesis, whiche was sent to Stoke and paid be T. Seynclow, xxvi*s*. viii*d*.[r] Now that chimneys were generally introduced, the mantel-piece became a principal ornament, especially in the banqueting-room or great chamber. Henry VIII. expended large sums on this feature of the royal apartments, and we find in an undated roll of that monarch an entry, "to certain ffrenche men workynge vpon the ffrontes of chemneys for the prevye chambre, vj*li*. xj*s*. xj*d*[s]." The chimney-piece was sometimes of tapestry. Among the furniture belonging to Henry VIII. at Wanstead, in Essex, was "an olde chymney piece of tapestrye[t];" and "a hanging clothe of tapestrye for the chimneys, of the storye of Danea," was at Hengrave Hall[u]. Over the chimney-piece, or at the sides, were usually affixed cressets, or candelabra, for the Paris wax and sizes, by the aid of which its adornments were fully displayed.

The chimney-piece was, however, frequently of stone, and formed part of the structure, as is evident from many existing examples. Sometimes it consists of a hood, with a bold projection; in other instances it is flat, and nearly flush with the surface of the wall, and ornamented with panelling, the opening being square, as at Cerne Abbas, Dorsetshire, where the opening is well moulded; there is a rich cornice above, and panelling between the cornice and the mouldings: the panelling in this instance is diamond-shaped, with cusps and foliage, and in the centre panel the initials of the abbot who built it. This custom of introducing the initials of the person who built this part of the house in the panels over the fireplace was

---

[r] Collier's Household Expenses of Lord Howard, page 285. Two other "aparyalls for chymenys," and "a tonne of Cane ston," were paid for on the same day.
[s] Rot. Reg., 14 B. iv. a.
[t] MS. Harl., 1,419, fo. 18. a.
[u] Gage's Hengrave, p. 27.

common in the fifteenth and sixteenth centuries. In Sherborne Abbey, Dorset, there is a good fireplace, with the usual Perpendicular panelling of the period, surmounted by a cornice and a battlemented moulding, after the fashion of that age, when battlements being less required for actual use, became a favourite ornament in all parts of the building, however inappropriate, such as the sills and transoms of windows, and, as in this instance, over the mantel-piece.

In the old house called "the Barracks" at Salisbury, there is a fine specimen of the fireplaces of this style, with a low square-topped opening, and an arch introduced in the panelling, as if to deceive the eye, and make the opening appear considerably higher than it really is. Shields are introduced in the spandrels and in the cornice, which have originally been painted with coats of arms, instead of inscribing the name or initials of the owner who built it.

CLUSTERED CHIMNEY-SHAFTS were of frequent occurrence about this time, yet Harison, writing at a much later period, says that the old men in his day noted how marvellously things were altered in England, especially in the multitude of chimneys which had been lately erected, whereas in their young days there were only two or three, if so many, to be found in the cities and towns of England. This account was probably somewhat exaggerated, and chimneys, even long before the fifteenth century, were more common than is usually imagined, as we have shewn in our previous volumes. From the Household-book of Sir John Howard, we learn that the cost of a chimney in 1465 was about twenty-six shillings[x].

---

[x] Household Manners and Expenses of the Thirteenth and Fifteenth Centuries, 4to. p. 261.

DOMESTIC ARCHITECTURE: SIXTEENTH CENTURY.

METTINGHAM, SUFFOLK.

ST. OSYTH, ESSEX.

DROITWICH, WORCESTERSHIRE.

LAYER MARNEY, ESSEX.

In the will of John Baret of Bury we have a curious and interesting description of his house in 1463. A short time previous to making his will, he appears to have enlarged his family residence, or "hefd place," by building a new house "with iij. tunys of chemeneyes" adjoining, and by his will he directs that this house should be formed into two tenements[y]. It is evident from the records of household expences of this century, that such alterations were frequently found necessary to meet the growing spirit of improvement.

Chimney-shafts, whether single or clustered, form one of the most ornamental features of the houses of the latter part of the fifteenth century and beginning of the sixteenth. In the earlier periods they are generally of stone, and frequently enriched with battlemented mouldings, as at Maxstoke Castle, Warwickshire: in the time of Henry VII. and VIII. they are commonly of brick, and richly moulded, and this fashion continued throughout the reign of Elizabeth. Very fine examples remain at Thornbury Castle, Gloucestershire; on the school-house at Tonbridge, Kent; at St. Osyth Priory, and Layer Marney Hall, Essex; at Droitwich, Worcestershire; on the town-hall at Wokingham, Berkshire, and in very many other places. In fact, no feature is more common or more picturesque in the landscape of many parts of England than these fine brick chimneys.

These details would appear trivial, were it not that all appertaining to the history of domestic architecture and manners derives additional importance from the fact that the tangible illustrations of this interesting subject are fast disappearing before modern utilitarianism. Many who cannot afford, or who have not the taste, to preserve

[y] Wills and Inventories from the Registers of Bury St. Edmunds, printed by the Camden Society, 4to., p. 22.

these architectural remains, find it convenient to rebuild, or to so alter them, that they lose their original character, and are no longer historical monuments by which the student can trace the history of his favourite science. Antiquaries have long had reason to deplore the vandalism and whitewash of churchwardens, and as to domestic antiquities, how numerous are the richly carved chimney-pieces, the quaint cupboards, and rare old furniture that have rotted in neglect, or been discarded as lumber. That which is recorded of Haddon Hall might be recorded of many mansions of the olden time. We are told that such of "the furniture of this mansion as was thought valuable was removed to Belvoir Castle, and at the same time, that which was not wanted was lodged in a barn on the north side of the hall, one end of which extended into what is provincially called 'a bye water,' being a branch of the river Wye. The whole quantity consigned to this miserable repository amounted to ten waggon loads. Here the furniture was kept till the moisture arising from floods and rain reduced the wood-work to a state of rottenness and decay, and then it was ordered to be used for fuel. Fifteen bedsteads were put into a long room near the house, which had been a granary, and after being left for a time to fall in pieces, they likewise were ordered to be cut up and burnt[z]."

As we have seen, the private room, whether used only as a dining-chamber, or for a parlour and bed-chamber, was handsomely furnished. The fine fireplace, and chimney-piece, the walls covered with wainscot, or richly painted and gilded, were further adorned by the windows being filled with painted glass, sometimes with figures taken from some popular romance, more often with shields of arms and diaper patterns.

[z] Rayner's Hist. and Antiq. of Haddon Hall, p. 51.

DOMESTIC ARCHITECTURE: FIFTEENTH AND SIXTEENTH CENTURY.

MAXSTOKE CASTLE, WARWICKSHIRE.

ASLACKBY, LINCOLNSHIRE.

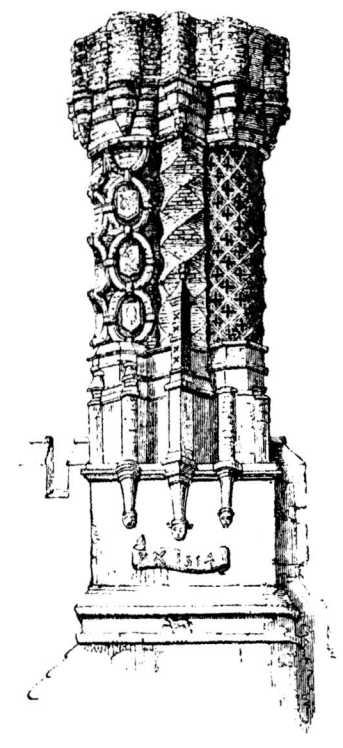

THORNBURY CASTLE, GLOUCESTERSHIRE.

TONBRIDGE SCHOOL, KENT.

THE CHAMBERS AND OFFICES.

GLASS WINDOWS were a luxury now fully appreciated, and casements were framed and fitted in the apertures hitherto protected with lattice-work and wooden shutters. We find in old domestic accounts several allusions to the cost of such alterations. Lord Howard, at Colchester, had to send to London for his glazier, who received four shillings and eightpence for fourteen days' labour; and at another time he was paid three shillings and fourpence "for werkynge on my lady Bernys chambre wyndow[a]," and my lady graciously gave the men two shillings to defray "theyr costes to London." For the glass the glazier was paid fourpence or fivepence per foot:—"For the glasyere for xiij. fote of glasse, the fote vd.[b]" Nevertheless glass windows, even at this period, were by no means common, but were regarded as objects of importance and value. Beryl and horn were still used:—

"The worke of wyndowe & eke fenestrall
Wrouȝte of beryle[c]."

We learn from the Household Book of the Duke of Northumberland, that when that nobleman left his town residence the glass windows were taken out and carefully laid by. In the inventory of goods belonging to Contarini, a Venetian merchant, who resided in St. Botolph's-lane in the sixteenth century, the glass windows of his house are mentioned as moveable furniture[d]. In the time of Henry VIII. the royal palaces and manors were furnished with glass casements, and in the accounts of the Surveyor-General we find minute descriptions of the cost of altering, glazing, and framing in new casements to the windows. The usual price of the glass was

[a] Howard's Household Book, edited by Collier for the Roxburgh Club, p. 188.
[b] Ibid., p. 467.
[c] MS. Cottonian, Aug. iv. fo. 29.
[d] Nichols' Illustrations, p. 118.

still about fourpence-halfpenny the foot[e]. But the quantities used for repairing some of the frames indicate that the panes were of small size. It is curious to read that in the king's chamber a broken pane was mended with a small piece of glass. Seventeen feet of glass was about the quantity used for a chamber window. The frequent repetition of such entries shews that glass windows were becoming common in the higher class of domestic buildings[f].

"And because throwe extreame wind the glase of the windowes of this and other my lord's Castells and houses here in this countrie doothe decaye and waste y[t] were goode the whole height of everie windowe, at the departure of his Lordship from lyinge at any of his said Castells and houses, and deuringe the time of his Lordship's absence or others lying in them, were taken down and lade appart in safetie; and at such time as either his Lordship or any other shoulde lie at any of the said places, the same might then be sette up of newe, with small charge to his Lordship when now the decaye thereof shalle be very costlie and chargeable to be repayred[g]."

The casements were usually made square or oblong, not arched or cuspated, but fitted within the frame of the window, whether that was of stone or wood, and secured by iron bars or bolts, of which the holes often remain, to shew exactly where the casements were fixed. They were also protected on the outside by iron stancheons and bars, which often remain, as at Yanwath Hall, Westmoreland. The windows were divided by mullions and transoms into several lights, each of which had its separate casement; and it was generally so contrived that all the casements might be of the same size, and might fit different windows, not only in the same house, but in

[e] Equal to about seven shillings of our money.

[f] See the curious volume of the Accounts of the Surveyor-General for 34 Henry VIII. among the Additional MSS. in the British Museum, 10,109, fo. 88, 114.

[g] Clarkson's Survey of Alnwick Castle, A.D. 1556.

DOMESTIC ARCHITECTURE: FIFTEENTH CENTURY.

BAY-WINDOW OF HALL.

IRON GRATING TO WINDOW OF STABLE,
YANWATH-HALL, WESTMORELAND.

different houses also, so that when a noble family removed from one seat or manor-house to another with all their household stuff and furniture, the glass casements formed part of the moveable chattels, until the time of Henry VIII., when they were ruled by the judges to be fixtures. In the stables and offices the windows were often not glazed, but protected by iron gratings or *grilles* only. Some good examples of these remain, as at Yanwath, but they are more common and more ornamental in France and in Belgium than in England.

Windows of churches of the fifteenth century were generally square-headed, and in the southern parts of England generally have dripstones or corbels over them; in the northern counties this feature is commonly omitted, which, to eyes accustomed to the relief of the dripstone, analogous to the eyebrow over the eye, gives a singularly bald and meagre appearance to the northern buildings. Hall windows, we need scarcely observe, have usually pointed arches, and at first sight appear exactly like church windows.

The use of painted glass was by no means confined to the hall or the chapel, or even to the principal chambers; the small private oratory was generally so ornamented, and casements for the bed-room windows were often also of painted glass[h]. The following extract shews that the windows of a small turret were so furnished:—

"Un jour estoie après diner
Alez, pour moi esbanoier,
Du paveillon haut à poier,

[h] "Les poutres et les solives des chambres du roi et de la reine étoient rehaussées de fleurs-de-lis d'étain doré, et les entre-voues de couleur en detrempe. Pour les murailles, elles étoient peintes en maniere de brique; les croisées treillissées de fil d'archal et de barreaux de fer, d'ailleurs obscurcies de vitres pleines d'images de saints et de saintes, ou bien des devises et des armes du roi et de la reine, dont le panneau revenait à 22 sols." — Sauval, t. ii. p. 279.

> En une tourele petite
> De verrieres painte et escripte,
> Bele et gente et de riche atour.
> Si vi j. tornoi tout entour
> Pourtrait et paint en la verriere:
> Dont j'oi merveille moult très-fiere,
> Combienque li veoir fist biaus[i]," &c.

In the romances the windows are now commonly mentioned as of glass:—

> "Square wyndowus of glas,
> The rychest that euer was,
> The moynelus was of bras,
> Made with manne handus[k]."

Indeed, the comparative cheapness of this material led to many alterations in old buildings. In place of the less commodious, but more elegantly designed, windows of the fourteenth century, new and larger ones were introduced, sometimes without much regard to the consistency of architectural design. Bay windows were a common feature in the chambers, and generally at one end of the dais in the hall[l]. In the household books of the period we often find incidental allusions to these alterations:—

"Item, to William Este, mason, for makyng of a Bay Window in the quenes chamber, xvi*li*.[m]

To Bauf Vnderwood, wyre drawer, for iij. lb. & a quarter of wyre of iren, for to hang w*t* verdours ayenst the grete Baye windowe[n].

Item, in rewarde to the werkman whiche made the wyndowe in my ladys chambre, v*s*.[o]

Payntyng of the grete wyndow in the closett and of wyndows in the gallerys of the coronasyon, lxxvi*li*. vii*s*. iiij*d*.[p]

[i] *Les Paraboles de Verité*, &c., par Watriquet, quoted by Francisque-Michel in his edition of Anelier's *Histoire de la Guerre de Navarre*, p. 496.

[k] Romance of Sir Degrevant, Thornton Romances, p. 238.

[l] At Sizergh Hall, in 1569, there was in the hall "a cuporde in ye baye wyndowe." Wills and Inventories, published by the Surtees Society, vol. iii. p. 221.

[m] Household Book of Henry VII., MS. Additional, 7,099, fo. 57.

[n] Wardrobe Account of Edward IV., MS. Harleian, 4,780, fo. 20. a.

[o] MS. Reg. 17 B. xxviii. fo. 10. a.

[p] An undated roll, about 1500, in the Museum. Rot. Reg. 14 B. iv.

THE CHAMBERS AND OFFICES. 125

Lydgate describes the casements as having flowers trained over them:—

> "And the housing full of habewynes,
> The ryche coynyng of ryche tablementis,
> Vinetis reunyng in ye casementis [q]."

We must not omit to mention that large class of windows which are constructed entirely of wood, not only the framework, but the mullions and tracery, being cut out of that material, and these are often quite as rich as those executed in stone. A few examples of wooden windows of the fourteenth century may still be met with, as at Baggeley Hall, Cheshire, described in our last volume. The hall of Smithell's Hall, Lancashire, bears

SMITHELL'S HALL, LANCASHIRE.

so close a resemblance to this, that it is generally considered to have been copied from it very soon afterwards,

[q] MS. Reg. 18 D. vi. fo. 22. b.

126 DOMESTIC ARCHITECTURE: FIFTEENTH CENTURY.

or erected by the same architect. The windows are very good examples, with ogee heads to the lights, and the mouldings are considered by Mr. Buckler (to whom we are indebted for the drawing of this remarkable window) to belong to the fourteenth century, but this is doubted by some other architects and antiquaries of equal eminence, and in such very plain work it is often difficult to decide the age of particular details, more especially as the mouldings of the fourteenth century were certainly continued or copied in late woodwork of the time of Henry VIII. and Elizabeth. Another example from Lewes,

HIGH-STREET, LEWES, SUSSEX.

Sussex, also drawn by Mr. Buckler, appears to have most distinctly the usual mouldings of the fourteenth century, but this also is doubted by some high authorities.

The city of Coventry abounds with timber-houses, many of which have very good Gothic windows, most of

DOMESTIC ARCHITECTURE: FIFTEENTH CENTURY.

ROOM IN A HOUSE AT WINGHAM, KENT.

which are of the fifteenth and sixteenth centuries, but one in the West Orchard is believed by Mr. Buckler to be of the fourteenth, and the forms of the tracery would agree very well with the time of Richard II.; but, as we have said, these forms were so often imitated in woodwork of a later period, that some doubt may reasonably be entertained on the subject.

In later examples in timber-houses the windows of the chambers, especially of the withdrawing-room, are often continued along the whole of one side of the room, as at Wingham, Kent, in this respect resembling the galleries or corridors which were frequent in the fifteenth century, and became extremely common in the sixteenth. The room at Wingham, of which we give an engraving, also affords a good specimen of the wooden panelled CEILINGS of the period.

It will be observed that this ceiling is divided into square panels by moulded ribs, with carved bosses at the intersections. Such ceilings were very common, and the effect of them is extremely good: they were enriched with painting and gilding. A good example of a ceiling of this kind occurs in the library of Merton College, Oxford, inserted by Warden Fitzjames late in the fifteenth century. A similar ceiling in the chapel has unfortunately been destroyed within the last few years. Ceilings of this kind continued in use for a long period, as might be expected from their manifest convenience. They are very common in the time of Henry VIII. and Elizabeth, but at that time the rich plaster ceilings were introduced, with pendants, and sometimes the two are combined, as in the drawing-room at Thame Park, Oxfordshire, where the cornices and the principal timbers of the ceiling are ornamented in plaster, with pendants at the intersections, while the panels are divided by wooden ribs. The walls, also, are chiefly of wooden panelling, but the upper part of plaster.

From the fourteenth to the end of the fifteenth century ARTICLES OF GLASS are seldom mentioned in inventories, unless indeed we are to regard of this material those described as of crystal, many of which are noticed in memoranda and inventories of the Exchequer[r]. It was long, however, esteemed as valuable as plate, and a single glass or cup is sometimes estimated at an extravagant rate. To serve wine in a glass was more complimentary than in silver. Perfumed water was a frequent presentation to royalty, and it was generally offered in a glass. In the wardrobe accounts of Edward IV. the only article of this material among his treasures was "a standynge glas[s]." Half a century later, and we find in the royal glass-house at Westminster an extensive collection of cups, bottles, ewers, lavers, and basins of glass. They were probably all importations from France and Venice. They are described as of various colours, some gilt with cyphers and the royal arms[t]. The manufacture of glass was not followed in England, although in a manuscript of the fifteenth century we have a receipt for softening glass, that it may "be cast ageyne[u]."

Among the glass of Henry VIII. was an "Hallywater stoppe of glasse withe a baille," and also "one rounde hollowe sesterne of glass, partilie guilte w^t the kynges armes[x]." These in former times were generally of gold and silver. Beaufort, Duke of Exeter, in 1426, bequeathed a great "holiwater stoppe" of silver, with a sprinkler (*aspersorio*) of silver[y]. In 1449 William Burges,

[r] Palgrave's Ancient Kalenders and Inventories of the Exchequer, vol. ii. p. 87.
[s] MS. Harl., 4,780, fo. 28. b.
[t] Ibid., 1,419, fo. 61, 62, 143, 146.
[u] "For to make glas nesche," MS. Sloane, No. 73, fo. 215.
[x] MS. Harl., 1,419, fo. 146, 148.
[y] Nichols' Royal Wills, p. 253.

THE CHAMBERS AND OFFICES.

Garter King of Arms, left "a gret halywater scoppe of silver with a staff[z]." They were often mentioned among articles of domestic use, and the supply of holy water is often alluded to in old household accounts. It was used for various purposes in the homes of our forefathers, who were taught to regard it as a specific in bodily disease, and a preservative against the machinations of witchcraft. Lord Howard paid to the "Alywater clarke for seruyng of my lordes place in London, xvi*d*.[a]" It was sprinkled over the apartments, and cast upon the bed. In "certen artycles" for the household of Henry VII. in 1493, the usher of the chamber, after making the bed, was to "knytt togedyr the corteynes, & a squyer of the body to cast hollywater on the bedde[b]." The piscina in Dacre Castle, Cumberland, mentioned in the second volume[c], was probably the stoup for containing it, and the drain which probably led beneath the hall was in accordance with the feeling of the age that the holy water should be thus allowed to escape to prevent its application to any profane use.

In describing the hall we have mentioned the custom of washing the hands, and the lavatories provided for that purpose, with their water-drains; the same customs were, of course, observed when the family

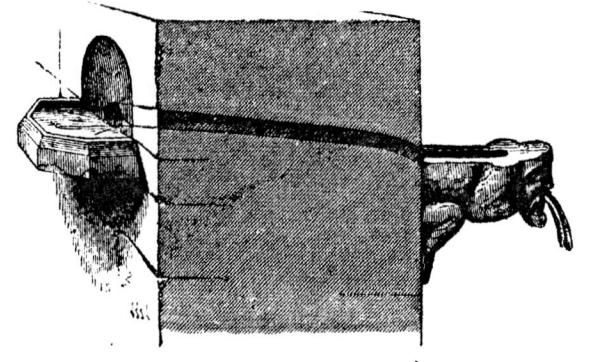

Water-drain, Abbot's House, Wenlock.

[z] Nicholas, *Test. Vetusta*, p. 266. The sprinkler was a brush with a metal or ivory handle. One is represented in the hand of a monk, who is sprinkling the corpse of St. Edmund, in MS. Harl., 2,278, fo. 22. b.

[a] Household Book of the Howards, p. 425.

[b] MS. Additional, 4,712, fo. 11. b.

[c] Vol. ii. p. 44.

dined in their chambers or dining-rooms, and water-drains often remain to shew where a lavatory has been, as in the Abbot's house at Wenlock, Shropshire, which is a very perfect example, having the basin or sink within, and terminating in a water-spout with a head at the end, like a gurgoyle; in our engraving we have shewn the section through the wall in order to make this more clear. Similar drains occur also in the offices, for the use of the servants, as in Warwick Castle, where the example given is now in a cellar, but this was probably originally the scullery; it is one of the range of offices connected with the kitchen.

Drain, Warwick Castle.

The lavatories and wash-hand-stands in the chambers are represented in manuscripts of the fifteenth century, as in Douce, 208 and 371; in the latter the arrangement is very complete, with ewer and basin and the towel all placed in the most convenient manner. These articles of furniture also shew the use of the turning-lathe, and that the work of the joiner was far from contemptible; this is further illustrated in 195, where a table is shewn ornamented with a band of pierced quatrefoils, on which stands a reel of thread, and a woman with a spindle stands near, with a man seated in an arm-chair at the other end.

DOMESTIC ARCHITECTURE: FIFTEENTH CENTURY.

FURNITURE, &c., FROM MSS. IN THE BODLEIAN LIBRARY.

WASH-STAND, BASIN, SOAP-DISH, AND TOWEL.

Douce, 371.

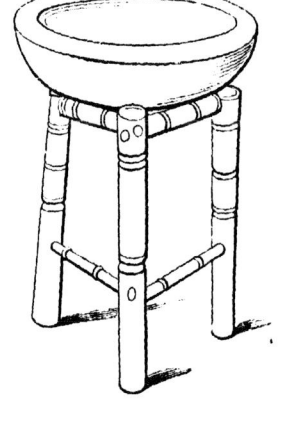

WASH-STAND AND BOWL.

Douce, 208.

SEAT, DISTAFF, SPINDLE, AND REEL.

Douce, 195.

THE CHAMBERS AND OFFICES. 131

In the fifteenth century we observe the almost universal introduction of CUPBOARDS, in addition to the simple chest and locker of earlier times. The history of this article of domestic furniture is interesting, and is associated with some curious customs. The distinction between the cupboard, the dressor, and the almery, has not been accurately defined, and the following remarks may not be altogether uninteresting. Cupboards were in use among the Saxons, and in our first volume we have engraved a representation of a long cupboard with doors, hung on foliated hinges, and enclosing a series of shelves, upon which pitchers are ranged[d]. Treasures were kept in such cupboards, and in the assessment made in 1300 all the valuables of Roger the Dyer and William the Miller were in their treasuries or cupboards[e]. They were also used in the days of chivalry for the safe keeping of the armour: among the Additional Charters in the British Museum there is a receipt of Geofry Poulin, for money for repairing, in 1419, the cupboard (*armoire*) of the Comte de Vertus, with a new key for the better security of the armour of the said Count[f]. During the fifteenth century the term cupboard was also applied to what we now call a sideboard or buffet[g], and stood in a conspicuous place: upon it were arranged the flagons, cups[h], and spice plate.

---

[d] MS. Cottonian, Nero, C. iv. fo. 17.

[e] Rot. Parl., vol. i. 243.

[f] Add. Char. No. 2,806.

[g] In old French the *buffet* and *dressoir* were synonymous.

[h] For a list of various cups, &c., usually found in the hall, see p. 69. We should also add the mazer bowl, and take the opportunity of inserting the following note:—An account is given of one of these maple, or mazer bowls, in the "Gentleman's Magazine," belonging to the Hospital at Herbaldown, near Canterbury, where it was used on all great occasions. The rims were of silver gilt, and in the bottom was a medallion representing Guy, Earl of Warwick, killing the dragon. An engraving is given in the Magazine, and the inscription made out to be—

"GY DE WARWYC : AD A NOUN :
ICCI OCCIS : LE DR A GOUN."

"The cupboarde w*t* coppys of golde & siluer[i],"

and

"The cupborde with plate shynynge fayre & clere[k],"

are the descriptions generally given by old poets. It was the most important piece of furniture in the hall and great chamber. To serve at the cupboard was a post of honour. It was often an object of envy from the wealth displayed upon its shelves, and its peculiar make and adornment denoted to those initiated in the etiquette of the court the rank and privileges of its owner. Alienor de Poitiers, a lady of the court of Burgoigne, has recorded with scrupulous accuracy the mysteries of this knightly office in *Les Honneurs de la Cour*[l]. Persons of high estate served spice and wine from the cupboards of royalty. The number of shelves in a buffet was a mark of distinction: two were allowed to the wife of a banneret, a countess claimed three in right of her superior rank, the buffet of a princess had four, and that of a queen had five shelves. This was a point of etiquette that does not appear to have prevailed in England, for the royal cupboards are generally described and represented as having but three shelves. According to the Lady Alienor, the canopy which adorned the buffet was to be made in accordance with certain rules of the court. Crimson cloth of gold was a luxury reserved for a queen; a countess might indulge her taste for display in a canopy of velvet, if it was not bordered with a different colour. The sanctuary laws of the age provided for the most minute details; even the texture and fineness of the napkins and cupboard-cloths were jealously defined according to the "estates." In the earlier ages the cupboard-cloths were generally of rich stuff, elaborately em-

---

[i] MS. Sloane, 1,315, fo. 6.

[k] Bradshawe's Lyfe of St. Werberge, published by the Chetham Society, 4to. 1848, Sign. E. viii. a.

[l] Printed in St. Palaye's *Mémoires sur l'Ancienne Chevalrie*, tom. ii.

DOMESTIC ARCHITECTURE: FIFTEENTH CENTURY.

POTTERY AND GLASS, FROM MSS. IN THE BODLEIAN LIBRARY.

Douce, 219.

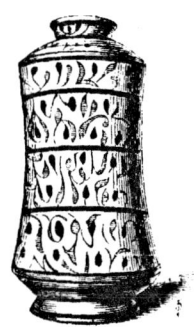

Douce, 219.

GLASS JUG.
Douce, 219.

Douce, 219.

FRUIT DISHES.
Douce, 219.

Douce, 219.

SAUCER.
Douce, 219.

FLOWER-VASE.
Douce, 311.

PLATE.
Douce, 219.

Douce, 219.

Douce, 219.

GLASSES.

broidered, but in the fifteenth century the usual covering was a cloth of white diaper or damask[m]. In a beautifully illuminated manuscript of this century the cupboards are similar to a modern whatnot, entirely open, and the shelves supported by a light framework: they are covered with white cloths[n]. The under shelf of the cupboard was generally carpeted, and from the size of the carpet we gain a knowledge of the dimensions of the cupboard. The carpets were of rich material: those of frame-work and "turkeye worke" frequently occur[o].

The ALMERY derives its name from being originally a receptacle for that portion of the provisions which, being left after the feast, was reserved for alms. It is evident from many passages in old writings that the viands once dedicated to that purpose were looked upon as sacred. The almery, or aumery, and also the alms-dish, were in ancient times in the charge of an officer called the aumerer:—

"The aumere a rod schall haue in honde,
As offyce of almes y understonde[p]."

Lydgate, too, in describing the charitable disposition of St. Edmund, says:—

"And humble compassion was his awmerer[q]."

In an inventory of furniture in the Marshalsea in 1483, we find "a litell olde Almery in the logge at the gate[r]," probably for the deposit of broken meat for the prisoners

[m] In the Household Roll of the Duke of Buckingham for 1444 we find the "cuppeborde clothes and portpayns" among the linen. Add. Charters in Brit. Mus., 5,962.

[n] MS. Harl., 2,278, ff. 13. b, 74. a.

[o] MS. Harl., 1,419, fo. 194. "Item, one olde cuppbord carpett of frame work, sore worne and moth eten, in length ij. yerds & iij. nayles, and in bredth iij. quarters of a yerde." In the inventory of Hengrave Hall we have "a large cupboard carpett for the cobarde of Turkeye worke," p. 26.

[p] MS. Sloane, No. 1,986, fo. 42.

[q] MS. Harl., 2,278, fo. 38. a.

[r] Additional Charters, No. 5,835, in Brit. Mus.

confined there. A passage in the statutes of Eltham shews that the same meaning was sometimes attached to this term in the reign of Henry VIII.:—

"And because hertofore relicts and fragments of meate and drinke haue not been duly distributed vnto poore folke by waie of almes, it is therfore the kinges pleasure that from hence forth speciall regard be had, that all the relicts and fragments be gathered by the *officer of the Almery*, and to be given to the poore people at the vtter courte gate by ouersight of the under Almerer[s]."

In old glossaries the almery is described as "a safe for meate," a "gardiviance[t]," a definition which is warranted from the fact that in old inventories of household goods under "The Buttery," we generally find an almery, or aumery, in addition to cupboards[u]. The original purpose of the almery was disregarded at the end of the fifteenth century, and the distinction between it and the cupboard appears to have been, that the former implied a cupboard secured by more than ordinary means, a secret receptacle, or little cupboard. In the "Antiquities of Durham Abbey" we have a description of one so contrived that "none could perceive that there was any almery at all[x]." This is the idea conveyed in the satirical allusion of Piers Plowman, who says:—

"Ther avarice hath almeries
And yren bounden cofres."

In an inventory of the fifteenth century we find "a close

---

[s] MS. Cottonian, Vesp. c. xiv. fo. 231. b.

[t] Among the goods of Sir John Fastolfe we find "i. gardevyant" in a chamber. *Arch.*, vol. xxi.

[u] Wills and Inventories published by the Surtees Society, vol. iii. pp. 42, 92, 134, 135.

[x] See Glossary of Architecture. In the "Ancient Rites &c. of Durham," mention is made of various almeries, from the description of which we learn that they were all enclosed and well secured; they were, in fact, the receptacles for the treasures of the monks. They are spoken of as "close" almeries, "safely enclosed," or "with locks and keys." See Reprint by Surtees Society, pp. 4, 11, &c.

almery[y];" and in the privy purse expenses of Elizabeth of York we have an entry of a payment for making " of almerys" in the queen's council-chamber, " for to put in the bokes[z]." Thus sometimes the buffet which stood in the hall or great chamber combined both the cupboard and the more secure almery. In 1530 Henry VIII. paid forty-three shillings " to a joyner for viii. cupbourds, some *with* ambreys and some *without*[a]." We also find similar articles described in the inventories of the furniture of that monarch; thus,—

"Twoo cuppbordes wyth ambries."
"A cupporde of waynscote w[t] ambries."
"A cupborde w[t] ij. smale ambries in yt[b]."

And in a roll containing an inventory of goods belonging to Sir Richard Newport in 1571, we find "a cupboarde with a closet in his painted chamber[c]."

This combination of both cupboard and ambry in one piece of furniture was probably introduced in the beginning of the fifteenth century. In a manuscript in the British Museum we have two beautiful representations of buffets or cupboards, with ambries in the middle, and a shelf above and below for the plate; the "leaves" of the ambries are carved, and secured with locks[d]. A passage in " Certen Artycles for the Regulatyng of the Housholde of Henry VII.," in 1493, illustrates the uses to which these three divisions of the buffet were applied:—

" Then schall the steward and the chambelayn come afor the cham-

[y] New Retrosp. Review, i. 102. In the accounts of the churchwardens of St. Michael's, York, in 1518, an entry occurs of " ij*d*. for payr of joutters to a ambre." Nichols' Illustr., p. 308.
[z] Page 96.
[a] MS. Additional, Brit. Mus., No. 20,030, fo. 49. a.
[b] MS. Harl., 1,419, fo. 56. b, 370. a. Cupboards with " tilles and drawers" are also described, fo. 139.
[c] MS. Additional, No. 10,128.
[d] MS. Cottonian, Aug. A. v. ff. 59. b, 334. b.

ber dore, and demande of the usher yff the spyce and wyne be redy for the kyng. Then they schall come into the chamber all togeder & go to the coppard. Then schal the usher take the kynges spyce plate and cuppe, and let them stande aboue the coppard. Then the usher and seruant of the seller schal sett the cuppes and wyne in the coppord, and all other spyce plates to stande beneathe the cuppord in order, after the estate be in degrees[e]."

In the fifteenth century cupboards that did not possess these little ambries or safes were termed livery cupboards, or dressors, and instead of being used like the court cupboard or buffet, for the display of plate, were for placing the dishes upon as they were brought into the hall. In the contract for building Hengrave it was specified that the hall was—

"To have ij. coberds, one beneath at the sper with a tremor, and another at the higher tables ende withoute a tremor, and y[e] cobards, they be made y[e] facyon of liuery y[t] is w[t]oute doors[f]."

This was the dressor on which the meat was placed by the server before it was taken to the high board by those of greater estate:—

"And if it be a day of estate ij. squyres for the body schal go to the Dressor, and bere ij. of the fyrst dysshes both att the fyrst course and the seconde[g]."

The DRESSOR, especially in the preceding century, was often placed behind the screen, or in the passage leading from the hall into the kitchen[h]. At Haddon Hall, in the middle of the passage leading into the kitchen, is a half door or hatch, with a broad shelf on the top of it, whereon to place dishes[i]. The term dressor, as applied to an article of kitchen furniture, occurs in the time of Henry VIII., when it was discarded from the principal apart-

[e] MS. Additional, 4,712, fo. 3. a.
[f] Gage's Hengrave, p. 42.
[g] MS. Additional, 4,712, fo. 9. b.
[h] In a Household Roll of the time we read of "j. dressorio et penticia" standing against the wall from the kitchen door.
[i] Rayner's Antiq. of Haddon Hall, p. 45.

THE CHAMBERS AND OFFICES.

ment. In the following extract the shelves in the scullery are called dressors:—

"Pullyng downe the rouf of the skowlery, with newe makynge of a rouf agayne for the same, laying in of a new grownsell pec there, and makyng of a new partycion within the same, selling and laying of newe dressors and shelves there, reparying and mendynge and makyng of diuerse weys in the kyngs privy kytchin[k]."

In the sixteenth century the term cupboard was applied to any enclosed recess; they were still regarded as moveable articles of furniture. In 1571 we find one or two cupboards in every room of an extensive mansion[l]. The only distinction between the chamber cupboards and those in the hall was that the latter were sometimes called standing cupboards. In the Surveyor General's accounts for 38 Henry VIII. we find specified the cost of making "standyng cupbords" in the "Bankest house[m]."

The cupboards were generally made of oak, or "estrichborde." The richly carved panels and back of the court cupboard or buffet denoted its foreign workmanship. The chests and cupboards used in England in the fifteenth century were imported from Flanders: this, in the reign of Richard III., was considered to act so prejudicially to the interests of English workmen, that a law was made "agaynst straunger artificiers," prohibiting, among other articles of furniture, the importation of cupboards[n].

In the domestic annals of this period we find allusions to many luxuries not found in those of a previous age, and many indications of a more refined and cultivated taste having been encouraged among the nobles. Incidental allusions to the fine arts and to literature are

[k] MS. Additional, 10,109, fo. 51. a.   [l] Ibid., 10,128, in Brit. Mus.
[m] Ibid., 10,109, fo. 83. a.   [n] 1 Rich. III. ch. 12. Statutes, vol. ii. p. 495.

more frequent than we might be disposed to imagine, and the effect of this improved taste is observable in the decorative arrangements of domestic life. The walls and ceilings of the apartments were more often painted with scenes from classical and romantic lore, and the books written for the use of the baron and his chaplain were more gorgeously illuminated. The most sumptuous volumes of this epoch, which adorn our national libraries, were transcribed for distinguished laymen. In the twelfth and thirteenth centuries we rarely meet with any indications of a literary taste among the laity; the books they purchased were more for ornament than use; but in the fifteenth century we find books mentioned in a manner which would seem to indicate that the laity were enabled to use them with pleasure, and that they were enabled to carry on their private correspondence without the learned aid of their chaplain. We have a private English letter preserved, of a date as early as 1399, written by the lady of Sir John Pelham; this is, probably, the oldest in existence. The large collection of letters belonging to the Paston family prove that a correspondence could be kept up with considerable vivacity and learning. Such items in household accounts as "Payd for paper, ynke and wax, 1d.°," are significant; and numerous sums paid to messengers for the conveyance of letters shew to what extent an epistolary correspondence was carried in private life. The charms of literature, too, were beginning to be appreciated: in times of peace the baron sought the solace of a book. In the year 1395, Alice, Lady West, left to Joan, her son's wife, "all her books of Latin, English and French[p]," terms which seem to denote no trifling collection. Books, indeed, were no longer buried in monasteries,

[o] Howard's Household Book, p. 131.   [p] *Test. Vetusta*, p. 137.

but became household comforts among the laity: many of the barons became as rich in literary treasures as the Oxford Student, who gloried in his

"Twenty bokes clothed in blacke and red."

Thus, from the Memoranda of Sir John Howard, we learn that that worthy knight could read at his leisure "an Englyshe boke callyd Dives et Pauper," for which and a "Frenshe boke," in 1464, he paid thirteen shillings and fourpence[q]. The library of this nobleman was sufficiently extensive to enable him to select therefrom, on the occasion of his going into Scotland, thirteen volumes for his solace and amusement on the voyage. A curious list of these has been preserved[r]. A member of the Paston family has left a little catalogue of his library[s]. Indeed, so important did the family collection of books in some cases become, that a little shelf or casket was insufficient to contain them, and an apartment became appropriated as a library. Such collections were not to be found in the mansions of a former age.

In the will of the wife of William Bowes, bearing date 1420, we find that she was possessed of the following books, which she bequeaths in these terms:—

"Lego Matildi filiæ Baronis de Hilton filiolæ meæ, j. romance boke [that] is called ye Gospelles.
Lego Matildi Rob. de Hilton Chev[r], unum romance boke.
Lego Dame Elinoræ de Wes-syngton, ye boke with ye knotts.
Lego Elizabethæ filiæ Whitchester, unum librum yat is called Trystram.
Do et lego Elizabethæ filiæ meæ, j. blak primer."

The legacy to the daughter of the baron is expressed singularly. In all probability it was an illuminated copy of the Gospels, which, as she could not read, she placed in

[q] Manners and Household Expenses, p. 260.
[r] Howard's Household Book, p. 277.
[s] Fenn's Paston Letters.

the same category with the well-known Sir Trystram, as a "romaunce boke," a common name at the period. This is more probable from the circumstance of her description of a book as "ye boke with ye knotts," shewing that she knew more of the exterior than of the interior of her literary treasures.

The widow of Lord Fitzhugh leaves behind her another kind of books, (1427):—

"And so I wyl yat my son Robert have a Sauter (Psalter) couered with rede velwet, and my doghter Mariory a Primer cou'd in rede, and my doghter Darcy a sauter cou'ed in blew, and my doghter Malde Eure a prim'r cou'ed in blew."

In the will of John Newton, Rector of Houghton-le-Spring, (1427), some curious books are bequeathed:—

"Lego ... unum librum vocatum Crisostimum super Matheum.
... unum librum de duodecim capitulis ricardi Ermes.
... unum librum vocatum Beliall.
... unum librum vocatum Vita Christiana."

In the will of Thomas Hebbeden, Rector of Meldon, we find the following books bequeathed, (1435):—

"Lego Librariæ ecclesiæ Dunelmensis unum librum vocatum Catho[t], alias Speculum Virtutis, ita quod dominus prior jam existens habeat usum illius libri durante vitâ suâ.
Lego Magistro Artays unum librum voc. Guydo de Columpna cum contentis in eodem.
Lego Isabella Eure unum librum gallicum vocatum Launcelot."

In the parlour of St. Mary's Guild at Boston are mentioned the following:—

"*A Bybill* prynted; the gyfte of Sir Robert Wyte.—A booke in prynt, called *Sermones*.—An old *Antiphoner*.—A booke called *Legenda Sanctorum*, wrytten.—A bigger *Antiphoner*.—An old buffet stoole[u]. A fyre-forke. A payre of tonges, and a fyre-*stommer*, 3 *racons*, with a payre of galows of yron."

[t] A book of metrical ethics attributed to Magnus Cato, or Dionysius Cato, much in vogue during the middle ages. It is mentioned frequently by Chaucer.
[u] See page 116.

DOMESTIC ARCHITECTURE: FIFTEENTH CENTURY.

FURNITURE, &C., FROM MSS. IN THE BODLEIAN LIBRARY.

Douce 195. Bodl. 283. Douce, 202.

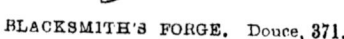

BLACKSMITH'S FORGE. Douce, 371.

SCULPTOR'S BENCH AND TOOLS. Douce, 371.

As these books were frequently of considerable size, a reading-desk or lettern became necessary in order to use them conveniently, and we accordingly find such articles of furniture frequently represented in the illuminations of manuscripts of this period, and they seem to have been equally convenient with any modern pieces of furniture of the same description. They were sometimes of wood, in other instances of metal; brass reading-desks of this century may frequently be met with, and these are richly ornamented, the forger and the sculptor in metal exerted his utmost skill in the ornamenting of the lettern. Good examples of letterns occur in Douce's Manuscripts, 195, 202, and 283, and of the forger and sculptor's bench and tools in 371. It will be observed that the forger used the double bellows for keeping up a continuous draught, and that the tools of the sculptor were very similar to those now in use.

It has been already mentioned that the hall was frequently on the first floor, with cellars or other vaulted apartments under it, and that the entrance from the court-yard was by an external staircase, or rather a flight of steps; in other instances it was by a winding stair round a newel in one of the turrets, but when this was the state entrance, it was by no means narrow and confined, on the contrary, it was a wide commodious staircase, as at Langley Castle, Northumberland. The other staircases were, however, much smaller, and often very narrow winding stairs, though even these were not practically so inconvenient as is commonly supposed. Besides the principal entrance to the hall at one end of the passage called "the Screens," there was usually another at the opposite end, leading by a staircase from the servants' court, and another short staircase led up into the music-gallery; this was usually close to the principal entrance. There was also frequently a straight flight of stairs down to the kitchen from the middle of "the Screens," passing between the buttery and the pantry, as in the hall of St. Mary's Guild at Coventry, where the whole of the original arrangements are still perfect, and in many of the colleges of Oxford and Cambridge, though the situation of the kitchen staircase of course varies with that of the kitchen itself, which is not always at the end of the hall, but rather at the back of it, and the staircase is then at the end of the Screens.

The primitive ladders by which formerly the solars, or upper chambers[v], were approached, were now discarded for STAIRCASES of a goodly size, flanked with curiously carved banisters of oak. External staircases were also frequently used; these are boldly corbelled out from the face of the wall, and covered with a pent-house roof, as in the Archbishop's Palace at Maidstone, Kent, in a part of the building now converted into stables, but probably of more importance originally: similar staircases occur in Berkeley Castle and many other instances, especially in the roof of a tower leading up to the watch-turret[x]. The steps leading out of the hall were sometimes of marble. In a manuscript of Lydgate's "Book of Troy" we have the following passage:—

> "Thorugh many halle and many ryche toure,
> By many tourne and many dyvers waye,
> By many *gree* made of marbyl greye,
> Hathe them conueyed a ful esy pas.

---

[v] Sometimes called a solier. In Caxton's "Golden Legend," fo. xxviii. edit. 1483, we read of "the solier where ye souper of Jhesu Cryst and of ye appostles was made."

[x] These watch-towers, called *aguas-seria*, (from the French *aguet*,) belong rather to the fortifications than to the domestic arrangements of a house. Still on all fortified houses of consequence they are to be found. See more than one illustration in the previous volume.

DOMESTIC ARCHITECTURE: SIXTEENTH CENTURY.

EXTERNAL STAIRCASE.

STABLES, ARCHBISHOP'S PALACE, MAIDSTONE, KENT.

DOMESTIC ARCHITECTURE: SIXTEENTH CENTURY.

PORCH,
WEOBLEY, HEREFORDSHIRE.

DOORWAY,
SHERBORNE, DORSETSHIRE.

THE CHAMBERS AND OFFICES. 143

> * * * * *
> And in his chambre englasid brizt and clere,
> That schone ful schene withe golde and azure,
> Of many ymage that was there in pycture[y]."

The porch to the hall has been already mentioned as the principal entrance to the house, but besides this there were numerous other doorways and doors, both external and internal, and so important a feature of the house was not likely to be left without ornament. The external doorway was frequently protected by a penthouse over it, or the projecting upper story served the same purpose, the door having the side-posts ornamented and carried up on spurs to support the overhanging beam, as at Sherborne, Dorsetshire, and Weobley, Herefordshire, and some rich examples at York have been already cited. The doorways also sometimes had canopies over them, with crockets and finials, like niches in a church, and the spandrels also filled with ornament, amongst which shields of arms were introduced, of which a very rich example remains in the doorway of a merchant's house in London-street, Norwich. There are several rich doorways of this class at Galway, of the time of Henry VIII. and Elizabeth, the ornament of which

Doorway, London street, Norwich.

[y] MS. Cotton. Augustus, iv. fo. 9, a.

is cut in the hard limestone with great skill. The wooden doors themselves are often worthy of notice as specimens of panelling or other ornament, although the rich ironwork of the earlier centuries has disappeared.

There is sometimes a sort of triangular PORCH on the outside of the door of the principal apartment, with two other doors opening from it, one to the bed-room in the turret, the other to the garderobe in a small turret in the angle, as at Saltwood Castle, Kent.

In the time of Henry VIII. a fashion was introduced of having an inner porch over the door of a principal apartment, such as the drawing-room at Thame Park, Oxon, an illustration of which has already been given: and this porch is often triangular also, that is, carried across the angle of the room over the entrance, and enriched with panelling and shields of arms, the same as the walls of the room. This fashion is common in Elizabethan houses, but it began earlier. In France we find the same fashion beginning at the end of the fifteenth century, and the porches of the Flamboyant style, both external and internal, are often very rich and elegant. The following extract from Sauval affords a good description of such a porch, and although he lived in the seventeenth century, he often describes buildings of earlier date:—

"On entroit dans les chambres et les salles, aussi bien que dans les chapelles, les galleries et autres lieux semblables, par un porche de menuiserie à trois, quatre ou cinq faces, haut de neuf et de douze pieds; d'ordinaire on le faisoit de bois d'Irlande; ils étoient couverts d'ornemens, et terminés de figures et autres enrichissemens gothiques; ils s'ouvroient de toutes parts, afin de pouvoir entrer et sortir plus commodément. Encore ils ressembloient à ces vieilles fausses portes de bois qui se voyent encore en quantité de vieux logis, et quoiqu'ils défigurent et embarrassent les lieux, nos vieillards pourtant ne s'en veulent point défaire et les conservent en dépit d'un chacun[z]."

[z] Sauval, t. ii. p. 278.

DOMESTIC ARCHITECTURE: FIFTEENTH CENTURY.

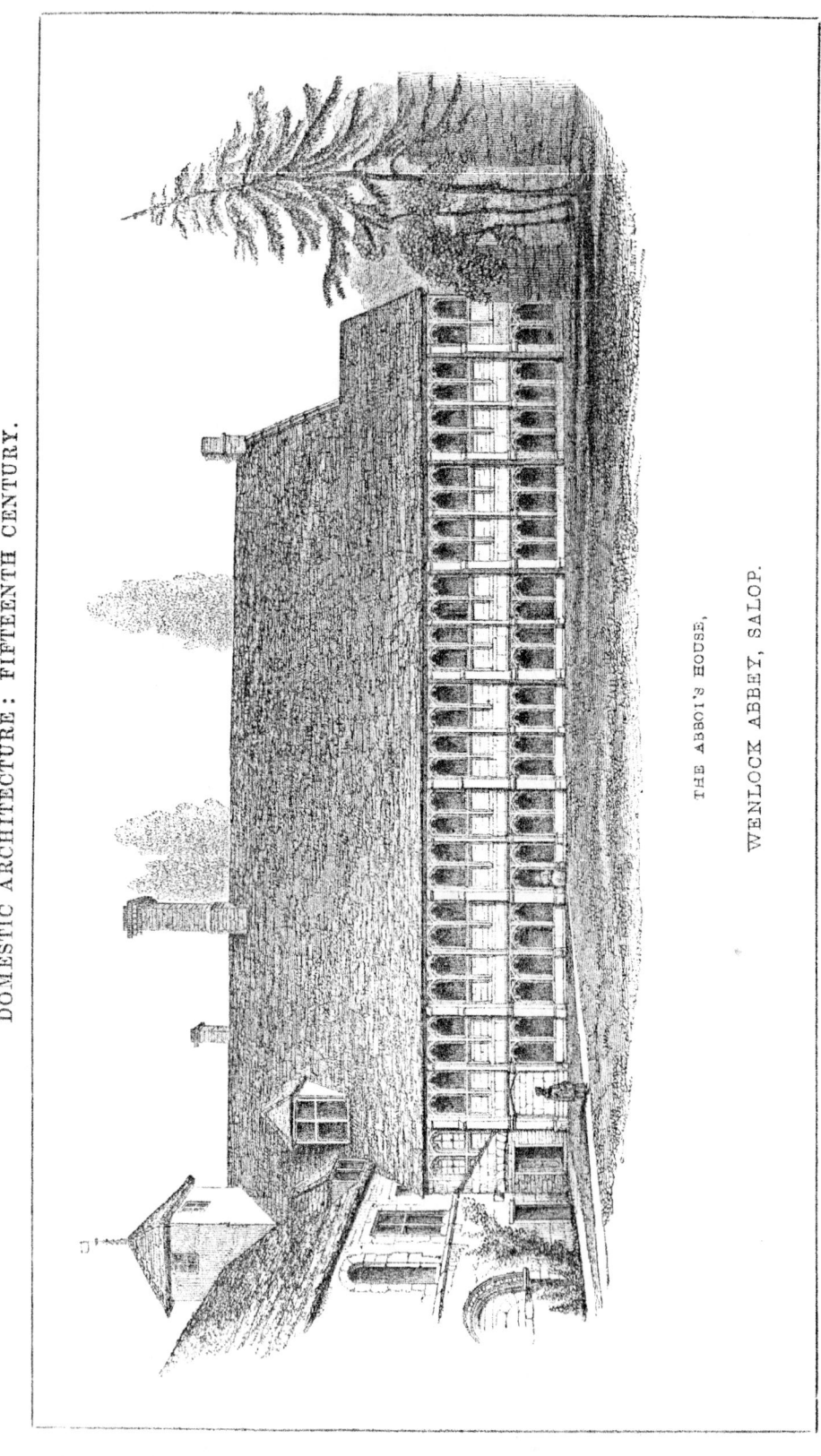

THE ABBOT'S HOUSE,
WENLOCK ABBEY, SALOP.

The PASSAGES and CORRIDORS are generally formed in the thickness of the walls, lighted sometimes by loopholes only, in others by windows, and in some cases, especially in timber houses, they are external, forming a sort of double cloister, one over the other. Of this latter arrangement perhaps the best example we have remaining is the Prior's House at Wenlock in Shropshire, which, although of a semi-ecclesiastical character, may still be taken as a fair example of a dwelling-house of the latter part of the fifteenth century of a person in a good position and a certain rank, as there is very little that is peculiarly ecclesiastical about it: the double cloister for the passages is by no means necessarily of that character; it never extended round the court, but was on one side only. A similar arrangement was continued very commonly in Elizabethan houses, and long afterwards, and even to our own day in country inns. Although the chief use of the corridors was for passages of communication, they were also used for other purposes. They often served as a sort of aisles or galleries to the chapel, as in Linlithgow Palace, where openings are provided from the passage into the chapel to enable persons placed there to join in the service, and in Hawarden Castle, where an upper passage has a sort of squint provided at the end of it opening into a small chapel in the thickness of the wall, which also had a door or arch with a screen into one of the principal chambers, where the family and guests might be assembled to hear mass and see the elevation of the Host, while the servants were enabled to attend in the corridor. In some cases there were curtains thrown across. In one of the inventories at Ewelme, already alluded to, we meet with

"A *travas* of purple tartren.—3 curteyns of green and blu paled tartran," &c.

This hanging across the passage is probably alluded to in Chaucer's "Merchant's Tale:"—

"Men drinken, and the travers draw anon."

The passages in the thickness of the wall often have the entrances to them in the recess of a window, as at Wetherall Priory, Cumberland. Such passages commonly lead to a garderobe only, with loopholes to give light, but in castles these also served to assist in the defence. Sometimes such an opening and passage leads to a bedroom in a corner turret, or to a staircase up to the roof; occasionally, and this especially in Ireland, by a descending stair to a small chamber, which seems to have been the dungeon or place of security for a prisoner of importance, the top of the tower-house being considered more secure than the bottom; and the only entrance to this chamber being from the principal state apartment at the top of the house, escape was almost impossible.

It was necessary to have a PROJECTION from the face of the wall, either a stone gallery at the top carried on a row of boldly projecting corbels, or a temporary wooden gallery thrown out from the face of the wall, for which corbels were often provided half-way up the wall, or merely supported on projecting timbers, for which the put-log holes often remain. The object of these projections was to enable the defendants to throw down missiles on the heads of the assailants, or to pour water on the faggots if they attempted to apply fire, and for this purpose the shaft from the well is often continued through the thickness of the wall up to the battlement. Sometimes, instead of a continuous gallery, small stone closets, called BARTIZANS or machicoulis, are thrown out on corbels immediately over the doorway, as in some of the pele-towers in Scotland. Similar projections also served

DOMESTIC ARCHITECTURE: FOURTEENTH CENTURY.

WINDOW MARKED A ON THE PLAN.

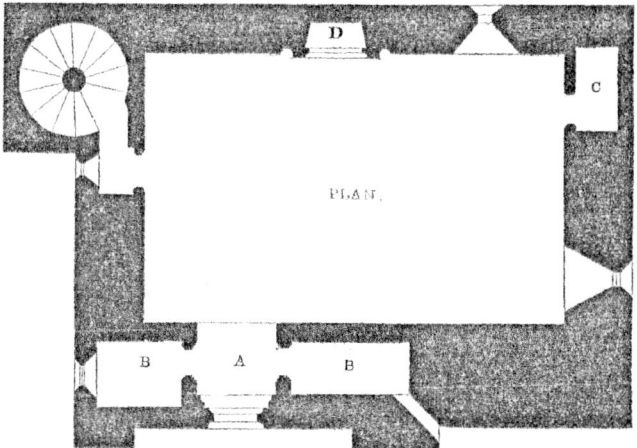

A. Window.   B. B. Two small rooms with external openings for watching.   C. Closet.   D. Fireplace.

ROOM OVER THE GATEWAY.

WETHERAL PRIORY, CUMBERLAND.

to protect the foot of the walls wherever they were liable to be attacked, and not the doorways only. At Conway there is a remarkable row of twelve of these closets, projecting from the parapet at the top of the wall, in one bay only, between two towers, of the town wall, and not in any other part. This arrangement is very singular, as the particular bay selected does not appear to be more exposed to danger than any other. It has been conjectured that these were merely garderobes for the use of the garrison, and it is observed that there is a remarkable absence of these conveniences in the other parts of the walls, both of the town and of the castle. It would appear that such projecting closets were used for both purposes, for defence when necessary, for convenience only at other times, and sometimes they appear to have been provided for convenience only, in situations where they could not have been wanted for defence.

In Ireland the bartizans are a prominent feature in most of the tower-built houses; they are usually round, and clasp one angle at the top of the tower, projecting from the battlement, but in some cases they project from the face of the wall about half-way up.

In Compton Castle, Devonshire, they are a very remarkable feature, from their extraordinary number; this appears to arise from there being no moat to protect the foot of the wall, which rendered this other mode of defending it the more necessary. They were clearly not garderobes, as there are garderobe turrets quite independent of them, and belonging to the same chambers as some of the bartizans, the opening of which is covered over by a wooden flap, making a seat in the sill of the window, and this appears to be an old arrangement.

The name of bartizan is commonly applied to these projections in England and in Ireland, and the corbels on which they are carried are called machicoulis; in France that name is applied to the whole structure: strictly speaking, it applies to the opening between the corbels which serves as a *coulis*, or gutter, or groove for throwing down stones and guiding them.

It seems probable, however, that the name of machicoulis was applied in the middle ages to the whole structure, as a part of the necessary fortifications, as appears from the following passages:—

"... quousque dicta villa perfecte fossatis et muris cum turribus et machicolamentis et barbacanis clausa pretit[a]."

The usual form of the royal license to fortify a house was:—

"Imbattellandi kernillandi, machicollandi," etc.

"Turris de mercato dicta S. Ludovici habet de alto computata fundamenta usque ad machacolladuram xi. cannas cadratas et 11 palmos[b]," etc.

Another mode of defending the foot of the wall from being undermined, when there was no moat, was by a covered way round the base of the tower exposed to danger. On the top of this covered way was a walk protected by a battlement, which served also to protect the entrance, which was from this walk; this served the purpose of a gallery, and an additional station for archers besides those on the top; and if the outer wall was undermined, the safety of the tower itself would not thereby be affected. A good example of this kind occurs at Rudesheim, on the Rhine, where the lofty round tower of the fifteenth century, with its very elegant battlement and cornice of Flamboyant work, has the base protected by a covered way of this kind, which remains perfect. One of the gatehouses of the small town of Tenby in South Wales has the covered way at the top quite per-

[a] Charta ann. 1346, ex Cod. Reg. 8,387. [b] Charta ann. 1382, ap. Ducange.

DOMESTIC ARCHITECTURE: FIFTEENTH CENTURY.

COMPTON CASTLE, DEVONSHIRE.

fect, and there are remains of it in several of the castles of that district.

A full supply of water was as necessary in the middle ages as it is now, and as well provided; the deep wells which they made in those days often remain in use to the present day. There was often also a shaft over the well through every story of the house up to the battlements at the top, with openings on each story, so that the bucket might be stopped wherever it was wanted. Good examples of wells with their shafts of this description remain in Rochester Castle, at Red Castle, in Shropshire, Carisbrook Castle, and numerous other places. At Dirleton Castle, Scotland, there are two such wells, one for the use of the kitchen, which was at the top of the house, the other for the more convenient use of the garrison in case of attack.

In other instances, when good water could not be obtained by digging wells, it was brought in pipes from some neighbouring hill, very much as in modern days. The very perfect system of pipes for the conveyance of water to every part of the great monastery at Canterbury so early as the twelfth century, is well known from the circumstance that the original plan, with all the water-courses drawn out in colours by a monk of the town, has been preserved in the library of Trinity College, Cambridge, and has been frequently engraved, though not very carefully. Professor Willis has thoroughly investigated the matter with his usual acumen, and has traced out the water-courses in the existing remains. It would be difficult to meet with another example equally perfect, but traces of similar arrangements may frequently be found.

In other instances, where the nature of the soil and the situation did not admit either of wells or of a supply

150 DOMESTIC ARCHITECTURE: FIFTEENTH CENTURY.

of water by means of pipes, arrangements were made to catch all the water which fell on the roof of the house or castle, and preserve it in a large reservoir provided for that purpose. A very fine and perfect example of a reservoir of this period has been preserved at Hawarden Castle, Flintshire, which stands on the summit of a hill of limestone. A large and deep reservoir is cut out of the rock, with a drain from it to the moat in case it should be ever full, and there are steps leading down to it on both sides, for the convenience of the servants, as it had offices on both sides protected by a sort of outwork of the fortifications. In early times, a frequent mode of taking a castle was by cutting off the supply of water, thereby compelling the garrison to surrender, and precautions to guard against this danger were afterwards adopted: there is a good original reservoir or cistern at Canon's Ashby, Northamptonshire.

Although it was sometimes necessary to catch all the water which fell on the roofs and convey it by pipes to

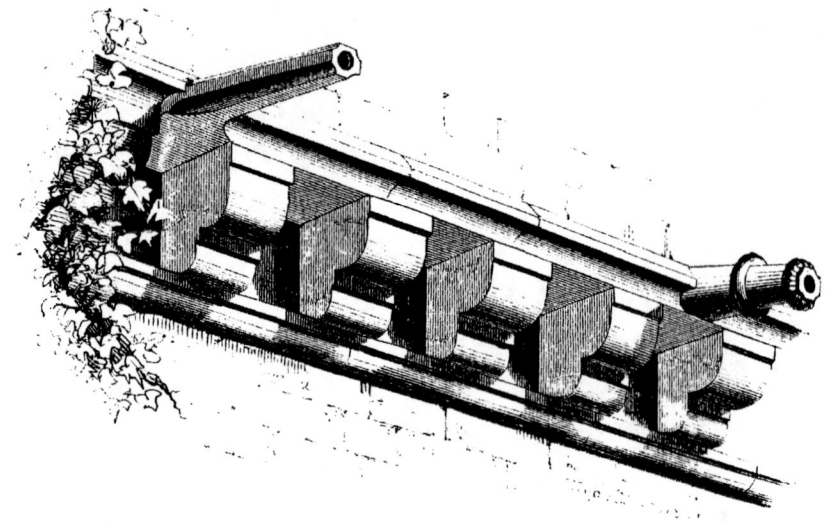

Water spouts, Kirk-Andrews-on-Eske, Cumberland.

the reservoir, it was more often necessary to throw it off as speedily as possible, and for this purpose gurgoyles or

DOMESTIC ARCHITECTURE: FIFTEENTH CENTURY.

KITCHEN,
STANTON HARCOURT, OXFORDSHIRE.

water-spouts are abundantly provided; these are sometimes ornamented with heads, as in churches, more often they are plain, and in disturbed districts they are made to resemble small cannons. In South Wales, especially in Bishop Gower's work, as at the bishop's palace, St. David's, large openings are left in the parapet at very short intervals, to allow the water to run off freely. In Ireland a similar plan is commonly adopted, but the openings are smaller and not so conspicuous; sometimes the projecting spouts like small stone cannons are used, as is also commonly the case in Scotland and in the north of England. A good example occurs at Kirk-Andrews-on-Eske, Cumberland, of which we have already given a general view, and here repeat the gurgoyles or spouts more at large.

The KITCHENS and MINOR OFFICES were usually in the preceding age detached from the main building, but they appear now to have been generally connected with it, and were frequently built with solars above. In a will bearing date 1463, we read of the "chambyr abovyn the kechene, with the draughth chambyr longyng therto[c];" and in a letter of Sir John Howard reference is made to the chambers "over the pantry and buttery."

There are many fine examples of kitchens of the fifteenth century remaining, either as distinct buildings or under other parts of the house. Of the former class, perhaps one of the finest is at the manor-house of Stanton-Harcourt, Oxfordshire: this is a square tower-like building, very lofty, with a fine open timber-roof, with lufferboards in the side windows at the springing of the roof, instead of the louvre at the top. The fireplaces and ovens remain, the roof is pyramidal, and surmounted by the family crest as a vane. It has an alure at the springing of the roof, protected by a parapet wall and

[c] Wills of the Register of St. Edmund's Bury, p. 22.

battlement, and approached by a newel staircase in a square stair-turret at one corner. Wykeham's kitchen at New College, Oxford, and Wolsey's kitchens at Christ Church and Hampton Court, are also of this class. When the kitchen is under other apartments it is usually vaulted for security, as at Warwick Castle, where it is under the principal state apartment, and forms one of a very fine suite of vaulted chambers, already alluded to: this is also the case in the Prior's House at Wenlock, Shropshire. In Berkeley Castle it is an hexagonal vaulted chamber, not detached, but forming part of the suite of buildings with the other offices connected with the lower end of the hall.

In the inventories of the period the kitchen is constantly mentioned: for instance, by the will of Roger Kyrkby (1412) we find that there were in his kitchen—

" vii. ollæ æneæ, vijs.
iv. patellæ, ijs. vid.
Unum veru (spit) ferreum.
ij. dresshyng-knives, vijd.
Unum plumbum continens xxxij. lagenas (gallons) cum tribus parvis plumbis, viijs.

ij. duodenæ vasorum de electro, (a mixed metal), xxs.
Una duodenæ vasorum veterum, vjs. viijd.
v. parapsides (dishes), x. disci (plates), ijs.
Unum fryingpan ferri, vjd.
Unum rostyng-iryn, iiijd."

From an inventory at Boston, Lincolnshire, we find that there were—

"IN THE KECHYN.—A hen cage, with a shelfe withyn. 2 tubs. 2 sowes, [large tubs]. A great boll & a lesser boll. A hogs-hed to put in salte. A market maunde (basket) with a coveringe. 12 brass pots, kettles, &c., weighynge together 167 lbs. A great yron spyt, weighynge 14 lbs. A payre of cobbards of yron, weighynge 23 lbs. Other spytts, droppyng-pans, frynge-pans, brandreths, &c., weighynge 86 lbs."

In the inventory of the Priory of Finchall (1411), in addition to articles mentioned above, we find—

THE CHAMBERS AND OFFICES.

"ii. posnetts (pipkins).
iii. zetlings (pans), videlicet ii. pro piscibus coquendis, et j. pro frixis (frying-pan).
xiii. salsaria antiqua.
xij. parapsides cum totidem salsariis novis.
j. machera pro carnibus levandis (probably the large iron fork for lifting the meat from the pot).
Unum mortariolum eneum cum pilo ferreo.
j. craticula ferrea (gridiron).
j. brandeyrne (probably a large gridiron or roasting bars for placing either on or in front of the fire).
j. potclames (pothooks or chains from which the pot was suspended).
j. por (poker).
j. falanga (a thick sort of pole, which men laid across their shoulders for carrying heavy goods, probably something like brewers use to this day).
ij. tubbs.
ij. calathæ (baskets) pro piscibus cariandis, et ij. minores pro ovis, et piscibus cariandis et aliis, ij. rakks (rakes) ferri debiles."

In the same kitchen, at a later date (1465), we find the same with some additions, such as—

"j. hausorium (bucket).
j. scommer.
ij. mortar lapedei.
j. par cleppis (pot-hooks?).
j. fleshaxs.
j. fleshcroyk.
j. dressyng knyff.
iiij. bus. farinæ avenarum.
vi. et dim lagenæ mellis.
Et j. qu. salis."

In royal and noble palaces the furniture of the kitchen was sometimes costly, as we read by the will of Richard, Earl of Arundel (1387), who leaves—

"Pur la cusyne trois dozeins des esquelx (dishes), deux dozeins des saucers, et quartre chargeours, tout d'argent."

The kitchen gear was sometimes of a more homely description, for my Lord Howard paid only eleven-pence "for two bolles for the kechyne, ij. rounde dysches, and xj. platers of tre to serve werkemen, and other gere[d]." In 1482, twopence was paid for "ij. erthen pannys." The use of pottery, however, even at this period, was not general. In 1463, John Baret of Bury by his will left to

[d] Howard's Household Book, p. 325.

his niece "a greet erthin potte that was my moderis[e]," but we do not find such household utensils often mentioned. In a manuscript entitled *Liber de Coquina* we read:—

"Take pejons and heu hom in vessel smalle,
Put hom in a *erthyn pot* thou schalle[f]."

Bottles and pots were made of leather. In the expences of the Howards several items occur for leathern pots and bottles, and at one time as much as seven shillings and eightpence was paid for "viii. leder pottes, vj. of a sorte, and ij. of a grettur sorte."

Perhaps the inventory of the goods of Sir John Fastolfe, taken about 1455, gives the best list of the usual contents of a kitchen of a large country-house:—

"j. gret bras pote.
vi. cours pottys of brasse.
iiij. lytyll brasse pottis.
iiij. grete brasse pottis.
iij. pike pannys of brasse (pans for dressing the fish of that name).
ij. ladels and ij. skymers of brasse.
j. caudron.
j. dytyn panne of brasse.
j. droppyng panne.
j. gredyren.
iiij. rakkis.
iij. cobardys.
iij. trevitts.
j. fryeying panne.
j. sclyse (large knife?).

ij. grete square spittys.
ij. square spittys cocnos (?)
ij. lytyll brochys rounde.
j. sars (sieve or cullender of brass).
j. brasyn morter cum j. pestell.
j. grate.
j. sarche of tre (cullender of wood).
i. flessche hoke.
ij. potte hokys.
j. payr tongys.
j. dressyng knyfe.
j. fyre schowle.
ij. treys.
j. streynour.
j. vinegre botell."

A much longer and more varied list of articles of furniture in the kitchen occurring in the inventories might be made, but enough has been given to shew that a

[e] Wills from the Register of St. Edmund's Bury, p. 23.
[f] MS. Sloane, 1,986, p. 60.

DOMESTIC ARCHITECTURE: FIFTEENTH CENTURY.

FURNITURE, &C., FROM MSS. IN THE BODLEIAN LIBRARY.

TABLE, FIREDOGS, AND FIREPLACE.

Douce, 195.

INTERIOR OF KITCHEN.

Canon. Liturg. 99.

kitchen was as well furnished with all necessary articles then as at the present day.

Before, however, concluding the list, a few words should be said about the ANDIRONS, or Fire-dogs (*chenets*[g]), which were originally used for the reredos or brasier in the middle of the hall, but afterwards were equally common in fireplaces. "A pair of andyrnes" is of constant occurrence in the inventories of the period, and although they have now been generally discarded from use in consequence of the introduction of coal, they may still be often found in old-fashioned houses, especially in districts where wood is abundant. Their use was not at all confined to the hall, they were equally convenient in the fireplaces of the chambers and kitchens before grates were introduced: representations of them are very common in the illuminations of manuscripts of this period, as in Douce's MSS. 99 and 195. Pokers and tongs are also frequently mentioned and represented. Thus we find in the Prior's chamber at Finchall, (1411):—

"ij. porrs (pokers) et forcipes (tongs) pro igne, videlicet j. pro camera Domini et j. pro camera ludencium[h]."

The large FIREPLACE is the usual mark by which to distinguish the kitchen; it generally, but by no means always, has a projecting hood over it: such fireplaces are constantly represented in the illuminations of manuscripts. They are also perhaps the most common feature to find remaining in the ruins of houses of the middle

---

[g] "Les chenets (des chambres royales) étoient de fer ouvré; en 1367, on en fit quatre paires pour les chambres de la reine au Louvre; la plus petite pesoit 42 livres, l'autre 60, l'autre 100, la plus grosse 198, et couterent 26 livres, 13 sols quatre deniers Parisis, à raison de 16 deniers la livre de fer. Les soufflets étoient tous chargés d'ornements. Les tenailles, les pincettes, les pelles et le traifen .... étoient de fer ouvré."— Sauval, *Ville de Paris*, p. 280.

[h] The chamber of the players, i. e. a chamber in the priory appropriated to the performance of mysteries and other dramatic entertainments.

ages of all periods, more particularly of the fifteenth century.

There is frequently a back kitchen situated at the back of the chimney-stack, with a doorway or small arch opening into it by the side of the kitchen fireplace. This seems to have been also used as the scullery, at least in some instances, as at Fawsley. The scullery is sometimes mentioned as a separate office, but less frequently than most of the others.

The PANTRY and the BUTTERY have been already described as the small chambers adjoining to the lower end of the hall, intervening between that and the kitchen[i]. The pantry, as we have said, was *usually* for the distribution of the bread, and the buttery of the liquors[k]. But these distinctions were not always strictly preserved, in the smaller houses one chamber often served both purposes, and the names of offices which were originally distinct are often confounded and mixed up together in the inventories of this period. The buttery (*botellarium*) and the cellar (*celarium*) became one. For instance, in the Finchall accounts, referred to in our last volume, we find first of all the inventories of the pantry and buttery separate; but when we come to the fifteenth century, on examining the details we find the cups, bowls, vessels, bread-chest, saltcellars, candlesticks, tankards, table-cloths, hand-towels, and knife for cutting the bread, all thrown together in one account, as if in one and the same chamber, and under the description of *pantaria et botellaria*.

Still later in the century (1465), and in the same series

---

[i] See vol. ii. p. 135.

[k] In the description of Durham Abbey the writer says:—"The victualls that served the said gessts came from the great kitching of the Prior, the bread and beare from his pantrie and seller."—Ancient Rites of Durham.

of accounts, we find the words pantry and buttery abandoned, and *promptuarium* supplying their place. The contents are now not so varied, consisting chiefly of table-cloths, jars, cups, spoons, and drinking vessels.

For the most part, the inventories are chiefly a repetition of those given in the last volume, but of course the utensils and implements are more numerous. A few, perhaps, may now be added of this century, which will exhibit the progress which had been made in household economy. From the will of Richard, Earl of Arundel, we learn—

"Je devise qe ma dite compaigne Philippe eit pur *le botellerye et celer* deux pottes d'argent, chescun contenaunt un potel (pint) ij. hanappes (bowls) d'argent, enorrez, enarmé (emblazoned), outre sa propre hanap appelle 'Bealchier,' un dozein de peces[1] d'argent, les deux salers (salt-cellars) d'argent enarrez, queux ma dite compaigne moy dona a moun aun doun (as my new year's gift) un chastel 'Philipp' et deux autres meindres salers d'argent, l'un ove coverture, et l'autre sans coverer. Deux chaundelers d'argent pur soper en yverne (two silver candlesticks for use during dinner in winter), ove haut pees, et mees eschochouns pendantz ove trois quartres sur meomes les chandelers et les suages (?) enbataillez et enorrez."

In the cellar proper of Sir John Fastolfe (1455), there is not much to be found, as far as appears by the roll:—

"In the SELER, certayn vessell whiche John Ouresby is chargid withe by an endenture, wherof the copy is annexed to this lese.—ij. pypes of rede wyne."

But in "the Bottre" we have a very complete list, which is worth noting:—

"ij. kerving knyves.
iij. kneyves in a schethe, the haftys of every (ivory), withe naylys gilt.

j. payre galon bottels of one sorte.
j. payre of potell bottellys of one sorte.

---

[1] *Pecia.* This word, as we have before mentioned, is used to denote any object made of precious metal. It answers to our expression, "a piece of plate."

j. nother potell bottell.
j. payre quartletts of one sorte.
iiij. galon pottis of lether.
iij. pottelers of lether.
j. trencher knyfe.
j. grete tankard.

ij. grete and hoge botellis.
xiiij. candylokys of laton (latten metal).
Certayn pecys of napre (table linen, &c.), according to a bylle endentyd annexed to this lese."

Then we have an account of the plate in the same buttery:—

"In primis iij. chargeres argenti de parvo sorte.
v. platers argenti.
xij. dissches argenti unius sort'.
viij. dissches argenti minoris sortes.
xi. sawseris argenti unius sortis.
iij. crateras argenti quarum.
j. dat' Margarete Hoddsone.
iij. covertories argenti enamelid and borage flours in les botimes (the knobs?).
vi. chacyd pecys gilte bi the bordurys with the touche of Paryce[m].
ij. pottis argenti potlers, percell gilte and enameled with violetts and dayseys.
ij. pottis of sylver, of the facion of goods enamelyd on the toppys withe hys armys.
j. quarteler argenti percel gilt, with j. chase a bough of rosys and levys (leaves).
j. rounde salt seler, gylt and covered with a wrethe toppe, with this wordys wreten 'Me faunt fere' abowght.
j. salt seler, pacell of the same fassion sengle.
ij. salt selers of silver, playne and small, with a double rose graven withthe armys.
j. basyn of silver, percell gylte, with a dowble rose, his armis enamelid in the bottom, bewith his helme and his crest."

In the inventory before alluded to, at Boston, and at a later date, we find—

"In the Buttre.—A playne armory, with three little chambers. A sprewce cheste. A dressynge-borde, with a pryck to hang clothes on. A brake to make *vergys* withall. A lyttell forme, and a bynke to sett ale potts on. A salt of tyn with a cover. 2 bell candelstyks. A quantitye of tabill linen, marked with this letter M, crowned. 2 dozen trenchers. Pewter plates, dishes and sawcers, amounting in weight to 114¾ lbs."

[m] Query the "handle of Parisian (workmanship)"—or (carved with the subject of) "the Choice of Paris."

In an inventory of the period (1412), we find that a clergyman's *celarium* (buttery) contained—

"Una mappa (cloth) cum uno manutergio (towel) de novo factis, iijs.

x. mappa veteres cum iij. manutergiis, ijs. vid.

xxxviii. ulni panni linei, xis. jd. (probably used as table-cloths).

iij. paria cultellorum (knives) argenti, vis. viijd.

ix. ulni panni linei de lake (lake, i. e. crimson colour), iiijs. vid.

ij. barels et iiij. standes, ijs."

In the inventory of the Prior of Durham, (1446) :—

" In Promptuario (pantry) sunt ij. coclearia argentea et deaurata, unius, sectæ, cum ymaginibus Beatæ Mariæ in fine eorundem.—xij. coclearia argentea cum glandibus in nodis, unius sectæ.—vij. coclearia argentea cum nodis deauratis.—ij. coclearia argentea cum 𝔓. 𝔍𝔬𝔥. insculptis cum longis stalkez (stems).—iij. murræ (murrain cups) cum cooperculis.

" Unum salsarium (saltcellar) rotundum, cum coopuerculo deaurato habente floridam circumferenciam cum 9 flo de luce (fleurs-de-lys).—Unum salsarium quadratum, cum cooperculo argenteo et deaurato cum armis, Johannis Wessyngton nuper prioris in summitate ejusdem.—Unum salsarium argenteum et deauratum longum cum nodo recurvo.—viij. salsaria argentea cum circumferentiis deauratis.

" Duo candelabra argentea concava oblonga, et deaurata in circumferenciis.—xij. candelabra de auricalco, quorum ij. cum ij. floribus."

A great proportion of the provisions were still purchased at fairs, although the increase of trade and general commerce had much encroached upon this custom. Lord Howard gave to Master Daniel money "to buy clothe at the fayre[n]." A glass, it does not say of what kind, was purchased for one penny, and in 1465 sixpence was paid "for a botelle of glasse bout at Ypswyche[o]." Utensils of glass, however, were still scarce and expensive. Earthenware is sometimes, although rarely, mentioned, the garniture of the table being principally composed

[n] Howard's Household Book, p. 99.
[o] Manners and Household Expences, p. 303.

of vessels of pewter. Many "a garnysshe of counterfet vesselys" were bought or exchanged with the pewterer of Colchester, at the usual rate of fourpence the pound[p].

In general, as we have before said, the place for washing the hands was behind the screen, but there was sometimes a separate office appropriated for this purpose, called the *lavatorium*, or EWERYE. Thus the Earl of Arundel leaves—

"Pur *l'ewerye* un paire basyns d'argent ennorrez de mes armes deux bassyns, deux ewers sengles d'argent et un paire bassyns, desquex etc est acustume a laver devant maunge et soper."

The LARDARIUM was the place for storing the potted meat which was preserved for winter use, the mouths of the pots being covered over with lard, as in the present day. Such preserved meats were extensively used in the middle ages, and the lardarium, or larder, was an important office, usually near to the kitchen.

It was in most cases the same as the SALSARIUM, in which salted provisions were stored, when it was necessary to provide so large a stock of provisions, both in castles in case of a siege, and in the manor-houses on account of the difficulty of obtaining a regular supply, from the badness of the roads and the scarcity of carts or wheel-carriages of any kind. Even in quite recent times it was customary in large establishments to lay in a stock of salted provisions for the winter supply.

The contents of the larder or salting-house, as given in inventories, will best explain the purpose of the building; and for this purpose reference is made to those already quoted.

"IN THE LARDYR-HOUSE.—A bultynge pype, covered with a yarde of canvesse. 2 bultynge cloths. A knedynge sheit of canvesse, con-

[p] Manners and Household Expences, pp. 279, 317.

THE CHAMBERS AND OFFICES. 161

teynynge 3 elles. A knedynge tubbe with a coverynge. 2 vergys barrels. A skeppe."

In Sir John Fastolfe's larder there were—

"iij. grete standere pannes.
j. bocher's (butcher's) axe.
ij. saltyng tubbes.
viii. lynges.
viii. mulwellfyche (haddock?).
j. barell dim aleč alb.
j. barell anguill unde car. cc. anguill.
j. ferkyn anguill hoole.
j. barell.
j. buschell salt albi.
j. quart alb. sal."

By this it will be seen that the larder contained chiefly salted fish for the observance of fast days. The ling, haddock, white herring, and eel seem to be the favourite fish. Similar to this are the contents of the Fynchall larder, during the different inventories which were taken.

Indications of progress are, however, observable in the provisions of the larder and store-chambers. Many delicacies were procured from foreign climes by the London merchants. Choice spices and fruits were obtained at moderate cost. Lord Howard sends to London for "a toppet of ffiggs[q]," and he is able to purchase a hundred and ten oranges at twopence the score. Twelve pence were paid to the "caryer for brengyng of prunys;" and almonds, raisins, currants, and cinnamon are supplied by "Sandys the grocer" in large quantities.

The BAKEHOUSE is generally situated near the kitchen. Sometimes the ovens are in the back kitchen, as at Haddon Hall; more frequently it is a separate chamber, and, having also the arch of a large fireplace in it, is frequently called a second kitchen, but the pair of ovens were usually placed under an arch of this kind. At Fawsley the whole arrangement is complete, the chimney-arch has the two ovens under it, all being original. In

[q] Howard's Household Book, p. 22.

Y

this instance the bakehouse is separated from the kitchen by the back kitchen or scullery.

The BREWHOUSE was an office of considerable importance and extent, which we commonly find among the outbuildings of houses, from the days of our Saxon ancestors to the present time. Brasenose College in Oxford, originally Brasenose Hall, owes its name to its having been built on the site of an ancient brewhouse, in Anglo-Saxon *brasen-huis*, just as the palace of the Tuileries owes its name to having been built on the site of a tile manufactory.

In the fifteenth century the brewhouse was not less important than at other periods. It is commonly joined on to the other offices, or forms part of the offices surrounding the servants' court, as at Fawsley, Haddon Hall, and Hurstmonceux. At New College, Oxford, the brewhouse is outside the walls of the college, but flanks the approach to it, from which it would appear not to have formed part of the original buildings of Wykeham, but to have been added soon afterwards. It is a large range of building, of the fifteenth century, and is connected with the other buildings of the college by a room over the street, which rests on an *askew* arch, of clever construction, built long before the difficulties of railway engineers were dreamed of.

At Merton College also the founder appears not to have supplied a brewhouse, and the college, in a subsequent age, to make amends for this deficiency, turned the sacristy of the chapel into a brewhouse, to which purpose it is still applied.

A malt-house seems to have been generally a necessary appendage to a brewhouse. But beer was not always brewed at home: the trade of a brewer had become one of importance. Hops were generally used.

Such items as "payd for ij. C. and xxi. lbs. of hoppes," at eight shillings the hundred-weight, are several times recorded.

In some instances the bakehouse and brewhouse are included under an inventory, as if the same chamber served for each, as in the Fynchall accounts we find—

"Pistrinum et Pandoxatorium.—Imprimis, iij. lebetes (cauldrons) magnæ.
Et iiij. parvæ in gylnghouse.
j. masfatt novum.
ij. saas (kind of tubs).
ij. fattis (vats).
ij. frogons ferri (forks used in raking the fire in the oven).
j. securis (axe) pro lignis secandis.
x. sacci ibidem et alibi.
ij. bulting-claythis (bowlting or sifting cloths).
j. temes (sieve) novum.
i. bulting ark (chest).
j. trow pro past (paste-trough) novum, et j. trow antiquum.

The kitchens, brewhouses, and bakehouses were no doubt supplied chiefly with wood for some time, but now COAL had become a large item in household expenditure. Roberd Gyrlynghouse was paid four shillings and twopence "for x. seme and a combe of collis[r]," and at a subsequent period twenty-four quarters of coal were bought at fourpence-halfpenny the quarter[s]. This did not include the cartage, for various sums were paid to the carters "ffor fettyng of coles from Wevenhoo." Coal-houses became necessary additions to the out-buildings, and we find an entry of fourpence being paid "ffor a locke for the cole hows dore[t]."

The trade in that useful article, coal, which we have already treated of, rose into importance only as chimneys became common. The citizens of London began to use coal in the reign of Edward i., but several of the nobility complained of it as a nuisance, and, after a commission of inquiry, a proclamation was issued, prohibiting the use of

[r] Howard's Household Book, p. 326.   [s] Ibid., p. 472.   [t] Ibid., p. 465.

sea coal[u]. But in spite of this royal interference the trade gradually increased, and we find that coal was used at the coronation feast of Edward II. Richard del Hurst petitions for the payment of ten shillings for sea coal supplied on that occasion[x]. On the 8th of January, 1308, John Fairhod, Thomas de Hales, Thomas Wastel, Roger le White, and John de Talworth, wood-merchants, received fifty pounds from the Exchequer, to provide wood and coal for the king's coronation[y]. The price of coal in the reign of Edward III. was six shillings and fourpence a chaldron. In the 38th year of the reign of that king 31*l*. 13*s*. 4*d*. was paid to John de Assehurst, for one hundred chaldrons of coals supplied for the king's use[z]. But charcoal, wood, and turf was the fuel most generally used for domestic purposes. The scholars of Magdalen College, Oxford, were allowed a certain time after meals to tarry round the charcoal fire[a].

In the romance of "William and the Werwolf" we have the following allusion to colliers:—

"And erliche on the morwe er the sunne gan shine,
Choliers that cary redon col come there bi side[b]."

The DAIRY may be mentioned, as it occurs in the old records, though the origin of the word may be open to dispute. We find the word mentioned in the account

[u] Pat. 35 Ed. I. m. 4. dorso. A grant of 34 Ed. I., printed by Hearne in *Liber Niger Scaccarii*, p. 480, illustrates this subject. The mayor and citizens of London were allowed to levy a toll of sixpence upon every shipload of sea coal passing under London-bridge. In the valuation made at Colchester, before referred to, a few of the tradesmen are mentioned as having a stock of talwood and sea coal, *carbon' marin'*, but it seems to have been used by blacksmiths, and not for domestic purposes. Rot. Parl., vol. i. p. 228.

[x] Rot. Parl., 15 and 16 Ed. II., vol. i. p. 405.

[y] Issue Rolls, Excheq. 1 Ed. II. Sea coal was used by David Atte Hope, the king's smith. Issue Rolls, Mich. 9 Ed. II.

[z] Issue Rolls, Excheq. Mich. 38 Ed. III.

[a] Chandler's Life of Waynflete, p. 205.
[b] fo. 37. a.

THE CHAMBERS AND OFFICES. 165

delivered to the prior and canons of Burcester (1407) by their dairy-man and dairy-maid:—

"Compotus Henrici Deye, et Johannæ uxoris suæ de omnibus exitibus et proventibus de "Dayri" domini prioris de Burucestre," &c.[c]

There are returns from selling cows, calves, hides, &c., but we find the chief to be—

"Venditio casci, et ob. receptis de caseo et *butiro*."

The GRANARY was another important office, in which the corn was kept after it was thrashed, and distinct from the barn in which it was thrashed.

The granary seems to have been often the same as the malt-house, one building serving for both purposes, as in the inventory of Roger de Kyrkby, 1412, we find, in GRANARIA:—

"x. quart. brasii (malt) mixti, xxxiijs. iiijd.
In frumento, ordeo (barley), avena (oats), et pisis (pease), nondum trituratis, viijl.
x. petræ ferri, vs.
Alia utensilia, xs."

In the inventory of the Prior of Durham, (1446):—

"GRANARIUM. In granario sunt lx. quarteria frumenti et extra lx. quarteria frumenti; precium qu. vjs., xxxvjl.
In braseo et ordeo ccc. qu., pr. qu. iijs., lxxiiijl.
In pandoxina pistrina et ustrina sunt diversa vasa et utensilia quorum aliqua sunt sufficiencia et aliqua debilia.
Unus equus pro frumento et braseo cariando, et apparatus competens pro eodem.
in prebendâ videlicet pisis, fabis, et avenis xl. quarteria."

The MILL was almost a necessary appendage to the manor-house at a time when the corn grown on the

---

[c] Some years after (1425) we find in the accounts, "De xxxvs. receptis de 'Dayeria' de la Breche ut patet per rotulum compoti. Johannis Deye et Margeria uxoris suæ." It will be noticed that the same name, "Deye," is retained, i. e. the name of the officer, as Hugo Dapifer, Henry Butler, and so John Day, i. e. the dairy-man.

estate was habitually consumed on the spot, the want of roads making it difficult to convey such a bulky article to any considerable distance. The same stream which formed the moat turned the mill, which was within the outworks. Such mills often remain still in use, though mutilated and altered in modern days, as at Great Chalfield, Wilts.

In other cases the ruins of them only are left, as at South Wingfield, Derbyshire, and Leeds Castle, Kent. Drawings of them may often be met with in the illuminations of manuscripts of this period, as in a manuscript of Quintus Curtius, 46, in the Bodleian Library.

Mill, with Sluice and Overshot Wheel. Quintus Curtius, 46.

The STABLES, as we have mentioned, formed a very important part of the offices of a house in the middle ages. In the small tower-built houses, or peles, in disturbed districts, they usually form part of the house itself, occupying the whole or part of the vaulted lower chamber or substructure. In the larger manor-houses the stables are sometimes in the inner court, as at South Wraxall, more often in the outer court, as at Tisbury,

DOMESTIC ARCHITECTURE: FIFTEENTH CENTURY.

FURNITURE, &c., FROM MSS. IN THE BODLEIAN LIBRARY.

LADIES' CARRIAGE.

CRADLE.
Douce, 195.

MILL, WITH SLUICE AND OVERSHOT WHEEL.
Quintus Curtius, 46.

TREASURE-CHEST.
Douce, 371.

SEAT. Douce, 371.

TABLE.
Douce, 371.

and frequently the stables and stable-yard are detached on the outside of the moat, as at Ightham, Kent. At Hampton Court the stables are banished to the opposite side of the green, where, however, they remain in nearly a perfect state, and of the same age as the palace itself. At Hurley Bottom, Berkshire, the stables are very remarkable, having stalls and woodwork of handsomely carved work of Jacobean character, but probably continuing an older fashion. At Yanwath, Westmoreland, the stable is on the opposite side of the court-yard to the house, and the window is furnished with a good iron grating of the fifteenth century.

FARM BUILDINGS and BARNS of the fifteenth century may frequently be met with in those parts of the country where the building-stone is of good quality, and the barns sometimes have fine timber roofs, as at Harmondsworth in Middlesex.

In general they differ little from modern barns, excepting that they usually have buttresses of Gothic character, and are cruciform, sometimes with two transepts, at the ends of each of which are the large folding doors with a four-centred arch over them, and generally a finial of the style of foliage used at this period, square leaved and angular, not so free or such flowing lines as on the barns described in our previous volumes.

At Place House, Tisbury, Wiltshire, the whole of the farm buildings are of the fifteenth century, and remarkably perfect.

The GRANGES belonging to the different abbeys were something more than farm-houses, they belong rather to the class of manor-houses, and have more often been preserved than most others, on account of the tenure of Church property by leasehold only.

It would be increasing the size of the present work

needlessly to minutely describe the usual contents of all the outer offices which were at this time common in the larger houses. It would be possible to find, from the inventories which are accessible to us, the contents of nearly all the various outbuildings which are found in a gentleman's mansion of the present day. The *porcaria* (pig-styes), *pultaria* (poultry-yards), the *domus fabri* (the smith's shop), *domus ortulani* (garden tool-house), besides the various storehouses in which were kept timber, gardening and agricultural implements, and means for repairing their carriages and waggons should any accidents befall them. It would not, at the same time, be an uninteresting study to trace the progress of agriculture through the middle ages, and a few extracts from the inventory attached to the will of the Prior of Durham, already so frequently mentioned, will exhibit in some degree the resources of a farmer of this period. In most cases, as throughout the inventories, the probable interpretation is appended to difficult passages. The name of the estate is attached to each portion, but in no case is the inventory given entire:—

"Wyvestowe. ij. equi pro carectis, xx*s*.—ij. arata cum toto apparatu tam ligneo quam ferreo pro xij. bobus et iiij. equis.—iij. harpicæ (harrows), pr. viij*d*.

" ij. carucæ cum toto apparatu videlicet jugis, tracez, et aliis necessariis, xiiij*s*.—j. plaustrum novum cum wholnwhelez et cum iiij. hoopez de ferro, pr. vj*s*. viiij*d*.—j. coupwayn (long cart) cum waynstryngez, pr. iij*s*.—j. carecta cum rotis iiij. hopis et viij. cartecloutez, pr. viiij*s*.

" j. whetridell (wheat riddler), j. bigridell, j. cribrum (sieve), j. modius, j. hopper (seed basket), j. barnshoile (barn shovel), ij. rastra, ij. yoke wymbils, j. restwymbyll, ij. grapez, j. shole (shovel) ligat' cum ferro, et xv. nekbandez, pr. iij*s*. vj*d*.

" Pittingdon. j. ventilabrum (winnowing fan); iiij. sacci pro semine; j. gret fatt pro granis conservandis.—iii. fattes minores; ij. reyngesevez (ring-sieves?); j. cribrum pro frumento; ij. cribra pro avenâ; ij. cribra pro ordeo mundando.—ij. hookes; ij. sholez (shovels)

THE CHAMBERS AND OFFICES.

pro orreo; ij. funes pro plaustris; ij. sholez; iij. grapez (dung-forks); j. securis; j. longa cista; ij. aratra cum toto apparatu pro xxiiij. bobus; vij. shakels (chains) ferri, unde ij. sine shakelpynnez (shacklepins) et v. cum shakylpynnez ferri.

"iiij. juga capitalia; ij. mukrakkez; j. mukforke (dung-fork); ij. magnæ ligaturæ ferri pro ostio cum iiij. crokez (crooks) de ferro.

"j. magna securis (axe); iij. yrinforkez; ii. wedehokez (weedhoe?); j. hambyr; v. rastra; j. hopper; j. modius; ij. langwaynez (long carts); ij. plaustra pro fimo cariando; iij. paria harpicarum et vj. axiltrenalez (axle-tree nails or bolts), &c.

"BEAULIEU. Una carecta ferro ligata cum toto apparatu pro iiij. equis trahentibus.—Una caruca cum toto apparatu pro viij. bobus; iij. harpicæ cum iij. tracez.

"FERY. Inter alia, ij. plaustra longa cum ij. rotis j. coupwayne sine rotis; iij. carucæ cum toto apparatu pro xxiiij. bobus; v. sevez; ij. scotelez (coal-scuttles); j. wyndow-cloth (winnowing-cloth); ij. yrnforkez; iiij. rakez; vj. wedehokes; iiij. grapez; ij. sholez; vj. harpicæ; vj. tracez cum j. hoper (basket)."

In the larger houses, as we have shewn, the number of offices was much greater, and it is not always easy to identify them. In the ground-plan of Haddon Hall, which we have given, a very good set of offices is exhibited, and the description of them, which we have copied from Lysons, is sufficient to enable the reader to distinguish them easily.

The following extract from Sauval's "Antiquities of Paris" shews, by the great number of names given to different offices according to their respective uses, that the French[d] were not behind us in the progress of social improvements, and may be useful for comparison with those already enumerated from English houses of the same period:—

[d] In France there are many examples of farm buildings of this period, some of them very perfect and interesting. The abbey granges are often remarkably fine and on a large scale, as at Maubuisson, and Ardennes, near Caen. Several others, in the department of Eure only, are described by M. Lemaitre, in M. de Caumont's *Bulletin Monumental*, vol. xv.

"Dans la plupart des basses-cours avoient été pratiquées la maréchaussée, la conciergerie, la fourille, la lingerie, la pelleterie, la bouteillerie, la sausserie, le garde-manger, la maison du four, la fauconnerie, la lavanderie, la fruiterie, l'eschançonnerie, la panneterie, l'hypocras, la patisserie, le bucher, la taillerie, la cave où l'on met le vin des maisons du roi. De plus, quantité de cuisines, quelques jeux de paumes, celliers, colombiers, galliniers, c'est-a-dire poulailliers; car nos rois, qui vivoient alors en bons bourgeois, tenoient leurs menages, et pour cela obligeoient les fermiers de leurs terres et de leurs domaines, à leur fournir poulets, chapons, pigeons, bled, vin, charbon... et enfin ces pigeons et ces poulets étoient élevés et nourris dans leur basse-cour, de même que chez les gentilshommes de campagne[e]."

Throughout what has been said it will be observed that considerable progress was made during the fifteenth century. In the previous centuries not only is the antiquary at fault whence to derive his information and where to find his examples, but there are clear indications that many of the luxuries which are in this century common were in the previous most rare, if indeed known at all. Many indications of new trades and callings are shadowed forth in the accounts of the period. Stationers, of whom parchment, ink, paper, wafers, &c., are bought, are mentioned more than once[f]. Sums were paid to plumbers, glaziers, and bed-makers, and we have an interesting notice of the " clokke maker of Kolchester," who was paid two shillings and fourpence "ffor mendyng of the clokke[g]."

In the fifteenth century not only the remains of the buildings are more frequently remaining and the inventories more numerous, but a large number of illuminated manuscripts throw much light upon the manners and customs of the period. For instance, in a manu-

[e] Sauval, liv. vii. t. ii. p. 279.
[f] Howard's Household Book, pp. 196, 352.
[g] Ibid., p. 167. Clocks are mentioned as part of the furniture belonging to Henry VIII. at his palace at Greenwich, MS. Harleian, No. 1,419, p. 58.

DOMESTIC ARCHITECTURE: FIFTEENTH CENTURY.

ILLUSTRATIONS FROM MSS. IN THE BODLEIAN LIBRARY.

FIREPLACE, SEAT, AND TABLE. Canon. Liturg. 99.

TABLE AND SEAT. Canon. Liturg. 99.

BAKEHOUSE. Canon. Liturg. 99.

SEATS, FROM MSS. IN THE BODLEIAN LIBRARY.

script in the Bodleian Library, Canon Liturg. 90, is an excellent representation of the bakehouse with the baker at work, taking the loaves out of the oven; the one which he holds in his pan is smoking hot. In the same manuscript is a man dining in the kitchen, with his back to the fire, and two servants waiting upon him; and above this is a *chamber* in which some person is warming his feet at the fire while the servant is preparing the table. Many others might be found, but one plate is sufficient to shew the information to be derived from this source.

In concluding this chapter on the Chambers and Offices, it may be remarked that there are few apartments in a modern house which cannot trace their existence to this century. It is true the purposes for which they were employed may have been somewhat changed, and their proportionate extent and importance altered, as years rolled on and requirements differed, but substantially they are the same. The dining-room is but a smaller hall, the withdrawing-room but a larger "solar;" the "lord's chamber" exists in the modern "study," the "lady's chamber" in the "boudoir." The sleeping apartments are scarcely more numerous in respect of the occupants of a house than they were, if we only allow for the difference that in the habitable room the bed was not an uncommon piece of furniture, as we meet with abroad at the present time; during the day-time it was covered with handsome tapestry, but at night was occupied, and so saved the necessity of another apartment. The "buttery and pantry" are now rolled into one, the latter name being used to designate the office in our large houses, the former being employed in colleges; but at the same time, the officer of the former, viz., the butler, is retained, and that of *pannetier* lost. The "cellars" existed as they do now, but by the introduction of glass bottles the space required for decanting the wines before they are brought to table is more limited. The cupboards in our houses for keeping linen and such like were in those days more extensive, as the stock was much greater and required separate chambers, called the "garderobe," but in many large houses a room is still set apart for this purpose. Of the "kitchen" we have said enough to shew that its importance was not less in those days than it is in these. As the trades of baker and brewer have sprung up, the "bakehouse" and "brewhouse," except in large establishments, are less frequent. The "butcher," too, now does away with the necessity of the large *lardarium* and *salsarium*, as a small room serves the purpose for the daily consumption, there being no need to lay in stores for months. The conveniences also, to which we have not alluded in this volume, but on which information will be found in the previous volume under the head of "garderobes," were not wanting in this century; indeed, it may be said that greater care was bestowed upon matters connected with the drainage of large houses then, than at the present time. Stables and farm buildings it was not necessary to speak of more than we have done, as, having been generally built of wood, nearly every trace of them has been swept away.

CHAPTER V.

THE DOMESTIC CHAPEL.

No particular variation of plan as to the situation of the DOMESTIC CHAPEL has been observed between buildings of the fifteenth century and those of earlier periods. The observation that "it was generally near to the hall, and connected with it by a short passage leading from the dais or upper end of the hall," which was made in our second volume (p. 79), holds good equally in the fifteenth century. It may be added, that it was frequently, at all periods, on a different level from the hall, and connected with it not only by a short passage, but by a staircase also, often in a corner turret, and leading up from one corner of the dais, or of the withdrawing-room behind the dais, to about half the height of the hall, which was usually of the height of two other chambers. The chapel sometimes formed the upper chamber in a separate tower, standing out at a right angle from the corner of the hall, sometimes only connected with it by the corner stair-turret, as at Kidwelly Castle, and the bishop's palace, St. David's. In other instances it is placed against one side of the hall, and separated from it by the wall only, as at Raglan Castle.

At the Mote, Ightham, Kent, the chapel of the time of Henry VII. is remarkably perfect, with its cradle roof, its screen, and stall-desks with their poppies. It forms part of the range of buildings round the court, by the side of the entrance, and is not immediately connected with the hall.

At Haddon Hall it forms one corner of the buildings of the outer ward, but here it was a parish church, and consists of nave and aisles, of earlier date, as well as chancel, the latter being, properly speaking, the chapel, and was connected with the hall by a passage, the hall itself standing between the outer and inner wards, and at right angles to the chapel, but at a short distance from it.

In Linlithgow Palace, Scotland, the chapel is separated from the hall by one of the corner towers: it is a room of considerable importance, and of good height, with a fine range of windows; on one side are two passages in the thickness of the wall, one over the other, and from the upper one are openings into the chapel, probably to enable the servants to see the elevation of the Host; but one of these openings led into the oriel or wooden gallery at the west end of the chapel, of which the corbels only remain.

In Hawarden Castle, Flintshire, the chapel is very small, and must have been either merely a private oratory, or, as seems more probable, the chancel or sacrarium only, separated by a screen from the principal chamber in the keep, and with also a "squint" or opening from the passage in the thickness of the wall, to enable persons thus placed to see the elevation of the Host. The piscina remains, which would hardly be required for a mere oratory.

In Warwick Castle the chapel is on a level with the hall, and connected with it by a groined passage: its situation is in a building projecting into the court, by the side of the withdrawing-room or state apartment, and it is connected by the passage not only with the hall, but with the whole suite of state apartments.

At Stanton Harcourt, Oxfordshire, the chapel forms

DOMESTIC ARCHITECTURE: FOURTEENTH CENTURY.

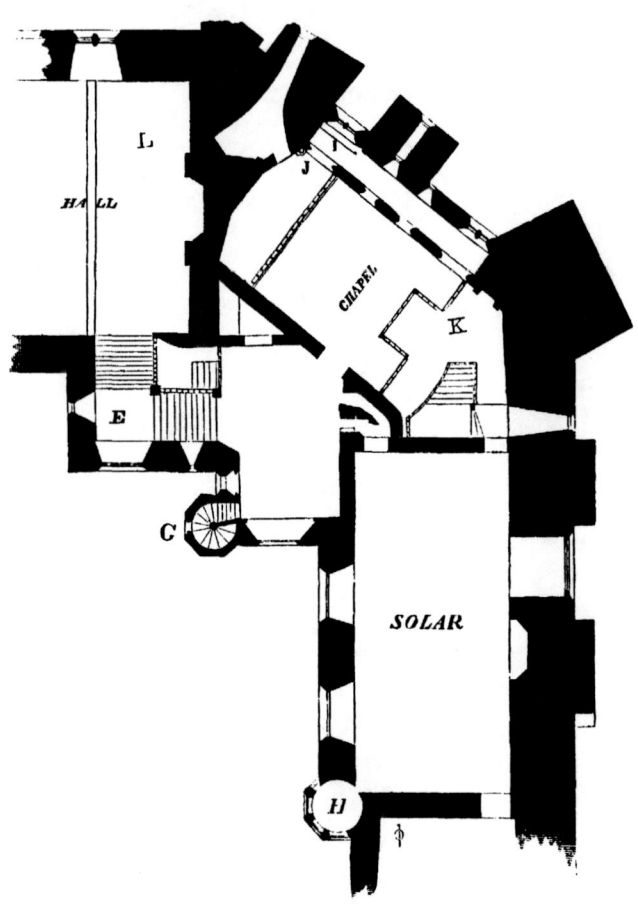

E *Staircase.*   G *Stair-turret.*   H *Closet-turret.*   I *Sedilia.*
J *Piscina.*   K *Gallery or Oriel.*   L *The Dais.*

PLAN OF CHAPEL, SOLAR, &c.

BERKELEY CASTLE, GLOUCESTERSHIRE.

the ground floor of a corner tower, and has a good groined vault, and a solid stone altar; but the latter

Domestic Chapel, Stanton Harcourt, Oxon

does not appear to be original, and probably belongs to the other furniture, which is modern.

At Cothele, Cornwall, the chapel is near the upper end of the hall, but separated from it by the dining-room, from one corner of which is a passage into the chapel, which is a good example of a late Gothic chapel, remaining perfect, but does not appear to have had any gallery or upper chamber.

The chapel often forms a separate wing of the house, joining on to the hall at one corner only, as at Lyte's Cary, Somersetshire; Bradley Manor-house, Devonshire; and in numerous other instances.

In Berkeley Castle it is placed at an angle with the hall, or at least it is not in a line with it, but forms one angle of the buildings in continuation of it round the court or inner ward.

In Trelawney House, Cornwall, it is at the lower end of the hall, behind the passage or screens, occupying the place usually assigned to the buttery and pantry, which are thrown to the back at the end of the passage. In this singular instance the chapel is the whole height of the house, and forms one wing of it.

Another situation in which we occasionally find the chapel is in the room over the entrance gateway, with an oriel window for the altar thrown out at one end, as at Prudhoe Castle, Northumberland, described in vol. ii. This appears to have been the case at Place House, Tisbury, Wiltshire, where there is an external stone staircase at the west end.

The chapel is sometimes a detached building standing in the centre of the principal court, as was the case with the Sainte Chapelle in the Palace[a] at Paris, and St. George's Chapel, Windsor. St. Stephen's Chapel, Westminster, was of two stories, like the Sainte Chapelle, but was connected with the upper end of the hall by a passage. It sometimes forms part of the range of buildings round the court, without any immediate connection with the hall, as in the colleges of Oxford and Cambridge.

In our second volume, pp. 79—81, it was shewn by several extracts from the Liberate Rolls, and by existing remains, that the chapel consisted usually of two parts; the sacrarium, in which the altar was placed, with its usual adjuncts, the Piscina and Locker; and the nave, or western portion, where the people assembled, and this was frequently divided into two stories or chambers by a floor, and separated from the sacrarium by a screen, which was the whole height of the chapel, and extended

[a] Now the Palais de Justice, but once the royal residence.

THE DOMESTIC CHAPEL. 177

in front of both the upper and lower chambers. The same arrangement was continued in the fifteenth century, and examples of it are more numerous and more perfect: the only example that has been noticed in which this arrangement is quite complete, with the screen remaining above and below, is at East Hendred, Berkshire; this is a plain and poor building, standing al-

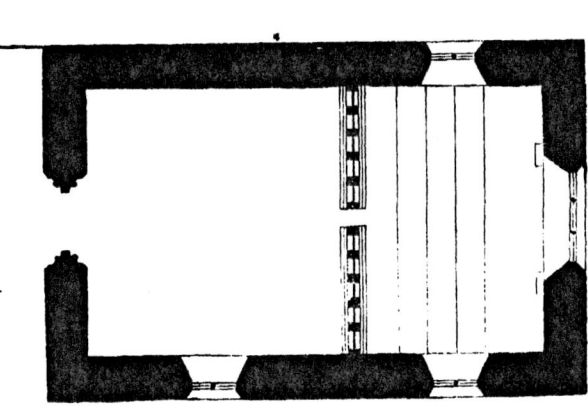

Section and Plan of Chapel, East Hendred, Berks.

most detached in the court-yard, close to the entrance, and had no internal communication with the house; there is a plain rude staircase from the lower chamber to the upper one, the windows are small and square-headed, and late in the fifteenth century. A cottage has been added on the north side, but it must have been originally a detached building, having windows on all four sides. Although this is the only instance known in which the screen remains perfect in front of both the upper and lower chambers, there are many examples in which it is evident that the same arrangement has existed, and in which the floor still exists. In Berkeley Castle the floor remains, and the screen in front of the upper chamber is slightly altered; the lower part is modern. There is a fireplace in the upper chamber, shewing that it was used for domestic purposes also, and it has a separate entrance from the lord's chamber or drawing-room, while the lower chamber is entered from a passage leading from the hall. The one at Chibburn, Northumberland, where the floor and the fireplace remain, and the windows clearly shew that this arrangement is original, was described and engraved in our last volume, p. 198. At Trecarrel House, Cornwall, the chapel stands in the courtyard, entirely detached from the house. Yet the western half is divided into two stories, with a fireplace and a garderobe to the upper chamber, clearly proving that it was used for domestic purposes as a habitation, and not merely a gallery to the chapel, although the east side of the chamber doubtless consisted of a screen and tapestry only, opening into the sacrarium.

In the ruins of Godstow Nunnery, near Oxford, the chapel is the most perfect part; and although the floors have been destroyed, the plastering on the walls clearly

ORIEL IN THE CHAPEL,
BERKELEY CASTLE, GLOUCESTERSHIRE.

THE DOMESTIC CHAPEL.

shews this arrangement of the sacrarium having been the whole height of the building, and the western part divided into two chambers by a floor. In Wigston Hospital, Leicester, and St. Thomas's, Northampton, the arrangement appears to have been the same.

At Sherborne, Dorsetshire, is an Almshouse or Hospital, founded by Bishop Neville in the reign of Henry VI., A.D. 1448, in which this old arrangement of the chapel is remarkably clear, from the construction of the building, although it has been entirely lost sight of in modern times. The sacrarium is the whole height of the building, with an east window high from the ground, and a window on each side at a lower level[b].

The Almshouse, Sherborne, Dorset. A.D. 1448.

[b] This is still used as the chapel, but the chancel-arch is filled up with a modern partition, and the small size of the chapel being complained of, it is now proposed as a great improvement, under the name of restoration, to destroy entirely the old arrangement by removing the floor in the western part, although it is evidently original, and the double range of windows in this part clearly shews that this was the original construction. A second floor has been in-

180   DOMESTIC ARCHITECTURE: FIFTEENTH CENTURY.

In the following passage the word oriel is evidently used in the sense of a gallery, and there are other instances of the word being used in this sense, as we have shewn[c]:—

"He dwellyd in a brewe house in St. Chadde's church-yorde, which afterwards was, and nowe of late dayes ys callyd the Colledge, and was burieed in St. Chadd's churche: who laf behynde hym a doughter of hys named Blase Tuptun, who cam by chance to be a leeper, and made the oryall to which she cam aloft to heare serveys throughe a doore made in the churche wall, and so passyd usually uppon the leades unto a glasse wyndowe, throughe which she dayly sawe & harde dayly serveys as longe as she lyvyd[d]."

Unfortunately there are no remains of this structure, but there are several instances of a projecting window, like what is usually called an oriel window, in the interior of a church, commanding a view of an altar, and it seems very probable that such windows were provided for the use of lepers, who were by no means always confined to hospitals nor belonging exclusively to the lower orders; as in the instance before us, a wealthy leper built a gallery, or family pew, with a window from it, and an external communication.

In Corpus Christi College, Oxford, the east end of the library opens by an arch into a sort of gallery at the west end of the chapel. In Magdalen College chapel there is an original opening through the south wall of the ante-chapel from a room in the bursar's tower. In France there are examples of oriel windows at the west end of churches at Harfleur, and Montivilliers, near Havre, in Belgium in Antwerp Cathedral, and there are many others both in England and on the continent.

---

troduced in the roof to form garrets, which ought to be removed, and if the chancel-arch was again opened a very commodious chapel would be formed by a real restoration of the original arrangement.

[c] Vol. ii. p. 82.

[d] The History of Shrewsbury, by Owen and Blakeway, &c., vol. ii. p. 257. London, 1825, 4to.

DOMESTIC ARCHITECTURE: FIFTEENTH CENTURY.

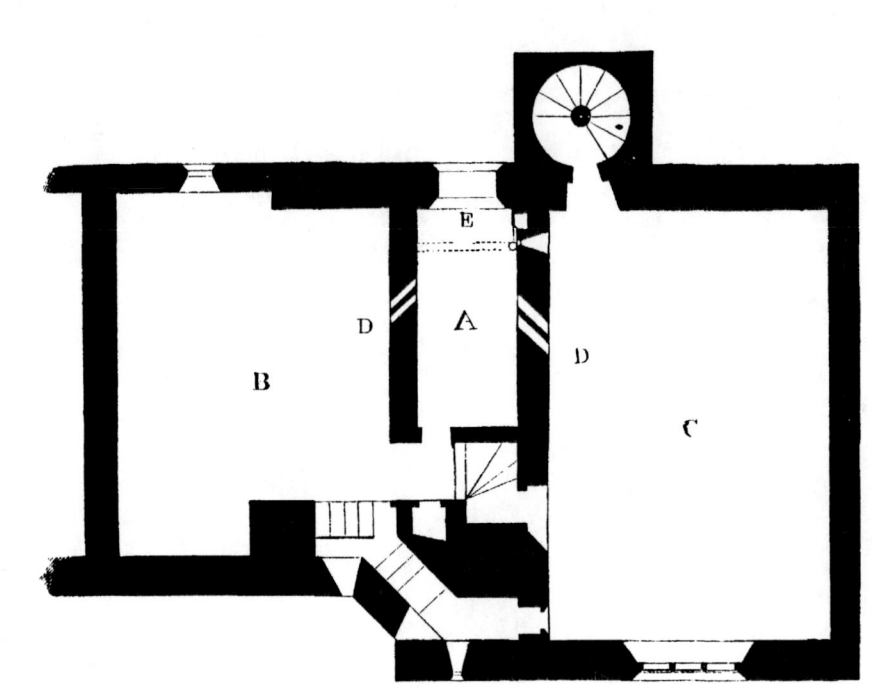

A *Oratory.*   B *Priest's Room.*   C *Lord's Bed-chamber.*   D D *The Squints.*   E *Altar.*
SECOND FLOOR.

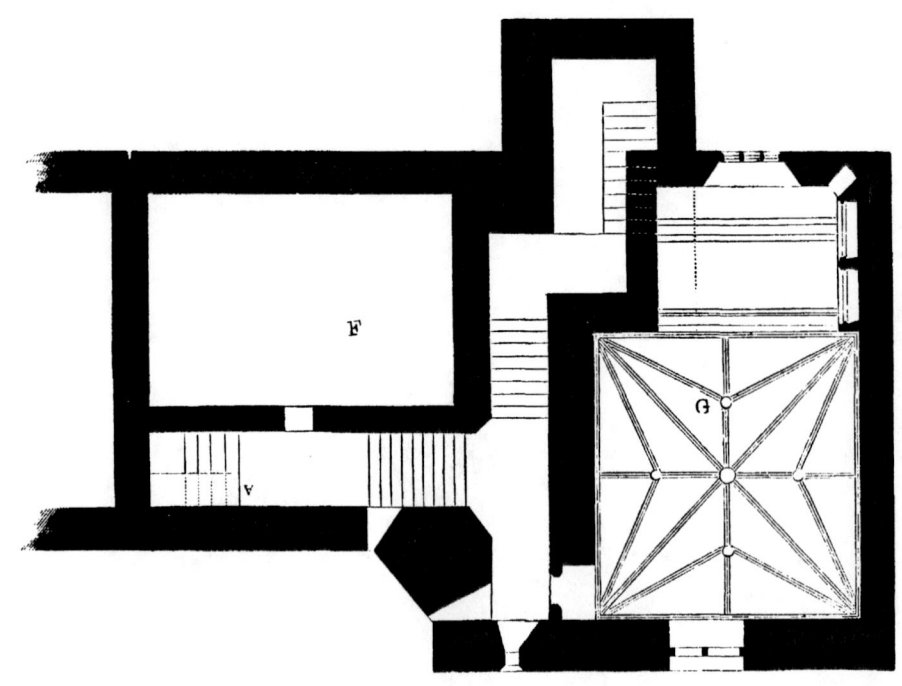

F *Parlour.*   G *Chapel.*
FIRST FLOOR.

BEVERSTONE CASTLE, GLOUCESTERSHIRE.

In Alnwick Castle, Northumberland,—

"Between the Constable's Tower and the Ravine Tower, was a faire chappell, of vii. yeards height of the wall, in length xix. yeards and vii. yeards of breadth, covered with slate, the windows well glazed, in all things well repaired (the seyling thereof onely excepted); betwixt the said chappel and the said curteyne wall ys builded one lytell house of two house height, of length viii. yeard; the nether part thereof called the revestry, the over part thereof a chamber wth a stone chimney, wherein the lord and ladie wth their children commonly used to hear the service (the oriel?). The same ys covered with slate, ye loft thereof would (should) be repayred.

"And before the said chapel door was a conduit, built of stone, and a cistern supplied with tryme and sweete water from one well called howlinge well, in pipes of lead[e]."

There was often a private oratory distinct from and in addition to the chapel, and often called the Lord's Oratory, as in Chepstow Castle, Monmouthshire, Brougham Castle, Westmoreland, and many others. It is usually at the top of a turret. In Linlithgow Palace, Scotland, the Queen's Oratory forms the interior of the upper floor of one of the octagonal turrets, and has a vault of rich fan-tracery on the exterior; it forms a sort of oriel window.

In Beverstone Castle, Gloucestershire, the oratory is in the upper part of the tower, immediately over the chapel, as shewn in the section annexed. The chapel itself is on the first floor, having a chamber with a stone vault under it, and is considerably larger than the oratory, or upper chapel; it has also a good groined vault and two elegant sedilia. In the oratory there is a piscina, which is rather unusual; but the chief peculiarity of the oratory consists in the remarkable squints, or hagioscopes, these are oblique openings, scarcely more than slits in the side walls which separate the oratory from the two adjoining

[e] Clarkson's Surrey, A.D. 1566.

bedchambers, probably to enable invalids in bed to see the elevation of the Host and join in the service. These openings are common in churches, and are always directed towards an altar, usually towards the high altar, but in domestic chapels they are rarely met with. Perhaps the opening through the wall at the side of the chapel in Broughton Castle, Oxfordshire, may be considered as belonging to this class.

Reference is constantly made to the ORATORY in the romances of the period. In the romance of "Parys and Vyenne," printed by Caxton in 1485, we find an interesting passage illustrative of a castle of this period, in which the private oratory is mentioned. Vyenne visits the parents of her lover, and—

"After all thys, the moder of Parys prayed hyr, that it myght playse hyr to come see the castell; and she answerd that she moche desyred it. Thenne the moder of parys shewed hir al the castel, and ledde hir in to an halle, al ful of armes and abylemens of warre for to fyght in battayll. After she ladde hyr to another halle, where was many hawkes, falcons, and many other fowles of chace. And after in to many other halls and chambers, rychely arayed, whyche were ouer longe to reherce. And after the moder of Parys shewed vnto hyr the chambre of Parys where that he slept, wherein were many abylments, whyche shold wel suffyse ye chambre of a grete prynce. And in the sayd chambre were two grete standardes couerde after the guyse of Fraunce. That one, was ful of clothe of gold and sylke, and that other, of harnoys[f] and of many other things."

The fair Vyenne searched this chamber, and

"Com on a syde of the chambre where they fonde a lytel dore, of whyche henge a lytel key by a thwonge, and anon they opened the dore and entred therin. And there was a lytel chambre whyche was xij. fote large, and was an oratorye wherein was the majeste of our Lorde Jhesu Cryst upon a lytel aulter, and at eche corner was a candelstyke of syluer, and thyder cam Parys for to make hys sacrefyce whan he aroos, and whan he wente to hys bedde[g]."

[f] Harness, i. e. armour.
[g] Storye of the Knyght Parys and of the fayr Vyeñe, printed by Caxton, 1485, Sign B. ii. b.

DOMESTIC ARCHITECTURE: FOURTEENTH CENTURY.

SECTION OF TOWER, SHEWING THE TWO CHAPELS.

A, the vaulted Lower Chamber.   B, the Chapel.   C, the Oratory or Upper Chapel.

BEVERSTONE CASTLE, GLOUCESTERSHIRE.

THE DOMESTIC CHAPEL. 183

The INVENTORIES of the furniture of the domestic chapel contain in most cases the same items as those of churches, &c., the list being chiefly composed of the different vestments for the priest and for the altars. Thus, in Sir John Fastolfe's inventory of goods (1455), we find,—

"j. vestement covered with crounes, gilt in the myddes with all the apparayle.
j. vestement hole of redde damaske warke.
j. vestement of black cloth, of gold withe the hole ornaments.
j. auter (altar) clothe with a frontell of white damaske, the trynete in the myddys.
j. vestement of tunekell.
j. cope of white damaske, with ye ornam[nts].
j. awbe (alb).
j. stole.
j. favon (fanon?) encheked white and blewe.
j. auter clothe.
ij. curtaynes of white sylke, withe a frontell of ye same, withe fauchonns of golde.
j. vestement of divers colurys, withe a crosse of golde to the bakke.

iiij. birdys quartelye.
j. crosse of sylver and gylt, withe oure Lady and Seynt John.
j. chales (chalice), sylver and gylt.
j. pax brede [h].
j. crucyfix, thereon withe oure Lady and Seynt Iohn, enamelyd and full of flour de lys.
ij. candylstykkis of sylver, the borduris gilt.
ij. cruettys of sylver, percell gylt.
iij. pyllowes stonding on the autre, off rede felwet, withe flowrys embrawderid.
ij. carpettis.
iij. cosschenys of grene worstede.
j. chayre in the closet of Fraunce fregid (of French cloth?).
j. cosschon of redde worsted.
j. sakeryng bell of sylver (the bell rung during the elevation of the Host)."

In the inventory taken at Ewelme in 1466 we find,—

"IN THE CHAPELL.—A tapyte of aras, of 15 signs of the Doom [i].
A tapyte of the story of Seynt Anna, of Aras.

A gret standard [k] of the chapell, bowden with ierne, with 2 lokks."

---

[h] The pix, i.e. the vessel in which the "pax brede" or consecrated wafer was kept. It may be mentioned here that in the inventory of the "bakehouse" in the same house mention is made of

"ij. payre wafer irens," i.e. the iron moulds or tongs in which the wafers were baked for the priest.

[i] Doom, the day of judgment as described in the Apocalypse, a very fa-

184   DOMESTIC ARCHITECTURE: FIFTEENTH CENTURY.

As the domestic chapel was generally hung with a great quantity of tapestry, we sometimes meet with the word "chapel" signifying simply the "hangings," in the same manner as when "la salle" was bequeathed, the hangings of the hall were meant. Thus Richard Earl of Arundel leaves—

"Nulle chose de moun dit devys, sinoun la *chapel* qe je avoie ovesq' ele ensemblement ove les litz, excepte la *chapel*, lit, et *sale* que je avoie de doun (received as a gift from) ma honure Miere de Norfolk. . . . . Item je devise a mon fitz Richard moun *chapel* ove tout appareil de drap velwet rouge ove angeles et archanngeles de enbroudez sur ycell."

It has been already mentioned that the origin of the ORIEL WINDOW was a recess for the altar of an oratory or small chapel, corbelled out from the face of the wall in order to give more space, and the earliest example known is at Prudhoe Castle, Northumberland, which is of the thirteenth century, and at the east end of the chapel, which is over the gateway. Examples also occur in the fourteenth, some of them remarkably beautiful, such as the well known one at Nuremberg, but they become much more common in the fifteenth century, and were then so frequently used for other purposes, that their original use seems to have been lost sight of, though they were still sometimes used for the same purpose[1]. In the Prior's house at Wenlock the altar stands in the recess of the bay window, the chapel or sacrarium being on the ground floor. Oriel windows are commonly used in this century over gateways; indeed, this fashion became so

---

vourite subject both for paintings on the walls of churches and for the hangings. In the hôtel de Bohème, at Paris, there was also, in 1408, a tapestry of the Doom. *Recherches sur les étoffes de soie.*

[k] A large chest, or trunk.

[1] There is a good example of this arrangement in the church of St. Mary-in-the-Capitol at Cologne, where an altar is corbelled out in an oriel at the end of each aisle by the side of the chancel, in order to give room in the side chapels.

DOMESTIC ARCHITECTURE: FIFTEENTH CENTURY.

ORIEL WINDOW AT

SHERBORNE, DORSETSHIRE.

W. Twopeny. del.　　　　　　　　　　　O. Jewitt, sc.

general, that some other origin besides that of the oratory has been sought for, and some antiquaries are of opinion that they had their origin in the machicoulis or bartizans of military architecture, which were generally used over the gateway in order to protect it from assailants; and this sort of projecting closet, when glazed in more peaceful times, assumed the form of the oriel window. Whatever their origin may have been, they are one of the most striking features of the domestic buildings of the fifteenth century, and they occur in various situations; not only over gateways, as in the colleges of Oxford and Cambridge and many other gatehouses, whether of houses or of monasteries, but in many other situations also, at either end of the front, as at Chalfield, in a gable end, as at Sherborne, Dorset, (now built into a modern house in imitation of the old style). They are almost always on the first floor, but occasionally they occur in the gable end of the upper story, as at Clifton Maybank, Dorset.

CHAPTER VI.

MEDIEVAL GATEHOUSES.

AMONG an infinite variety of examples, and even of classes, GATEHOUSES fall naturally under two great divisions; those which stand as detached erections, and those which are brought into close contact with other buildings. Both however would include a great number of subdivisions. The former chiefly consists of the gateways of monasteries. In designing a monastic erection space was for the most part little regarded, and defence was a secondary consideration; the gateway might therefore, if desired, stand alone by itself, connected with the other buildings by nothing more than a blank wall. And, standing thus detached, it might be built of any size and shape that the architect might think good. Consequently the various forms assumed by monastic gateways are nearly infinite.

In a castle, on the other hand, in a great private house, in an academical college, the case was different. In a great medieval castle mere space was certainly of no more consequence than in a monastery; but then the gateway was naturally a chief point of attack and defence, which it was necessary to bring into the closest connexion with other parts of the building. In a medieval house again, of sufficient consequence to possess a gatehouse of any architectural character, defence, though not a primary consideration, was more thought of than in the case of monasteries; domestic reasons would also co-operate to make the whole building as compact as pos-

DOMESTIC ARCHITECTURE: SIXTEENTH CENTURY.

LAYER MARNEY, ESSEX.

sible. In a college built in a town every inch of ground was precious, and the buildings could not be allowed to straggle unrestrainedly like those of a great abbey. In all these classes therefore the gateway was brought much nearer to the other buildings than was necessary in the case of a monastery. The result has been that the gateways of castles, houses, and colleges, present some points of resemblance to each other, though of course the general type assumes forms of considerable diversity according to the class of buildings to which it was applied.

This type is that which places the actual aperture of the gate between two towers or turrets, which, though not universal, is decidedly characteristic of the three classes of buildings, castles, houses, and colleges. It is also found in a great number of monastic edifices; but there it is only one form used indifferently among others, and is in no way characteristic of the general class of structures.

The aspect of the genuine military gate, such as we see in many of the Edwardian castles, is sufficiently familiar. The outer side presents the gate itself between two massive round towers, leaving no more space between them than is actually necessary for the aperture. Rhuddlan, Flintshire, exhibits this type in its most strictly military state, without the intermixture of any purely architectural modifications. At Tunbridge Castle we have the same idea, as strictly military as anywhere, but with its character somewhat altered by the extreme beauty of the masonry and execution. Chepstow, Pennard, Penrice, the Burgesses' Tower at Denbigh, and numerous other instances, exhibit this type in its perfection. The town-gate at Rye, though not strictly that of a castle, is also a fine example of the same class. Most, if not all, belong to the Edwardian period. At

Carisbrooke, which seems later, the towers are less massive, the space between extends a little beyond the mere gateway, and a little more of purely architectural ornament is introduced. At Llawhaden, Pembrokeshire, where the towers are still very massive, square-headed windows with mullions and transoms cause some deviation from the pure military type. So at Allington Castle, Kent, we find plain tolerably massive round towers, but the gateway itself has a square spandrel and a square-headed window over it.

In the interior of these gateways the towers are generally much more slender; the space between is wider, and admits a somewhat greater amount of strictly architectural enrichment. This may be very distinctly seen at Tunbridge. It is easy and interesting to trace the steps by which this purely military type was changed into that of the fine domestic and collegiate gateways of the fifteenth and sixteenth centuries. Whenever the flanking towers cease to be round, there is a deviation from the purely military idea. Defence may still be contemplated, and may even be primary, but strictly architectural considerations are no longer excluded. The gateway of the Bishop's Palace at Llandaff, of the thirteenth century, is flanked by two enormous square towers with their angles chamfered off. This particular example does not itself depart from the purely defensive type[a], but it evidently exhibits the germ of the octagonal turrets of a later period. In the superb gateway of Denbigh Castle, of the fourteenth century, we find a further advance. The towers are octagonal, and the

---

[a] Bishops' Palaces of course vary according to their position. This of Llandaff, standing neither in a town nor in a fortified close, approaches more nearly than usual to the head of purely military architecture. It is in fact an episcopal castle, like Llawhaden and others.

GATE HOUSE, CHURCH HALL, METHAM.

whole is a grand display of architecture. The detail is mostly destroyed, but the arch of the gate itself and an elaborate niche with a statue over it shew that we have reached a state of things quite different from Rhuddlan or even from Tunbridge.

Raglan Castle, of the fifteenth century, has less enrichment than Denbigh, but, from its better preservation, we can more safely judge of its general effect. The gate is flanked by two comparatively slender hexagonal towers. Though there is but little ornament, the execution is excellent, and evidently shews the presence of the architect and not of the mere engineer.

The inner gate of the Palace at Wells exhibits nearly the same stage. Octagonal towers are formed by giving that shape to the extremities of the whole mass on each side. In the actual gate we see for the first time in this series the square head and spandrel.

The magnificent gateway of Herstmonceux Castle marks the turning-point between military and domestic structures. The turrets—we can hardly any longer call them towers—have become much more slender, though less so than in still more advanced examples; their lower part is octagonal, but the upper stages are round. Machicolations and eylets are still very prominent, but the height of the whole gatehouse, the additional height of the turrets—a smaller stage being raised above the machicolations—and the large windows over the gate itself, shew that the domestic idea prevails, and that the military features are little more than a decaying tradition.

In the gateways of Cowdray, Sussex, and Oxburgh, Norfolk, of more advanced Perpendicular, we may look upon the change as fully accomplished. Military details still exist; there are eylets for instance, but they have very much less prominence than at Herstmonceux, and the whole genius of the thing is purely domestic. At Cowdray four equal octagonal turrets occupy the four corners of the gatehouse. There are large windows over the gate, but unluckily very little of the details can be made out, a great deal being broken down, and a great deal concealed by the favourite plague of ivy.

Oxburgh is a noble example of brick architecture. It is not merely the material, as at Herstmonceux, but it completely influences the style. The gateway is of a great height; two lofty turrets flank the gate, and rise a good way above the battlements, though less so than at Herstmonceux. They are covered with a sort of panel-work in brick, and the battlements have corbie-steps. There are two large square-headed windows over the gate. Within, the effect is more massive and less enriched. The two great turrets of the exterior exist only in the form of much smaller ones perched on the battlements. There is no great window over the gate, but a tall slender turret or lofty oriel, containing three stages of small windows, is placed on each side of it. Those at Layer Marney, in Essex, another grand example of brick-work, develop into actual turrets, rising above the rest of the gatehouse. The actual angles are splayed off into a quasi-octagonal form. Instead of the oriels of Oxburgh, these turrets contain a great number of small distinct windows, arranged in eight stories. Unlike Oxburgh, also, there are two large square-headed windows over the gate itself. These examples at once lead us to the familiar type of the Perpendicular gateway, flanked by two slender octagonal turrets and commonly presenting no military feature whatever. In houses and colleges the whole gatehouse assumes something of the character of a tower, and rises more or less over the buildings on each side. The variations in proportion,

DOMESTIC ARCHITECTURE: FIFTEENTH CENTURY.

GATEWAY OF JESUS COLLEGE, CAMBRIDGE.

detail, and amount of ornament are nearly infinite. In some cases we meet with two openings, a large wide gate for carriages, and a smaller one by its side for foot-passengers; internally, the two are most frequently thrown into one of enormous width. The great gate of Trinity College, Cambridge, is one of the finest examples. But it is more common to find only a single opening. Of this class none would probably have been more admirable than the magnificent gateway which still remains unfinished near the chapel of King's College. As far as it is completed it is covered with ornament of the best style of the period. The outer gateway of the Palace at Wells is a good specimen, with much enrichment in the way of windows, niches, and panelling. In a house at St. Pierre, Monmouthshire, is a much plainer, but very well-proportioned example. The town-gate at Lynn, though really a military structure, and standing quite detached, has more of the character of these domestic and collegiate gates than of the old castellated type. It is, however, much more massive, and its turrets, though octagonal, are not equilateral.

In all these examples the arch of the main gate is four-centred, and in several of them it has a square spandrel, often very richly adorned. The smaller gate, when it occurs, has often a more pointed arch, and in Cambridge there is a tendency to cover it with rich ogee canopies and similar ornament, as at Jesus College.

The gateway of the Palace at Norwich may be placed with these, but it has some peculiarities of its own. The turrets—if they are to be so called, being something between turrets and buttresses—are flat, except a single octagonal one on their side. The whole is much lower than usual. Externally there is a double gate; the great gate and the inner one are obtusely pointed, with a very rich spandrel, in marked contrast to the plainness of the remainder of the building.

This example leads us to those domestic and collegiate gateways which have dispensed entirely with turrets, except perhaps a single one at a corner for a staircase. This is the prevalent type in the college gateways in Oxford. Every one who has compared the architecture of the two Universities must have observed how much more prominently the gateways at Cambridge stand out as distinct portions of the building. At Oxford the gateway-tower is generally only distinguished from the rest of the building by its masonry rising as high or a little higher than the apex of the high roof on each side; prominent turrets form no part of the type; except in the late and anomalous, though magnificent gateway of Christ Church. The double entrance never occurs. Over the gateway is often a large oriel window, which frequently marks the rooms originally designed for the Head of the College.

The gateway towers of William of Wykeham have a peculiar character of their own, arising from the manner in which the corner turret is set on the angle of the square mass and rises above the battlement. The towers themselves are a story higher than the mass of the building, but not otherwise distinguished from it by any projection until they rise above the roof. There are two of these Wykeham towers at New College, Oxford, two at Winchester, one remaining at Windsor, and a few others in different places, which may be distinguished by their peculiar turrets, even though it may not be known that Wykeham was the architect of them.

A very fine gateway which may be referred to this class, is that of the Hospital of St. Cross. It has a stair-

DOMESTIC ARCHITECTURE: FOURTEENTH CENTURY.

GATEHOUSE.
MACKWORTH CASTLE, DERBYSHIRE. c. 1350.

case-turret at one corner, the rest have buttresses reaching to the top. The proportions are massive, but it rises considerably above the roof of the buildings on each side. Two plainer examples occur at Crickhowell, Brecknockshire, (called Porth Mawr,) and Itton Court, Monmouthshire. Both have only a square turret rising from the battlement; both have single and rather tall pointed arches. At Itton the battlement has the corbel-table characteristic of the military church-towers of the district.

This leads us to Tretower Court, Brecknockshire, where the architecture is ruder and more defensive, but where the gateway-tower is still less marked without, though it is very conspicuous within, the range on each side of it being a merely defensive wall, connecting it with other parts of the house. There is a double gate, but the smaller one is not within the tower. Finally, in the Bishop's Palace at Bosbury, Herefordshire, (unless indeed, as is quite possible, the building has been lowered,) there is no tower at all, but the gateway is placed in a range of a very uniform height. It consists of an unusually lofty pointed arch reaching the whole present height of the building, with a smaller one. The two stand between two large flat buttresses. The arch on the inner side of the gateway is of wood. Similarly, in the College at Higham Ferrers, the gateway is merely placed in the ordinary range, like a large doorway, without at all assuming the character of a distinct portion of the building.

We may here add a few very anomalous domestic gateways.

The gatehouse of Mackworth Castle, Derbyshire, is of anomalous character; it is a complete house in itself, and the archway is little more than a doorway: it has two round turrets projecting from the two outer corners, and a good chimney, which has an earlier look than the rest of the work. The windows are square-headed, with labels over them; these, and the ogee head to the doorway, and the moulded battlement, appear to be late work. Some antiquaries of eminence consider the gatehouse to be as early as the middle of the fourteenth century, but its general aspect seems more like the end of the fifteenth.

In many of the larger castles the gatehouse is quite a complete house in itself, of which Saltwood Castle, Kent, is a very fine example: this is generally the case also in the larger castles of South Wales, as at Oystermouth.

The gatehouse at Athelhampton, Dorsetshire, is a fine example of rather late date. It is a complete house in itself, and rather out of proportion to the manor-house to which it forms the entrance. It has a good gable end, with the family crest for a finial, and corner buttresses amounting almost to turrets, one being corbelled out to avoid the wall which joins on to it, and both are terminated by figures: the archway is small, and has an oriel window over it, and a closet boldly corbelled out by the side of it.

We now turn to the monastic gateways, including some collegiate and other ecclesiastical examples erected under similar circumstances. The Close of a cathedral or other great secular foundation had the advantage of space just like a monastery, and was very different from a college built in a street of Oxford or Cambridge. Indeed, as the inhabitants did not live cœnobitically, but occupied their own private houses, the gateway of a secular cathedral might be a still more independent building than that of a monastery. But, for that very reason, it lost in architectural splendour. The buildings

DOMESTIC ARCHITECTURE: SIXTEENTH CENTURY.

GATEHOUSE, ATHELHAMPTON, DORSETSHIRE.

within such a Close did not form so much of an architectural whole as those of a monastery. They were more like a small town with a wall and gateway, and such is often their character.

As was before said, the gateways of monasteries, which might stand thus independent, assumed any form which the designers thought good. But, on the other hand, though they might stand almost detached, they also might, and often did, stand in close connexion with other buildings.

Some stand quite detached, or connected only by a wall. Such are the two magnificent gateways at Bury St. Edmunds. The well-known Norman tower is a gateway and campanile in one. But for the lower story, where the actual gateway is formed, it would be a very fine example of a Norman church-tower, and might just as well have been attached to one of the three churches which it helps to enclose. It is strikingly analogous to the superb campanile at West Walton in Norfolk, which stands quite away from the church, and whose lower portion similarly forms a magnificent approach to the churchyard. Walton is indeed a mere parish church, with no other buildings connected with it, so that the tower merely makes a sort of magnified lichgate; but architecturally the arrangement is remarkably similar.

The other gateway at Bury, that known distinctively as the Abbey Gate, is as grand a structure and one as completely independent as the Norman tower; but it is totally different in date and character, being in form a massive oblong, and in style an example of enriched Decorated work. It is, in fact, a large oblong mass, completely unbroken except by flat buttresses which are doubled at the angles, but which do not assume the character of turrets or rise at all above the general battlement. It consists of the actual passage and a story over it. In length it forms three bays, with an intermediate arch between the first and second bay from the outside. The outer arch is segmental with an ogee canopy; the inner one is pointed, and much higher and wider.

In these Bury gateways, the actual opening of the gate is still the main thing, and the whole design has direct reference to it, whatever there is above and beside it being chiefly intended for its support and ornament. But in some other instances the actual gateway is little more than a mere aperture in a large distinct building. Thus the Priory gate at Malvern now stands quite detached, and can hardly have at any time had more than a wall, as at Bury, connecting it with other parts of the monastery. It is an oblong building, in the Perpendicular style, rich with panelling, with the gateway in the centre. But this gateway is made no more of than a large doorway; it is not the architectural centre of the whole. On each side of it is a window; in the upper stage there are three, that over the gateway itself being an oriel, but not brought into any special relation with the arch itself.

Not altogether unlike this is the gateway of Castle Acre Priory, Norfolk, though it is much plainer, and as there is a large and a small archway, it is less symmetrical than Malvern. Both archways appear on the inner side, the smaller one having a distinct passage, instead of being, as usual, thrown into one inside. The gateway called the Newark, at Leicester, is a large quadrangular building, with a large and a small gate in one corner, and square-headed windows irregularly disposed as they were wanted. In the Canongate at Chichester, the two archways fill up nearly the whole width, but the build-

THORNTON ABBEY.
EAST SIDE OF GATEWAY.

ing is of the same oblong form, with small windows over the arches. These arches are of the same height but different widths, being very obtuse. They reappear, as at Castle Acre, though there is no separate passage. They are clearly late Perpendicular, but from the early vaulting within they must be a mere casing of an older building. The gateway of Malling Abbey, Kent, has one large pointed archway, the full height of at least the present building, and beside it a smaller one with a square-headed window over it. In all these examples the style is Perpendicular.

One of the grandest and at the same time most imposing of monastic gateways is that of Thornton Abbey, Lincolnshire: it has two side archways, rather lower than the central one, over which is a fine oriel window, and on the inner face are four tall slender octagonal turrets, and there are wings on each side with battlements on corbie steps: its date is near the end of the fourteenth century.

The great gatehouse of Maidstone College, also Perpendicular, joins on to the collegiate buildings, on one side at least, forming a range from which it does not at all project, though in height it rises considerably above them. It is, like so many others, a distinct large oblong building, without buttresses or turret, with a large pointed archway in the middle and a smaller one on one side, with square-headed windows above and on each side.

In some cases a gateway, instead of finishing square at the top, has a gable. A noted case of this is St. Æthelberht's Gate at Norwich[b], a well-known and beau-

[b] The other gateway of the Close—the Erpingham Gate—seems unfinished; it presents, in its proportions and treatment, the appearance of a gigantic Perpendicular *doorway*, being most unusually lofty.

tiful example of the Decorated style, and remarkable as exhibiting some of the best and earliest specimens of the characteristic Norfolk flint panelling, combined, on the outer side, with rich niche-work. It consists of the gate itself—single with a pointed arch—and a story over, formerly a chapel[c]. It has no turrets nor even buttresses of any great consequence.

This St. Æthelberht's Gate stands quite detached, but at Kingswood Abbey, Wiltshire[d], a gateway gabled in this manner stands in the centre of a range of buildings. This example is the more valuable, as shewing that this form was deliberately employed[e], and thought capable of a high degree of ornament, the gable being adorned with large crockets and finished with a rich finial. The gateway itself has a niche on each side and a pointed window. The style is Perpendicular, with some singularities of detail. A gateway of a somewhat similar arrangement occurs at Bayham Abbey, Sussex.

Not unfrequently again monastic gateways reproduce, as one of their varieties, the collegiate or domestic type. Such, for instance, is the magnificent Decorated gateway of Battle Abbey, which stands in the midst of a long range of buildings, above the apex of whose roof—now lowered—it only rose by the battlements. In this it resembles the Oxford type; but in its greater width, its double archway, and the four turrets at the angles, it approaches to those at Cambridge. The details are well worthy of study. There is also a Perpendicular one at Montacute Priory, Somersetshire, whose appearance is still more collegiate. The adjoining buildings here re-

[c] One of the town-gates at Winchester still has a church over it, and there was one so placed at Canterbury.

[d] A detached part of the county, locally in Gloucestershire.

[e] Sometimes the gabled form is due to alterations, as at Llanthony, where the gable was evidently introduced when the gateway was converted into a barn.

DOMESTIC ARCHITECTURE: FIFTEENTH CENTURY.

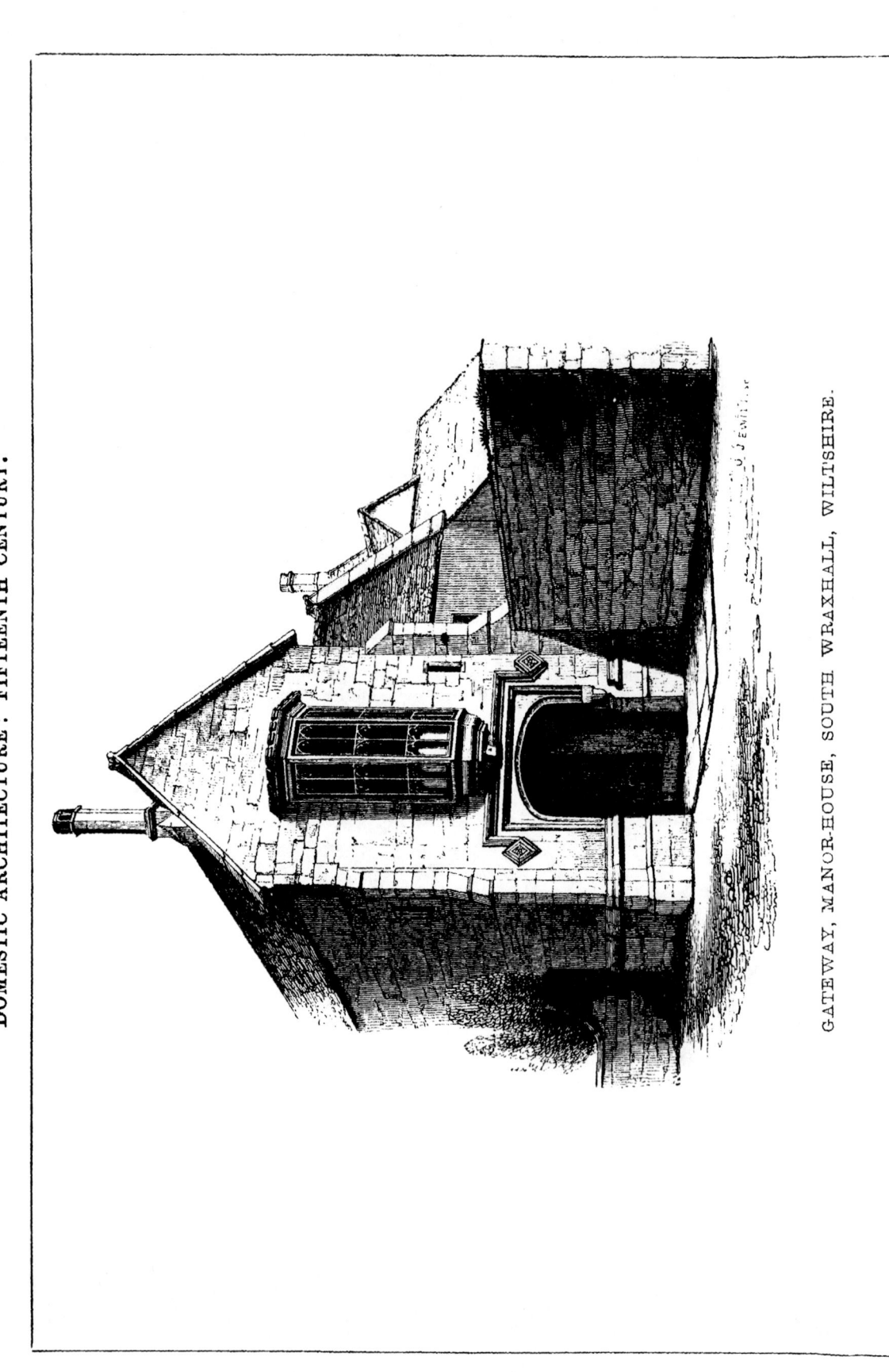

GATEWAY, MANOR-HOUSE, SOUTH WRAXHALL, WILTSHIRE.

tain their high roofs, so that the gateway-tower rises very little above them. Over the archway is a fine oriel; there is a bold staircase-turret on one side, and one not reaching the full height on the other.

Of the numerous gateways at Canterbury the two finest will come in here. Christ Church Gate, late Perpendicular, is a massive rectangular structure, with turrets at the angles, not rising above the battlements. The two archways occupy but a small proportion of the height, which is filled up with a gorgeous display of niches, panel-work, and heraldic ornament. The beautiful Decorated gateway at St. Augustine's Abbey forms, in its light and airy proportions, the most marked contrast to the massive solidity of that of Christ Church. It is flanked by two turrets rising far above the battlements; the arch is single; the whole is well known as an example of the most beautiful ornamental detail of its own date.

The gatehouse of Congleton Court, Warwickshire, is worthy of especial mention as a fine example in good preservation of a grand tower gatehouse, with tall turrets standing up clear above the parapet, and an oriel window between, thrown over the archway. This belongs to a room of some importance, now used as the drawing-room. We have before observed that there is frequently a room of considerable dimensions and importance in this situation, the use of which is not clear. Sometimes it was the chapel, but this does not seem to have been the usual arrangement. It may have been the guest-chamber, and strangers may have been lodged altogether in the gatehouse.

A plain example with a gable occurs at the manor-house of South Wraxhall, Wiltshire. The gable is quite plain, with a chimney on the slope of it: the arch is four-centred, with a square label over it, and a fine oriel window. The room over the archway has been one of some importance, and has remarkable squints or small windows, commanding the approach so far as to see who was coming, but it has scarcely any vestiges of the military character, the defences are calculated only to resist a band of robbers.

The above seem to be the most marked and important among the various classes of gateways; but doubtless there are other classes, as there certainly are individual examples which cannot be reduced to any of them. Nowhere does the individual genius of the architect appear to have been allowed freer scope: even among those which evidently exhibit the same leading idea, there is the widest difference in proportion and consequently in general effect.

Printed in the United States
993000001B